Windows 32-bit API Programming
THE USER INTERFACE

Dr. Dobb's
JOURNAL
**INTERACTIVE
CD-ROM-BASED
WORKSHOP**

Windows 32-bit API Programming
THE USER INTERFACE

Copyright © *Dr. Dobb's Journal*, 1997

Version 1.0, January, 1997

All rights reserved. No part of this online workshop or accompanying software may be copied in any form without prior written consent of *Dr. Dobb's Journal*. The only exception is that you may copy the lab exercise and sample program software for use in your own programs.

Dr. Dobb's Journal makes no guarantee that the material in this workshop is correct and assumes no responsibility for any errors contained within.

All trademarks are owned by their respective companies. Microsoft, Visual C++, Windows 95, Windows NT and Microsoft Windows are trademarks of the Microsoft Corporation. Borland and Borland C++ are trademarks of Borland International, Inc.

You can contact *Dr. Dobb's Journal* at:
650-358-9500
fax: 650-358-9749
email: hvessichelli@mfi.com
World Wide Web: http://www.ddj.com

Dr. Dobb's Journal
411 Borel Avenue, Suite 100
San Mateo, CA 94402

Welcome to the Online Workshop!

Thank you for selecting the best computer-based learning environment available! This online course features plenty of graphics, audio, quizzes and hands-on lab exercises. But the real focus in this workshop is in solid technical information and time-proven instructional techniques. After completing this course, you *will* be a productive Windows programmer!

System Requirements

The workshop requires a computer running Windows 95 or Windows NT 4.0 (or later) with a 10MB free disk space.

You will need a Windows C++ compiler and development environment to do the lab exercises. The lab documentation is written for Microsoft Visual C++, but you should be able to adapt the labs to other Windows C++ compilers.

You need a Windows-compatible CD-ROM player (double speed or better).

For the voice-over feature to work, you need a Windows-supported sound card.

For best viewing, we recommend a display resolution of 1024x768 with 256 colors. That will let you position several of the online course windows next to each other. Higher display resolution is better!

Installing the Workshop

To install the workshop, run the SETUP.EXE program from the installation CD-ROM. Be sure to have the CD-ROM handy so you can enter your unique CD key as required by the setup program. Once you have installed the course, you can start it by choosing **Windows 32-Bit Programming Workshop** from the Descriptor Systems entry on the Start menu.

Be sure to check the README file on the CD-ROM for late-breaking information.

Configuring the Workshop

Before you start taking the online course, you should take a quick moment to configure the course to your preferences. Your basic choices concern whether the voice-over should play automatically or not, and which program should be used to view the lab exercise documentation (which is also printed in this book). To configure the workshop, choose the *Settings* button on the Viewer Tool Palette window.

Getting Started

The Descriptor Systems On-Line Course Viewer lets you take an interactive, computer-based workshop. The Course Viewer displays two initial windows: the main display window, and the Viewer Tools window that contains buttons that you can press to navigate the workshop, ask for help and so forth. You can browse the online help by pressing the F1 key at any time.

Sizing the Course Viewer Window

When you change the size of the Course Viewer window, the Course Viewer re-sizes all of the elements on the page. For example, if you enlarge the window, the page title text and any pictures on the page will also be larger. This lets you set the Course Viewer's window size to the size that looks best to you.

However, the online course has been designed to look best if the Course Viewer window has the same shape as a piece of paper laying sideways: 11 inches by 8.5 inches. So you will see the best presentation if you set the Course Viewer window's size to that shape. Otherwise, you may see extra blank space at the top, bottom or sides of the page.

The Course Viewer window "remembers" its size and position when you close it and resets itself to the previous size and position. All of the secondary windows, such as the Chapter and Page List Window do the same. This lets you arrange the windows in a pleasing manner – the program will reset itself to that state when you restart it.

Navigating Through the Workshop

The Viewer Tools window contains buttons that let you navigate the workshop:

- « Changes to the previous page.
- » Changes to the next page.
- L Changes to the last viewed page.
- ▢ Displays the *Chapter and Page List* window from which you can change to any page in the workshop.

Please refer to the online documentation for more information.

The Contents of This Book

This book has two major components:

- The workshop pages
- The lab exercise documentation

This first part of this book contains half-size listings of all the workshop pages. We provide it so you can take notes on the workshop as you view the pages. Each page also shows as much of the voice-over text as would fit on the printed page.

The second section in this book contains the write-ups for the lab exercises. We provide this primarily as a convenience, since the online course lets you view and print the lab documentation.

Please note that this book is *not* a replacement for the online course – it is merely an adjunct (a useful one, we hope). The workshop's primary instructional media is the CD-ROM itself.

How Long Will it Take?

It's very difficult to predict how long it will take you to complete the course, since it depends on your background and your diligence (and how many coffee breaks you take!). But as a guideline, most chapters should take about 30 minutes to an hour and a half if you study them carefully. And as a rule, the lab exercises take about an hour and a half.

Getting the Most Out of the Course

To maximize your learning, we recommend that you go through each chapter in the course at least twice. The first time, listen to the voice-over and write notes in this workbook. The second time, study the text and any sample programs in the chapter, then work on the chapter's lab exercise (not all chapters have exercises). Before you go onto the next chapter, be sure to take the quiz! We recommend that you don't leave the chapter until you can get at least 90% of the quiz questions correct.

One other note: it's been our experience in almost 20 years of teaching technical topics that many people learn more and faster, if they take a class with a partner. So we encourage you to find someone else with whom you can take the class with and compare notes as you go (our legal people say to remind you that its against the law to copy the course materials). That will also help you as you go through the lab exercises. Also remember that each lab exercise has a solution.

Technical Support

If you have any problems with the course, or have technical questions, or if you just want to chat, send email to jbarnum@netins.net. (That's how to tell us about typos and bugs, too.)

Go For It!

So with out further ado, fire the course up and happy learning!

Chapter 1: Intro to Windows Programming

- History of Windows
- 16 and 32-bit Programming Differences
- Windows Development Environments
- Other Resources for Windows Programmers

The History of Microsoft Windows

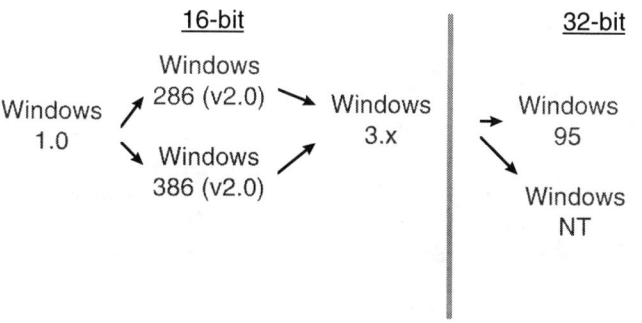

- Up until Windows NT and Windows 95, all versions of Windows presented a 16-bit interface to programmers
- Windows NT and Windows 95 share a common set of system calls -- the Win32 API

Windows 1.0 was designed to run on computers that had an Intel 8088 or 8086 microprocessor and 256 K of memory and no hard disk. It supported windows that didn't overlap each other, called tiled windows -- each window touched four other windows or the edge of the screen. When you changed the size of one window, Windows 1.0 resized all of the rest. Even though Windows 1.0 was not very popular, it established the event-driven programming techniques and many of the system calls that we still use today.

Windows 2.0 came in two flavors: Windows/286, which ran on 8086, 80286 and 80386 computers, and Windows/386, which ran on the same set of chips, but took particular advantage of the 80386's Virtual 8086 mode. It's interesting to note that Microsoft subtitled these versions "Windows Presentation Manager: consi...

Windows: A Developer's View

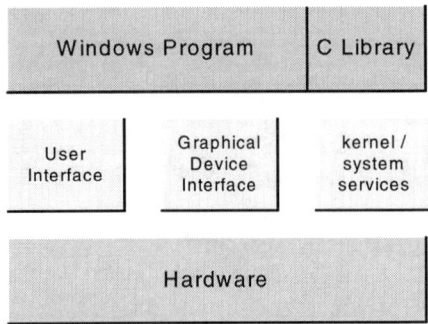

- The user-interface component provides system calls (API) to manage windows and dialog boxes
- The Graphical Device Interface (GDI) provides API to perform device-independent graphical output
- The kernel/system services component provides memory management, tasking and so forth

We can think of Windows as consisting of three major components: the User Interface component, the Graphical Device Interface (GDI) and the Kernel or System Services component. Each component exports a set of system calls that Windows programs can call. For example, the User Interface component provides the CreateWindow system call that opens a window on the display.

Windows has other subsystems besides the three shown here. These include the multimedia subsystem, pen subsystem and so forth.

A typical C or C++-language Windows program contains application logic, calls to Windows functions and calls to the C runtime library (strlen and so forth). Windows programs do not typically access hardware devices directly. For example, to draw a line in a window on the display, a Windows programs calls the GDI LineTo function, which calls the display's devi...

32-Bit and 16-Bit Windows API

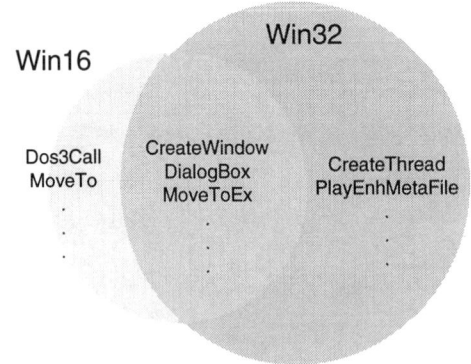

- Many system calls are common to Win16 and Win32, but there are some that unique to each
- This workshop covers only the 32-bit system calls (green and blue areas in picture)

This diagram shows the APIs provided by 16 and 32-bit versions of Windows. The blue area represents the system calls available only in 32-bit Windows. The yellow area shows the calls that work only in 16-bit versions of Windows. The green area shows the common system calls. The diagram is not really to scale -- the green area should be the larger of the three.

The largest percentage of system calls work the same in 16 and 32-bit Windows (the green area). However, there is a set of 16-bit specific system calls that are obsolete and not supported in Win32 (the yellow area). If you are porting a 16-bit program to Win32, you must remove these calls and replace them with 32-bit equivalents. The Windows programming documentation has conversion charts to aid in this process.

Win32 supports many new kinds of functions that weren...

16 and 32-bit Programming Differences

In Win32:

- No memory models (e.g. small and large)

- No near and far types of function calls

- No need to export window and dialog box procedures

- All handles are 32-bits. For example, window handles and pointers to memory

- New capabilities, including threads, graphics transforms, enhanced metafiles and so forth

Unless you have previous experience with 16-bit Windows programming, you can pretty much ignore this page.

If you do have a 16-bit Windows background, you'll be happy to know that 32-bit Windows programming is actually much easier! You don't have to worry about Intel 8086-style segmentation issues anymore: no more memory models, near and far pointers and such.

If you need to port a 16-bit Windows program to 32-bits, it's also nice that 32-bit compilers ignore most of the keywords like near and far that we used in 16-bit programming. That makes it easier to convert 16-bit code. However, you will still need to convert the differences in system calls as discussed on the last page, and you may also need to modify any 16-bit code that assumes that handles are 16 bits (especially in processing the WM_COMMAND message).

Windows Development Environments

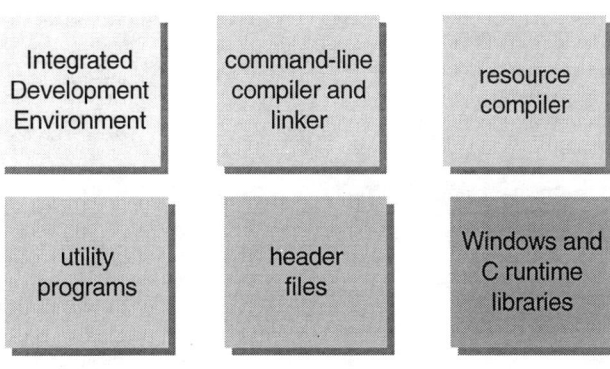

- Development environments like Microsoft's Visual C++ and Borland C++ provide everything you need to write 32-bit Windows programs

- Since the environments include an integrated editor and debugger, you never need to leave the environment!

In the bad old days of Windows development, you needed to buy both a compiler and a Windows Software Development Kit (SDK). Nowadays, most compiler vendors such as Microsoft or Borland bundle the SDK with the compiler so you only need to purchase and install a single package.

In addition, the integrated development environments in such packages have made great strides in usability. In fact, unless you have a favorite editor that you simply cannot give up, there's really no reason to ever resort to the command line.

Windows C++ Class Libraries

Windows Program	C Library

Microsoft Foundation Classes or Borland's Object Windows Library

User Interface	Graphical Device Interface	kernel / system services

- Microsoft, Borland and others provide C++ class libraries that hide some of the complexities of Windows programming
- This workshop doesn't cover such libraries, but instead focuses on the Windows API itself

1-6

To make Windows programming easier, Microsoft, Borland and other companies have developed C++ class libraries. These libraries act as a layer between the Windows program and the Windows API.

The libraries do simplify Windows programming, but there are some downsides to using class libraries that you should be aware of:

a. They tend to increase a program's size and make it load and run slower.
b. Before you can use one, you must know C++ quite well.
c. They are proprietary to a particular compiler vendor.
d. They sometimes hide too much -- it may be difficult to do things that are not directly supported by the library.

That being said, we believe that class libraries are a useful part of a Windows programmer's repertoire. However, we also believe that a thorough knowledge of the underlying API will make any...

Windows Header Files

\msdev\include
　windows.h
　　windef.h
　　winbase.h
　　wingdi.h
　　winuser.h
　　winerror.h
　．
　．
　．

```
#define STRICT
#include <windows.h>
    .
    .
    .
HWND hwnd;

hwnd = CreateWindow ( ... );
if ( hwnd == 0 )
    DWORD dwErr = GetLastError
();
    .
    .
    .
```

- Each development environment provides a set of Windows header files that include all of the types, constants, macros and function prototypes for Windows development
- The STRICT definition causes the compiler to perform more stringent type checking

1-7

Your Windows development environment most likely creates an INCLUDE directory that contains the WINDOWS.H file and any other Windows header files. In earlier versions of Windows programming toolkits, almost all of the information was contained in the single WINDOWS.H file, but in current versions, WINDOWS.H itself includes other subsidiary headers.

In the sample code shown on this page, the program allocates a variable of type HWND, which is a type defined by WINDOWS.H -- holds a 32-bit window handle. The program then calls the CreateWindow function, which is prototyped by WINDOWS.H.

The header files are compiled differently if you define the STRICT symbol before including WINDOWS.H. With that symbol defined, the compiler performs stronger t...

Other Windows Programming Resources

The Microsoft Developer Network

This is a subscription service that sends you one or more CD-ROMs four times each year. Each CD is filled with documentation, technical articles, sample code and so on.

Internet News Groups

Point your newsreader toward:

comp.os.ms-windows.programmer.win32
comp.os.ms-windows.programmer.ole
comp.os.ms-windows.programmer.tools.mfc
comp.os.ms-windows.programmer.tools.owl
comp.os.ms-windows.programmer.winhelp

Microsoft's Developer Web Page

Point your Web browser toward:

http://www.microsoft.com/msdn

Your development environment probably contains documentation for the Windows system calls and the C runtime library and that's really all you need to get started with Windows programming. However, you occasionally may need more information than the documentation provides, or you might have a question that's not addressed by the documentation. If that's the case, you can use one or more of the resources shown on this page.

Lab Exercise 1: First Windows Program

In this lab, you will write the smallest possible working Windows program. The idea is to give you experience with your Windows development tools and to provide a foundation for future lab exercises.

To view the lab exercise instructions, press the "Lab Write Up" button. This will display the lab document and let you print it if you wish. When you are finished with the lab, you can continue by taking the review quiz on the next page.

Review Quiz

Before you move on to the next chapter, you should test your comprehension of this chapter by taking the review quiz. The quiz assumes that you have already done the lab exercise.

The quiz will be displayed in a separate window so that you can page through the chapter to help you find the answers. In other words, this is an open book quiz!

After you have answered all of the questions, press the button at the bottom of the quiz window to see how you did. If you didn't score as well as you think you should, you should review the chapter before continuing on.

Chapter Summary

- Windows NT and Windows 95 have a common programming interface called the Win32 API. Programs that adhere to the Win32 API should work on either operating system, provided that they do not use specific features of either.

- Windows 3.x uses a 16-bit version of the Win32 API. While it is mostly compatible with Win32, there are differences.

- Windows development tools such as Microsoft's Visual C++ and Borland C++ provide everything you need to develop 32-bit Windows programs, including a compiler, linker, editor and debugger.

- All C or C++ Windows programs include the WINDOWS.H header file, which defines the constants, macros and function prototypes required for Windows programming.

Chapter 2: What is a Window?

- ◆ User's View of a Window

- ◆ Programmer's View of a Window

- ◆ The Default Window Procedure

2-0

User's View of a Window

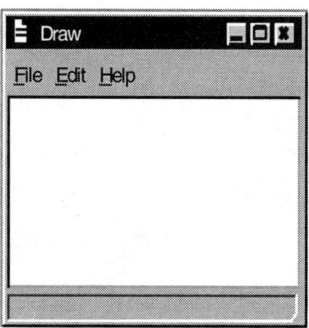

This sample displays a blank client area, but can be sized.

Depending on your system and the program creating the window, the window may look a little different than the one depicted here. For example, this window has the Windows 95 appearance and has a status bar, but no scroll bars.

- A typical Windows program creates one or more windows to display text or graphics
- The user can manipulate the window by clicking the mouse or pressing keys

Introduction to Messages

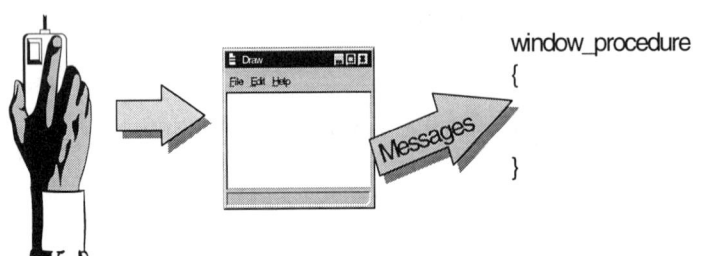

Whenever the user clicks the mouse or types a keystroke on a window, Windows calls a window procedure. The window procedure can then react to the event.

Your job as a Windows developer is to write window procedures and process these events, which are referred to as messages.

- Every window has an associated window procedure that Windows calls when the user interacts with the window
- This call to the window procedure is called a message -- Windows defines values with symbolic names for each kind of message

2-2

Anatomy of a Window

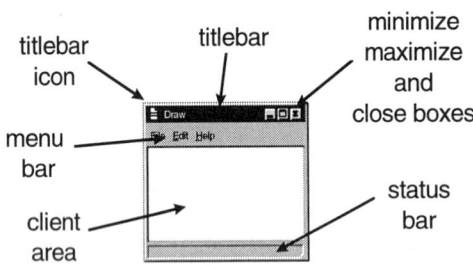

The window shown here has both a client area and a set of non-client components. Your window procedure only has to process messages for the client area -- Windows handles the rest.

- A window consists of two main parts: the client area and non-client area
- Windows itself normally draws and handles the non-client area
- Application developers write the window procedure to control the client area

2-3

Programmer's View of a Window

Window Data Structure

hwnd → [Win Proc Address / Size / Position / etc.]

Win Proc Address → window_procedure { }

Messages

When the user interacts with a window, Windows must find the associated window procedure. To do that, Windows maintains an internal list of data structures, each of which describes a window, including its window procedure address. We refer to the structure as the window data structure.

Since the window data structure is internal to Windows, we cannot access it directly. However, we can manipulate the window data structure and the associated window using a window handle. Windows gives you the window handle when you create the window.

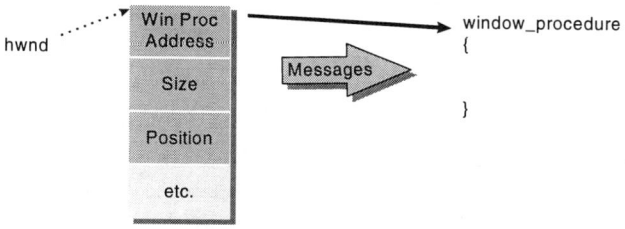

- To the developer, a window consists of a data structure and the window procedure
- Windows allocates and maintains the window data structure, but developers can access it if they need to
- Whenever a program creates a window, Windows assigns a unique window handle, which is a 32-bit number you can use to manipulate the window. For example, to remove a window, call the DestroyWindow system call, passing the window handle

2-4

The Default Window Procedure

```
LRESULT CALLBACK WndProc ( HWND hwnd, UINT iMsg
                         , WPARAM wParam, LPARAM lParam )
{
    switch ( iMsg )
    {
        default:
            return DefWindowProc ( hwnd, iMsg, wParam, lParam);
    }
}
```

Every window procedure you write should have these arguments and return value. Click on the underlined words for a description of each.

You can use the window procedure shown here as a skeleton or template for your own window procedures.

The default window procedure provides the minimum processing for all messages, but essentially does nothing in response to mouse clicks or keystrokes on the client area. Thus, a window procedure, like this one, that does nothing except call the default window procedure, will have a pretty boring window. The user will be able to move, size and close the window however, since these are non-client actions. The default window procedure does all of the processing for the non-client components.

- Windows defines hundreds of message types -- a typical window procedure only handles a few and passes the rest to the default window procedure
- The default window procedure handles all non-client processing and default processing for the client area (blank window)

2-5

Creating a Window

```
WinMain ( ... )                 WndProc ( ... )
{                               {
  HWND hwndMain;                    switch ( iMsg )
    .                               {
    .                                   case WM_CREATE:
  hwndMain =                                .
      CreateWindow ( ... );                 .
    .                                       return 0;
    .                                       .
}                                           .
                                        }
                                }
```

- A program can call the CreateWindow system call to create a new window
- As part of CreateWindow, Windows calls the window procedure with the WM_CREATE message
- In this message, the window procedure can open files, initialize variables and so forth

WinMain is a function that's required in all Windows applications -- it replaces the main function found in C or C++ programs. The Windows program loader calls WinMain when the user starts the program. You can code many window procedures in a Windows application, but you can have only one WinMain function.

In WinMain, a typical application program creates one or more windows in which to display text and graphics.

Notice there are two places where you could code your program's initialization -- in WinMain or in the WM_CREATE message in the window procedure. The general rule is that you code window-specific initialization in WM_CREATE and general program initialization in WinMain. This makes more sense if you remember that a Windows application can have many window procedures.

At the end of each message case in the window procedur...

2-6

Destroying a Window

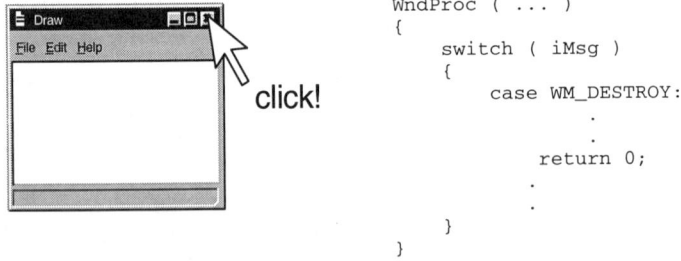

click!

```
                                WndProc ( ... )
                                {
                                    switch ( iMsg )
                                    {
                                        case WM_DESTROY:
                                            .
                                            .
                                            return 0;
                                            .
                                            .
                                    }
                                }
```

- When the user closes a window (or a program calls DestroyWindow), Windows calls the window procedure with the WM_DESTROY message
- In this message, the window procedure can clean up: close files, deallocate memory and so forth

The user can close a window by clicking on the "X" button on the titlebar. When the user does, Windows passes a WM_DESTROY message to the window procedure.

To be more precise, when a user closes a window, the window procedure first receives the WM_CLOSE message. But if the window procedure passes WM_CLOSE to the default window procedure, DefWindowProc calls the DestroyWindow system call, which gets rid of the window and generates the WM_DESTROY message. So most of the time, the window procedure receives WM_DESTROY as its last message.

Windows ignores the return value from the WM_DESTROY message, so in this example, we just return the value 0.

2-7

Drawing to the Client Area

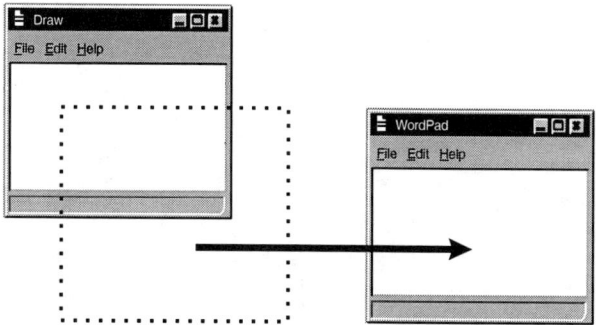

- Whenever it's time for a window to draw its client area, Windows calls the window procedure with the WM_PAINT message. In this example, the Draw window will receive a WM_PAINT message when the user moves the WordPad window so that it no longer overlays the Draw window
- In WM_PAINT, the window procedure can call Windows system calls, for example, TextOut to draw text or Rectangle to draw a box

Every window that displays text and graphics needs to process WM_PAINT, since this is Windows' command to the window to draw itself. This process is quite different from text-based environments, such as MS-DOS, where the program decides when to perform screen output.

In the example shown, Windows transmits WM_PAINT to the Draw window procedure when the user moves the overlaying WordPad window. The WordPad window procedure will not receive WM_PAINT in this case because Windows will copy it's image to the new location. Windows can't do that for the Draw window, since part of it was obscured -- instead, the Draw window must refresh its display during WM_PAINT.

2-8

Window Coordinates

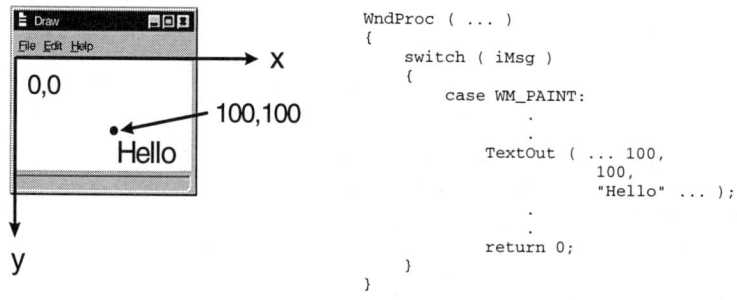

- Each window has a coordinate system that the window procedure can use to position text and graphics
- By default, the coordinates are in pixels and the origin is in the upper-left corner of the client area. In this example, the "Hello" text is at x=100, y=100

This window procedure draws the "Hello" string in the client area.

Each client area has a coordinate origin in its upper left corner. By default, x coordinates grow larger to the right, and y coordinates grow larger down. Again by default, the units are in pixels.

This coordinate system is called the MM_TEXT mapping mode, but it's not your only choice. A program can use a different coordinate system by calling the SetMapMode system call. For example, a program might prefer to position its output in terms of millimeters instead of pixels. We will cover this notion in a later chapter.

2-9

Built-in Window Procedures

Examples:

Button	Edit control	List box
OK	this is a test	entry 1 / entry 2 / entry 3 / entry 4

- Windows itself provides several pre-written window procedures for common windows such as buttons, edit controls and so forth

- These pre-written procedures are called public window classes -- a developer can use them by simply creating a window and specifying the class name

These built-in window procedures are especially useful in dialog-box programming. In fact, even though a dialog box is a window, you don't normally need to write much of a window procedure for a dialog box, since most of the components on dialog boxes have pre-written window procedures. Instead, the dialog window procedure just needs to respond to messages from the buttons, listboxes and so forth.

The built-in window procedures are included in Windows Dynamic Link Libraries (DLLs) that ship with each version of Windows. Since they are dynamically linked, you can use them in your program without increasing the size of your program's executable file.

Review Quiz

Before you move on to the next chapter, you should test your comprehension of this chapter by taking the review quiz. The quiz assumes that you have already done the lab exercise.

The quiz will be displayed in a separate window so that you can page through the chapter to help you find the answers. In other words, this is an open book quiz!

After you have answered all of the questions, press the button at the bottom of the quiz window to see how you did. If you didn't score as well as you think you should, you should review the chapter before continuing on.

Chapter Summary

- In this chapter, you learned that a minimal Windows program requires two functions -- a WinMain function that the Windows loader calls, and a window procedure that responds to messages.

- WinMain normally creates the program's window(s) and then enters a message loop (covered in the next chapter).

- The window procedure can either provide custom processing or call the default window procedure for generic processing.

- Every window that draws text or graphics to its client area does so during the WM_PAINT message.

Chapter 3: The WinMain Function

- Structure of a Windows Application
- Introduction to Message Queues
- A Flowchart for WinMain
- Running Multiple Instances

Structure of a Windows Application

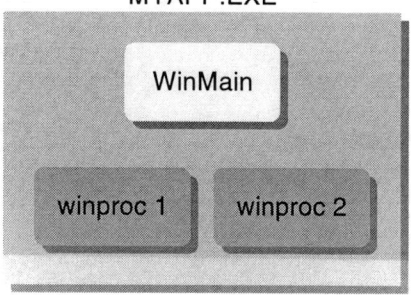

This figure shows the pieces of a typical Windows program. WinMain is the program's entry point and Windows calls the window procedures when the user interacts with their associated windows.

- Every Windows application needs a function named WinMain that the Windows loader calls when the program is started
- Windows programs also normally contain one or more window procedures -- one for each distinct kind of window that the program creates

WinMain Argument Signature

```
int PASCAL WinMain ( HINSTANCE hInstance
                   , HINSTANCE hPrevInstance
                   , LPSTR     lpszCmdLine, int nCmdShow )
{


}
```

As you've already learned, WinMain is the entry point for a Windows program -- it replaces the main function found in C-language programs. WinMain must accept the arguments shown here -- click on each for a description.

A 16-bit Windows program can determine if it's already been in memory by examining hPrevInstance -- if that argument is zero, then this is the first instance. If it's nonzero, it's actually a pointer to the previous instance's data segment. In Win32 however, hPrevInstance is always zero. That's because Win32 runs each Windows application in its own process address space.

We will discuss the command-line arguments in more detail in later chapters.

- For Windows programs, WinMain replaces the C-language main() function
- Click on each argument to WinMain for more information

3-2

Introduction to Message Queues

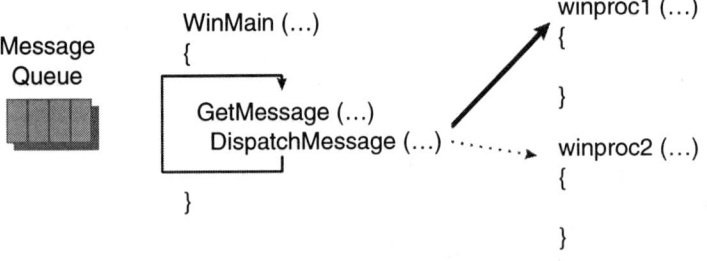

Whenever the user manipulates one of a program's windows, Windows creates a data structure describing the event and places it in the application's message queue. GetMessage dequeues the message and DispatchMessage calls a window procedure, which then processes the message and returns control back to the message loop.

A Windows application needs only one message queue, even if it creates many windows or has many window procedures -- the DispatchMessage system call uses the window handle to route the message to the correct window procedure.

- Before the Windows loader calls WinMain, it creates a message queue for the program
- WinMain must contain a message loop that pulls message data structures from the queue and dispatches them to a window procedure

The default size of the queue is 8 messages, but Win32 automatically expands the size as required. Win16 applications can change the queue size by calling SetMessageQueue.

3-3

The WinMain Function

A Flowchart for WinMain

```
// register a window class
  if ( hPrevInstance == 0 )
  {
     .
     .
     .
     RegisterClass ( ... );
  }

// create and show the window
  CreateWindow ( ... );
  ShowWindow ( ... );

// message loop
  while ( GetMessage ( ... ) != FALSE )
    DispatchMessage ( ... );
```

- The next few pages examine each WinMain section in more detail

The steps shown here are for a typical, simple Windows program -- a more involved program might have other steps.

We first register a window class for the program's main window, then create the window and make it visible. Then we enter the message loop so that Windows can route messages to the window procedure.

Note that in Win32, since hPrevInstance is always zero, the if statement checking it is rather redundant. However, the code shown here is backward compatible with Win16, where only the first instance of a program should register a class.

3-4

Registering a Window Class

```
WNDCLASS    wndclass;                    // class structure

    if (!hPrevInstance)
    {
        wndclass.style          = CS_HREDRAW | CS_VREDRAW;
        wndclass.lpfnWndProc    = WndProc;
        wndclass.cbClsExtra     = 0;
        wndclass.cbWndExtra     = 0;
        wndclass.hInstance      = hInstance;
        wndclass.hIcon          = LoadIcon ( 0, IDI_APPLICATION );
        wndclass.hCursor        = LoadCursor ( 0, IDC_ARROW );
        wndclass.hbrBackground  = (HBRUSH)
                  GetStockObject ( WHITE_BRUSH );
        wndclass.lpszMenuName   = NULL;
        wndclass.lpszClassName  = "Template";

        if ( !RegisterClass ( &wndclass ) )
            return FALSE;
    }
```

- Before you can create an application-defined window, you must register its window class
- We will discuss the class styles in later chapters

This code fragment is part of WinMain in a simple Windows program. It allocates and initializes a WNDCLASS structure, and then calls RegisterClass. Click on each field for a description.

If RegisterClass returns FALSE, that means it failed for some reason, probably due to an incorrect field in the WNDCLASS structure. If it fails, this simple program returns from WinMain, which terminates the program. A more robust program might log an error to a file or display a dialog box window indicating the failure.

The key field in the WNDCLASS structure is lpszClassName -- as you will see on the next page, when you create a window, you must specify a class name string. The string must reference an application-defined class as shown here or a class predefined by Windows, such as a listbox. We choose the ...

3-5

Creating and Showing a Window

```
hwnd = CreateWindow (
      "Template"           // class name
    , "Hello"              // window caption (title)
    , WS_OVERLAPPEDWINDOW  // style
    , CW_USEDEFAULT        // initial x
    , CW_USEDEFAULT        // initial y
    , CW_USEDEFAULT        // initial cx
    , CW_USEDEFAULT        // initial cy
    , 0                    // no parent
    , 0                    // no menu
    , hInstance            // instance handle
    , NULL );              // no create parameters

if ( hwnd == 0 )
    return FALSE;


ShowWindow   ( hwnd, nCmdShow );
UpdateWindow ( hwnd );
```

- We will discuss the window styles in more detail in later chapters

CreateWindow allocates and initializes a window of the specified class and calls the window procedure with the WM_CREATE message so the window can initialize itself. CreateWindow returns the new window's handle, or zero if the call fails.

In this example, we create a window of the "Template" class, which was registered on the last page.

This window has the style WS_OVERLAPPEDWINDOW, which is actually a composite of several other styles, including WS_OVERLAPPED, WS_THICKBORDER, and so forth. Window styles are different than class styles because each window has its own style flags, whereas class styles apply to all windows based on a class. We will discuss styles in more detail later.

We use CW_USEDEFAULT to specify the new window's position (x,y) and size (cx,cy) -- this causes Windows to calculate a "random" initial si...

3-6

The Message Loop

```
MSG         msg;

while ( GetMessage ( &msg, NULL, 0, 0 ) != FALSE )
{
    DispatchMessage ( &msg );
}

return msg.wParam;
```

- GetMessage retrieves a message from the message queue and places it in the MSG data structure
- The return value from GetMessage is a BOOL -- GetMessage only returns FALSE if the dequeued message is the WM_QUIT message

Every Windows program has a message queue -- this bit of code extracts messages from the message queue and routes them to a window procedure for processing.

We stay in this loop until GetMessage returns FALSE, which it does only when it dequeues the WM_QUIT message. The program itself should put a WM_QUIT message in the queue when the program's last window closes.

When that occurs, we return from WinMain, which causes the program to terminate, just like exiting from main terminates a normal C program.

If the queue is empty, GetMessage turns control over to Windows so that other programs can run. It's quite important for Windows programs to call GetMessage often, or else Windows will not multitask well, if at all. This is...

3-7

The WinMain Function

Closing a Window

```
WinMain (...)
{
    .
    .
    while (GetMessage (...) != FALSE)
        DispatchMessage(...);
    return msg.wParam;
}

winproc (...)
{
    case WM_DESTROY:
        PostQuitMessage (0);
        return 0;

    default:
        DefWindowProc (...);
}
```

click! → WM_CLOSE

When the user closes a window, Windows passes the WM_CLOSE message to the window procedure. In this example, the window procedure doesn't process WM_CLOSE, but instead passes it to the default window procedure. A more sophisticated program might ask the user if it's OK to close the window before passing the message to DefWindowProc.

When DefWindowProc detects the WM_CLOSE message, it issues DestroyWindow to get rid of the window that the user closed. DestroyWindow sends the WM_DESTROY message to the window to let the window procedure clean up after itself. This window procedure calls PostQuitMessage to terminate the entire program.

A program typically calls PostQuitMessage to enqueue WM_QUIT only when the user closes its last window. PostQuitMessage takes a single argument, which it places in the wParam field of the resulting MSG data struc...

- To process WM_CLOSE, the default window procedure issues DestroyWindow, which generates the WM_DESTROY message
- This window procedure terminates the application when its window closes by calling PostQuitMessage to insert WM_QUIT into the message queue

3-8

Accessing the Command Line

```
extern int     __argc;
extern char ** __argv;


int PASCAL WinMain ( HINSTANCE hInstance
                   , HINSTANCE hPrevInstance
                   , LPSTR    lpszCmdLine, int nCmdShow )
{

}
```

The lpszCmdLine argument to WinMain is rather useless, since it is a "raw" command line. Most C and C++ programmers are used to having the main function receive "argc" and "argv" parameters that contains a parsed command line and a count of command-line arguments. If you use lpszCmdLine, you must parse it yourself.

Luckily, Windows programmers can access the parsed command line by defining the external variables shown on this page. Note that the syntax of these externs depends somewhat on your compiler -- check your compiler's documentation for more information. These externs work for Visual C++.

- There are two ways to access command-line arguments -- the unparsed command-line string via lpstrCmdLine and parsed arguments via external variables
- The syntax for external command-line variables are compiler specific. These are for Microsoft Visual C++

3-9

Running Multiple Instances

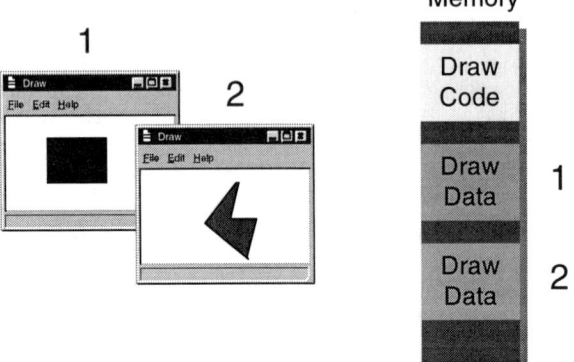

- If the user runs the same program more than once, Windows loads a unique copy of the program's data for each instance, but shares the code
- In 16-bit Windows, subsequent instances received a handle to the previous instance's data in the hPrevInstance argument. In Win32, hPrevInstance is always zero

In Windows, the user can run a program more than once -- we call each copy an instance. To save memory, Windows doesn't load a complete image of each instance into memory. Windows loads a single copy of the program's code, but creates a new set of data memory for each instance. That guarantees that the instances run independently of each other.

In Windows 3.x, the hPrevInstance argument to WinMain is a handle (pointer) to the previous instance's data memory -- if hPrevInstance is zero, there is no previous instance in memory. So conceivably, an instance of a Win16 program can read or write the data memory belonging to another instance. That works because Windows 3.x runs all Windows programs in a common address space.

But that can't happen in Win32, which runs all programs, even instances of the same program, in their own completely separate ad...

Lab Exercise 2: Complete Windows App

In this lab, you will write a simple yet complete Windows program. You will write the WinMain function and the window procedure.

You will also gain experience processing errors returned from system calls, as well as using the debugger.

To view the lab exercise instructions, press the "Lab Write Up" button. This will display the lab document and let you print it if you wish. When you are finished with the lab, continue to the next page to take a review quiz.

Review Quiz

Before you move on to the next chapter, you should test your comprehension of this chapter by taking the review quiz. The quiz assumes that you have already done the lab exercise.

The quiz will be displayed in a separate window so that you can page through the chapter to help you find the answers. In other words, this is an open book quiz!

After you have answered all of the questions, press the button at the bottom of the quiz window to see how you did. If you didn't score as well as you think you should, you should review the chapter before continuing on.

Chapter Summary

- Every Windows program needs a WinMain function that the loader calls when the program is loaded.

- WinMain typically calls RegisterClass to register one or more program-specific window classes, and then calls CreateWindow to create one or more windows based on the registered class(es).

- After creating a window or two, WinMain then enters a message loop, which dequeues messages and dispatches them to window procedures. The program stays in the message loop until GetMessage dequeues the WM_QUIT message, which usually happens when the user closes the program's last window.

Messages

Chapter 4: Messages

- The Message Data Structure
- Retrieving Messages
- Example: WM_LBUTTONDOWN
- Example: WM_SIZE
- Example: WM_TIMER
- Transmitting Messages
- Example: Sending a Message

4-0

What is a Message?

This page is a review from an earlier chapter. It reminds you that a message consists of an event, followed by a call to a window procedure.

In this chapter you will learn that there's also a data structure that describes the event -- when the event occurs, Windows builds the data structure and writes it into a message queue.

- Every window has an associated window procedure that Windows calls when the user interacts with the window
- This call to the window procedure is called a message -- Windows defines values with symbolic names for each kind of message

4-1

The Message Data Structure

```
typedef struct tagMSG
{
    HWND      hwnd;
    UINT      message;
    WPARAM    wParam;
    LPARAM    lParam;
    DWORD     time;
    POINT     pt;
} MSG, *PMSG;
```

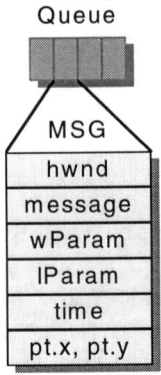

- Whenever an event occurs, Windows allocates and initializes a data structure that describes the event and inserts it into a program's message queue

- The contents of wParam and lParam are different for each kind of message

The message queue is actually a list of message data structures, each of which describes an event.

Windows defines a symbolic message ID for each kind of event that can occur. For example, WM_LBUTTONDOWN is the symbolic ID for the message generated when the user presses the left mouse button on the client area and WM_SIZE is the ID of the message generated when the user changes a window's size.

The wParam and lParam fields contain further information about the message. For example, if the message ID is WM_LBUTTONDOWN, lParam contains the coordinates of the mouse click. If the message ID is WM_SIZE, lParam contains the client area's new width and height. As you can see, the actual content of wParam and lParam depends on the message ID -- whenever you decide to process a message in your window procedure, you must look in a Windows prog...

Retrieving Messages

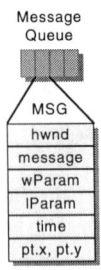

```
WinMain(...)
{
    MSG msg;

    while (GetMessage (...&msg..) )
        DispatchMessage ( &msg );
}
LRESULT WndProc ( HWND hwnd, UINT iMsg
                , WPARAM wParam
                , LPARAM lParam )
{

}
```

- Every Windows program contains a message loop that dequeues messages from the message queue and routes them to a window procedure
- DispatchMessage uses msg.hwnd to find the destination window procedure's address, then calls it, passing msg.hwnd, msg.message, msg.wParam and msg.lParam

GetMessage retrieves a message data structure from the program's message queue and then DispatchMessage calls the destination window procedure, passing the first four fields of the MSG data structure as arguments.

The message queue is actually ordered by message priority. For example, user-input messages such as WM_LBUTTONDOWN have a higher priority than WM_PAINT messages. All this really means is that if both kinds of messages are in the queue at the same time, GetMessage will dequeue the higher priority message first.

Notice that the window procedure does not receive the message time and point as arguments -- that's because most programs don't care about them. If you do care, you can retrieve them by calling GetMessageTime and GetMessagePos.

Example: WM_LBUTTONDOWN

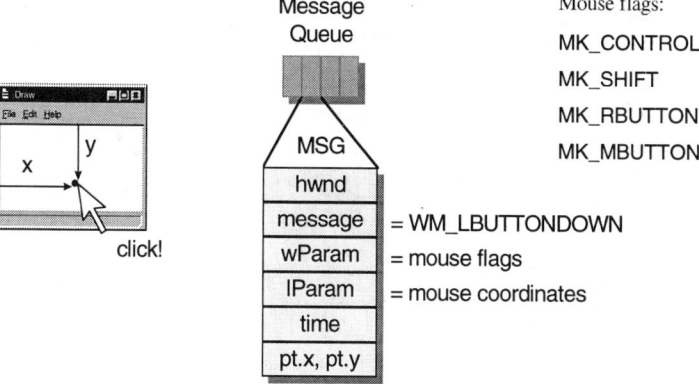

Let's now take a look at the WM_LBUTTONDOWN message. Remember that Windows passes the first four fields of the message data structure to the window procedure.

For WM_LBUTTONDOWN, the wParam field contains bit-flags that indicate if the user was pressing any keys while clicking or if the user pressed more than one mouse button at the same time. The flags are:

MK_CONTROL - user was pressing the control key
MK_SHIFT - the user was pressing the shift key
MK_RBUTTON - the user also was pressing the right mouse button
MK_MBUTTON - the user also was pressing the middle mouse button

You can ignore these flags if your program doesn't care about them.

The lParam field contains the mouse-click coordinates (x,y), each of which is a 16-bit pixe...

- When the user presses the left mouse button, Windows initializes a message data structure describing the event
- The coordinates of the mouse click are in pixels, relative to the client area's upper-left corner

---

WM_LBUTTONDOWN, Continued

```
LRESULT CALLBACK WndProc ( HWND hwnd, UINT iMsg
                         , WPARAM wParam, LPARAM lParam )
{
  switch ( iMsg )
  {
    case WM_LBUTTONDOWN:
    {
      POINT   pt;
      HDC     hdc;

      pt.x = LOWORD ( lParam );
      pt.y = HIWORD ( lParam );

      hdc = GetDC ( hwnd );
      TextOut ( hdc, pt.x, pt.y, "a", 1 );
      ReleaseDC ( hwnd, hdc );
    }
    return DefWindowProc ( hwnd, iMsg, wParam, lParam );
}
```

This is a fragment of a window procedure that responds to the WM_LBUTTONDOWN message.

As you saw on the last page, Windows packs the lParam of WM_LBUTTONDOWN with the mouse coordinates -- the least-significant 16 bits contain the x-coordinate, the most-significant 16 bits hold the y-coordinate. To help us extract the 16-bit values from the 32-bit lParam, the Windows header files define some handy macros -- LOWORD and HIWORD. The LOWORD macro extracts the bottom 16 bits from a 32-bit number, while HIWORD extracts the most-significant 16 bits. While it's certainly possible for you to write your own C code to extract the coordinates, we recommend that you use the macros; they make your code more readable and more portable.

This program calls the TextOut system call to display a singl...

- This program displays an "a" character at the coordinates where the user presses the left mouse button

Example: WM_SIZE

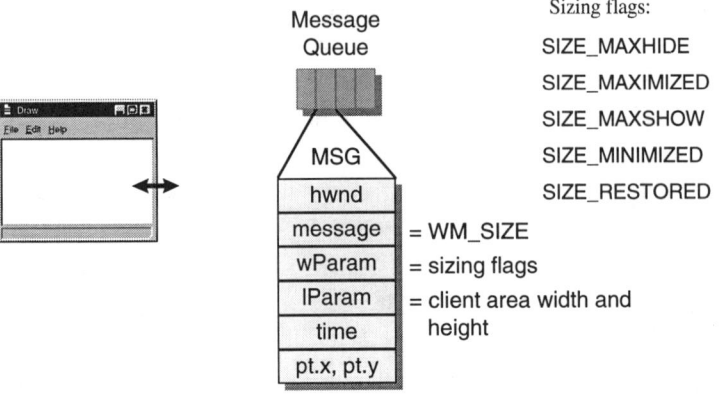

Sizing flags:

SIZE_MAXHIDE
SIZE_MAXIMIZED
SIZE_MAXSHOW
SIZE_MINIMIZED
SIZE_RESTORED

Now let's examine the WM_SIZE message, which Windows sends when a window's size changes. A program could use this message to scale its graphics to the new window size or to display a different amount of text.

The wParam field contains bit-flags that indicate the sizing operation:

SIZE_MAXHIDE - another window was maximized
SIZE_MAXIMIZED - this window was maximized
SIZE_MAXSHOW - another window was restored to its previous size
SIZE_MINIMIZED - this window was minimized
SIZE_RESTORED - this window was restored to its previous size

Many programs ignore the sizing flags completely.

The lParam field contains the client area's new width and height, both of which are 16-bit values. Windows packs the width into the least-significan...

- Whenever the user changes a window's size, Windows initializes a message data structure describing the event
- The client area width and height are in pixels

4-6

WM_SIZE, Continued

```
LRESULT CALLBACK WndProc ( HWND hwnd, UINT iMsg
                        , WPARAM wParam, LPARAM lParam )
{
  switch ( iMsg )
  {
    static  int nWidth, nHeight;

    case WM_SIZE:
      nWidth  = LOWORD ( lParam );
      nHeight = HIWORD ( lParam );
      return 0;

    case WM_PAINT:
    {
      PAINTSTRUCT    ps;
      char           sz[100];

      BeginPaint ( hwnd, &ps );
      sprintf ( sz, "width = %d, height = %d", nWidth, nHeight );
      TextOut ( ps.hdc, 0, 0, sz, strlen ( sz ) );
      EndPaint ( hwnd, &ps );
    }
    return 0;
}
```

This program fragment responds to the WM_SIZE message by extracting the client area's width and height and storing them in the nWidth and nHeight variables. The WM_PAINT message case then formats the width and height into a string, which it then displays with TextOut. So if you run this program, it will continually draw its current client area width and height in the client's upper left corner.

It's important to note that we used the C-language static keyword to define the width and height variables -- that ensures that the storage for the variables isn't discarded when the window procedure hits a return statement. Compilers typically allocate non-static variables on the stack when a procedure is called and then throw them away when the procedure returns -- that won't work here since we initialize the width and height variables in WM_SIZE and use them in ...

- This program displays the client area's width and height and updates it whenever the user changes the window's size

4-7

Example: WM_TIMER

`SetTimer ( hwnd, idTimer, nMilliseconds, pfnCallback )`

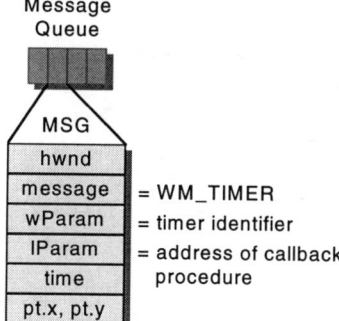

= WM_TIMER
= timer identifier
= address of callback procedure

- The SetTimer call causes Windows to periodically place a WM_TIMER message into the message queue
- Timer messages are not a very accurate measure of time, because the receiving window may not dequeue the time message right away

The next message we will examine is the WM_TIMER message, which lets a program respond to periodic events. For example, a graphical clock program might set up a timer to go off every second so it could move its second hand.

The SetTimer call lets you schedule the periodic event. Windows signals the event either by placing a WM_TIMER message in the window's message queue, or by calling the application-provided callback function. Since this chapter is on messages, we will ignore the callback feature for now and concentrate on the WM_TIMER message. To disable the callback feature, pass NULL for pfnCallback in the SetTimer call.

If a window starts multiple timers, it should give each a unique timer ID. When any timer goes off, Windows queues the WM_TIMER message and wParam contains the timer's ID so you can tell which timer expired. ...

4-8

WM_TIMER, Continued

```
const    int idTimer1 = 1;
const    int idTimer2 = 2;

switch ( iMsg )
{
  case WM_CREATE:
    SetTimer ( hwnd, idTimer1, 500, NULL );
    SetTimer ( hwnd, idTimer2, 100, NULL );
    return 0;

  case WM_TIMER:
  {
      POINT   pt;

      HDC hdc = GetDC ( hwnd );
      int     idTimer = LOWORD ( wParam );
      char    *psz;
      if ( idTimer == idTimer1 ) psz = "1"; else psz = "2";

      pt.x = rand() % nWidth; pt.y = rand() % nHeight;
      TextOut ( hdc, pt.x, pt.y, psz, 1 );
      ReleaseDC ( hwnd, hdc );
  }
  return 0;
```

- This program displays characters periodically at random locations in the client area

This program starts two timers; one with an ID of 1 and an interval of 1/2 second, the other with an ID of 2 and interval of 1/10 of a second. We start the timers in the window procedure's WM_CREATE message. The Full Sample Source listing shows that we stop the timers in the the window procedure's WM_DESTROY message by calling KillTimer on each ID.

In the WM_TIMER message, we initialize a string pointer to point one of two strings, depending on which timer clicked off. We then use the C-language rand function to calculate a random coordinate for displaying the string. We use the modulus operator to ensure that the coordinate is within the bounds of the client area.

The nWidth and nHeight variables contain the client area's width and height -- they are initialized in the WM_SIZE message case, which is not ...

4-9

Transmitting Messages

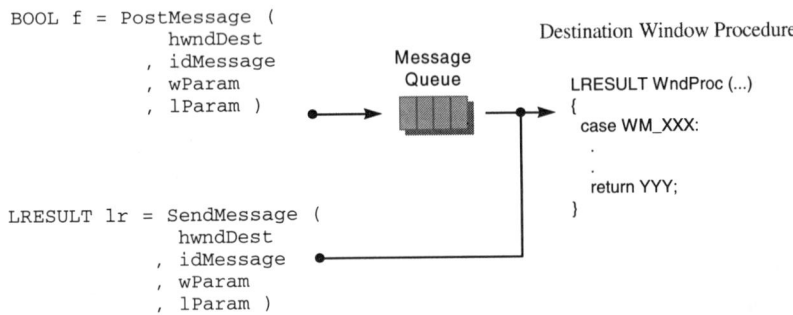

- A program can transmit a message to itself or another window procedure by calling SendMessage or PostMessage
- For example, if the user clicks the mouse on a button, the button transmits WM_COMMAND to its parent window
- PostMessage queues a message data structure, while SendMessage acts like a direct call to the destination window procedure

Transmitting messages is a very common programming technique in Windows. You will learn much more about messaging with predefined window classes such as buttons, edit boxes and list boxes when you study the chapters on dialog controls.

Transmitting a message is the opposite of receiving a message -- when you receive a message, Windows passes you the message ID and the message parameters. You must then unpack the message parameters. When you transmit a message, you must supply the message ID and package the message parameters for the recipient. To make that easier, the Windows header files have macros to help you construct message parameters, for example, MAKELONG, which builds a 32-bit number from two 16-bit numbers. You will see an example in a page or two.

There are two different ways to transmit a message -- sending and posting. When you post ...

Messaging with Other Windows

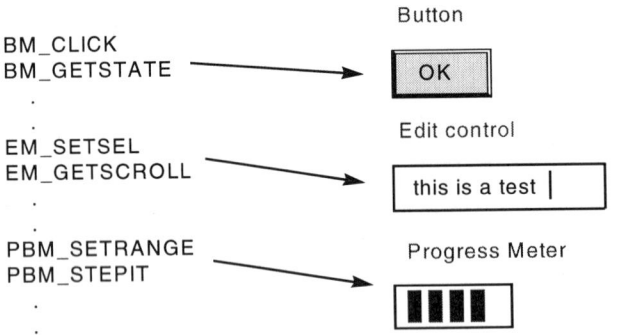

- Most predefined window classes respond to special control messages that let a program control their behavior
- Many predefined window classes generate notification messages to inform the parent window of significant events (for example, mouse clicks)

This page shows only a few of the types of windows that Windows provides. We will cover many of them in more detail in later chapters.

The developer of a window class like a button writes the window procedure so that it recognizes messages from other windows. These messages, called control messages, are typically used to interact with the child windows found on dialog boxes. For example, a dialog box procedure might send the EM_SETSEL message to an edit box window to pre-select the text in the edit box.

Notice that each kind of window has its own set of messages that it recognizes -- and there are more messages for each control than shown here! Refer to your Windows programming reference for a list of all of the messages for each window class. The messages are specific to each window class. For example, ...

Example: Sending a Message

```
case WM_CREATE:
  {
    hwndProgress = CreateWindowEx ( 0, PROGRESS_CLASS
        , NULL, WS_CHILD | WS_VISIBLE
        , 10, 10, 200, 50, hwnd, 0, hInst, NULL );

    LPARAM lp = MAKELONG ( 0, 100 );

    SendMessage ( hwndProgress, PBM_SETRANGE
        , 0              // unused (wParam)
        , lp );          // range (lParam)

    SendMessage ( hwndProgress, PBM_SETSTEP
        , 10             // step increment (wParam)
        , 0 );           // unused (lParam)
  }
  return 0;
```

- This program creates a child progress window and updates it periodically
- The progress window class is a predefined window class that responds to messages like PBM_SETRANGE

This code fragment shows creating a progress meter window as a child and then initializing it by sending messages to it. See the Full Sample Source for the rest of the code.

A progress window is a good way to show the user the progress of an operation, say downloading a file. The window draws a series of boxes as each increment of the job is finished. Actually, the progress window doesn't know what the program is doing at all -- it simply responds to messages that initialize the progress window and messages that tell the progress window that an increment is finished.

In WM_CREATE, this program first calls CreateWindowEx to create the progress window as a child of the main window. There are a lot of arguments to this call, but the most important (for now) are the second, which specifies the window class, the fourth, which specifies the new window's style, and the next ...

Lab Exercise 3: Messages

In this lab, you gain experience receiving messages in a window procedure and sending messages to a child window.

To view the lab exercise instructions, press the "Lab Write Up" button. This will display the lab document and let you print it if you wish. When you are finished with the lab, continue to the next page to take a review quiz.

Review Quiz

Before you move on to the next chapter, you should test your comprehension of this chapter by taking the review quiz. The quiz assumes that you have already done the lab exercise.

The quiz will be displayed in a separate window so that you can page through the chapter to help you find the answers. In other words, this is an open book quiz!

After you have answered all of the questions, press the button at the bottom of the quiz window to see how you did. If you didn't score as well as you think you should, you should review the chapter before continuing on.

Chapter Summary

- Windows programs communicate with other windows (and themselves) by transmitting messages -- a message consists of a data structure describing an event and a call to a window procedure.

- The message data structure that describes a message contains the destination window's handle, the message identifier and two message parameters -- wParam and lParam.

- Windows provides two ways to transmit messages -- posting a message enqueues a message data structure into a message queue, while sending a message bypasses the message queue and directly calls a window procedure.

Chapter 5: Icons

- Creating an Icon
- What is a Resource?
- Writing a Resource File
- Loading an Icon

What is an Icon?

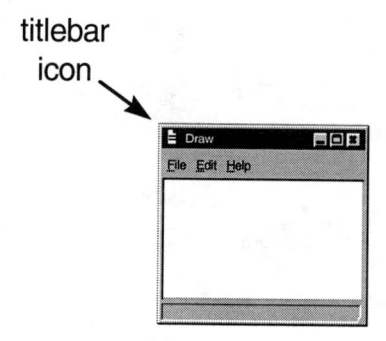

titlebar icon →

- An icon is a small picture that represents a program or a window
- Windows programs can bind the icon's data into the .EXE file

Icons are actually a kind of bitmap -- they differ from bitmaps in that they can have transparent areas (bitmaps always obscure whatever is underneath them). In this chapter, you will learn how to associate an icon with a program.

Different version of Windows use program icons in different ways. In Windows 3.x and Windows NT 3.x, you see a program's icon if you minimize the program. You also see the icon if you install the program as a Program Manager item, or if you display the directory containing the EXE file in the File Manager.

In later versions, such as Windows 95, you see the icon displayed in the window's upper-left corner, as well as in the taskbar. You also see the icon in the Explorer or if you install the program in the Start menu.

Creating an Icon

To create an icon, you can use an icon editor that comes with your compiler. The icon editor lets you draw your icon, and then save the icon's data in a file.

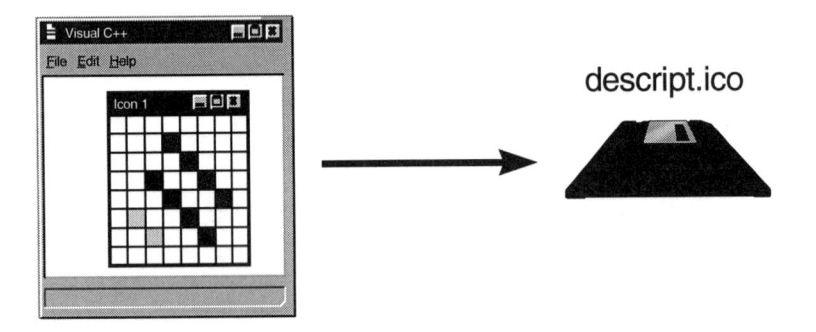

- Most Windows development environments contain a tool that lets you draw an icon and save its data in a file

5-2

What is a Resource?

Most Windows programs define their icons, menus and dialogs in a resource file that you compile separately from the program's source code. Since menus and dialogs contain text, by defining them in a separate file, you avoid recompiling the entire program if you change the text, perhaps translating it to another language.

An .RC file is a text file that you can create with your normal program editor -- you will examine one on the next page. Alternatively, your compiler might contain a tool to interactively generate the .RC file for you. The .RES file is a compiled version of the resources; it's a binary file.

Your Windows development environment contains the resource compiler that compiles the .RC file into the binary .RES file. In Win16, you then need to run the resource compiler again to bind the resources to the .EXE -- in ...

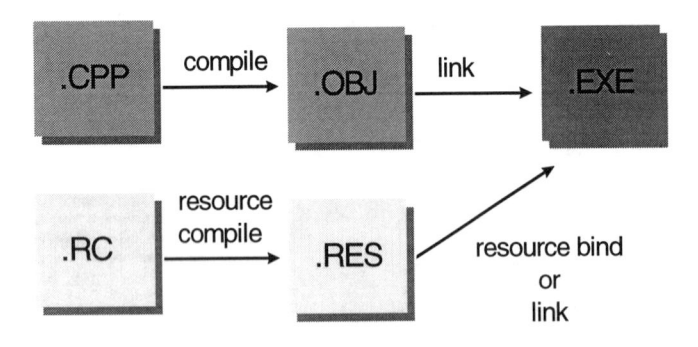

- A resource is a set of data that's compiled separately from a program's source -- for example, icons, menus and dialogs
- By defining the resources in a separate file, you make it easier to translate text resources to other national languages

5-3

Writing a Resource File

TEMPLATE.RC

```
#include <windows.h>
#include "resource.h"

IDI_MYICON   ICON   descript.ico
```

- An .RC file lists the resources that will be bound into the .EXE -- in this case, just an icon
- For each resource, you list the resource ID (IDI_MYICON), the resource type (ICON) followed by resource-specific syntax -- in this case, the icon's file name
- Some development environments, for example Visual C++, will write the resource file for you!

This is a simple resource file that defines only one resource -- an icon. The syntax of the icon statement is the icon's ID, here a symbolic constant, the keyword ICON and the name of the file that contains the icon's data. The icon file name can specify a full path name, so you can reference icon files from other directories.

You can define more than one icon in an RC file, but each icon needs a unique ID.

The icon ID can either be a number or a string. The resource compiler first looks for a #define for that symbol, and substitutes a numeric value if it finds one. If there is no #define, the resource compiler assumes that the symbol is a string. You will see in a moment that a program can load an icon using either an icon string or an icon numeric ID. Here we have defined the numeric icon ID in a header file named RESOURCE.H that we include into the RC file.

Using numeric IDs saves a li...

Resource Identifiers

RESOURCE.H

```
#define IDI_MYICON 100
```

TEMPLATE.CPP

```
#include "resource.h"
.
.
.
```

TEMPLATE.RC

```
#include <windows.h>
#include "resource.h"

IDI_MYICON   ICON   descript.ico
```

- You can assign a symbolic ID name for each resource -- it's best to define the IDs in a separate header file so you can refer to them in the .CPP source file, too
- Windows also allows resources to have string names instead of numeric IDs, but the string names are slightly less efficient

This figure shows three of the files used by a program that uses an icon resource. The RESOURCE.H header file contains symbolic constants, TEMPLATE.CPP is the program's source, and TEMPLATE.RC defines the program's resources, in this case, an icon. We include the header file into both the program source and the resource file so that both can refer to the icon using its symbolic ID.

Visual C++ will create both the .RC and RESOURCE.H files for you -- just tell VC++ that you wish to create a new "Resource Script". You can then add an icon to the script and edit the icon. When you choose Save from the File menu, VC++ will create the .RC and .H files for you. If you wish to edit an existing script, you can open .RC file in VC++ and edit existing resources or add new ones.

The traditional name for the ...

Loading an Icon

TEMPLATE.CPP

```
if (!hPrevInstance)
{
       .
       .
       .
  wndclass.hIcon = LoadIcon ( hInstance
                    , MAKEINTRESOURCE ( IDI_MYICON ));
       .
       .
       .
  if ( !RegisterClass ( &wndclass ) )
      return 0;
}
```

- You can associate an icon with all windows of a class by loading the icon when you register the window class
- The MAKEINTRESOURCE macro converts the numeric ID to the string resource format that LoadIcon expects

5-6

This code fragment is taken from a program's WinMain.

When you register a window class, you specify the icon to be used for windows of this class by setting the WNDCLASS structure's hIcon field to the icon handle. You can retrieve the icon handle by calling the LoadIcon system call.

LoadIcon expects a string for the second argument, but if you have defined the icon with a numeric ID, you can use the MAKEINTRESOURCE macro, which casts the numeric value to a string.

The first argument to LoadIcon specifies the instance handle of the module to which the icon resource is bound. In this example, we specified hInstance, which the loader passes to WinMain -- in other words, we are loading the icon from the current instance's executeable file. That works fine because this program's makefile binds the .RES file to the .EXE.

Lab Exercise 4: Icons

In this lab, you gain experience creating an icon and associating it with a window class.

To view the lab exercise instructions, press the "Lab Write Up" button. This will display the lab document and let you print it if you wish. When you are finished with the lab, continue to the next page to take a review quiz.

Review Quiz

Before you move on to the next chapter, you should test your comprehension of this chapter by taking the review quiz. The quiz assumes that you have already done the lab exercise.

The quiz will be displayed in a separate window so that you can page through the chapter to help you find the answers. In other words, this is an open book quiz!

After you have answered all of the questions, press the button at the bottom of the quiz window to see how you did. If you didn't score as well as you think you should, you should review the chapter before continuing on.

Chapter Summary

- Windows programs can define resources, which are blocks of data, such as icons, bitmaps, menus and dialogs. You define the resources in a .RC file rather than the program's source.
- The resource compiler translates the text-file .RC into a binary file that we then bind to the .EXE or a .DLL.
- A Windows program can specify the icon for all windows of a class by loading the icon when the program registers the window class.

Chapter 6: The Graphical Device Interface

- What is a Device Context?
- GDI Drawing Objects
- Drawing Lines
- Drawing Rectangles
- Drawing Text

What is the Graphical Device Interface?

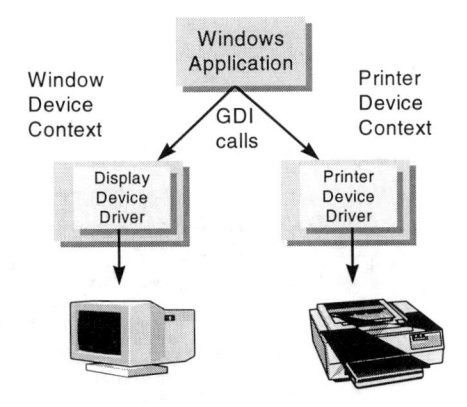

- The graphical device interface (GDI) provides Windows programs with a device-independent interface to graphical output devices such as a display window or a printer
- GDI contains commands to draw lines, rectangles, text, bitmaps, metafiles and so on

Performing graphical output under Windows is much different than in MS-DOS programs. Since MS-DOS provides no built-in graphics calls, each program must "roll their own" graphics. That means that DOS programs must be able to detect different kinds of displays and printers, since each output device has it's own specific command set for graphics.

In contrast, in Windows, the application program doesn't need to worry about which display or printer the user has connected. Instead, the Windows application program calls generic GDI output commands -- these commands are intercepted by a system-level device driver that translates the commands to device-specific output. Of course, for this to work, the user must install the correct device driver for their display and printers.

Windows programs do not in...

What is a Device Context?

```
LineTo ( hdc, 10, 10 );
```

Drawing Attributes

Attribute	Used By:	Default Value
current position	lines	(0,0)
font	text	system font
text color	text	black
mapping mode	all	MM_TEXT
pen	lines	BLACK_PEN
brush	rectangles	WHITE_BRUSH

Device Context

hdc → Device Driver Instance

Current Drawing Attributes

- The device context presents an abstraction of an output device and acts as a target for GDI calls
- The device context is the repository for drawing attributes, such as the current position, text color and so on

A device context is a chunk of memory that represents an output device, such as a display window or a printer. The device context acts as a connection to the device driver and also stores a set of drawing attributes, such as text color, font and so forth. When you issue a GDI call such as LineTo, the device driver queries the current attributes from the DC to perform the output. For example, LineTo uses the current position from the DC as the starting point of its line.

When a program requests a device context, Windows returns a DC handle. At this point, Windows also sets all of the attributes in the device context to the default values shown in the table.

Since a device context occupies memory, it must be allocated and deallocated. Windows handles the low-level memory management, but programs must tell Windows when they are finished with a device context so Windows can ma...

6-2

Drawing to a Window

DRAW.CPP

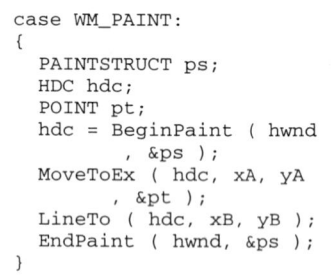

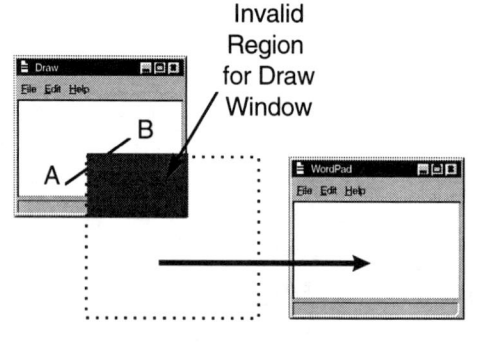

```
case WM_PAINT:
{
  PAINTSTRUCT ps;
  HDC hdc;
  POINT pt;
  hdc = BeginPaint ( hwnd
          , &ps );
  MoveToEx ( hdc, xA, yA
          , &pt );
  LineTo ( hdc, xB, yB );
  EndPaint ( hwnd, &ps );
}
```

Invalid Region for Draw Window

- Whenever Windows determines that any portion of a window needs refreshing, Windows queues a WM_PAINT message
- In WM_PAINT, the window procedure must restore the window's contents

In the figure, the user has moved the WordPad window so it no longer overlays the Draw window. This leaves a portion of the draw window (shown here in red) that the Draw window needs to refresh. We say that the Draw window is invalid when this happens.

Whenever a window has an invalid region, Windows enqueues a WM_PAINT message in the window's message queue. In response to WM_PAINT, this program calls BeginPaint to retrieve a window device context handle and then draws a line from point A to point B. Don't worry too much about syntax here -- we will cover lines in more detail in a moment.

BeginPaint not only retrieves a window device context handle, it also:

1. Sends the window a WM_ERASEBACKGROUND message, which you normall...

6-3

The Window Coordinate System

DRAW.CPP

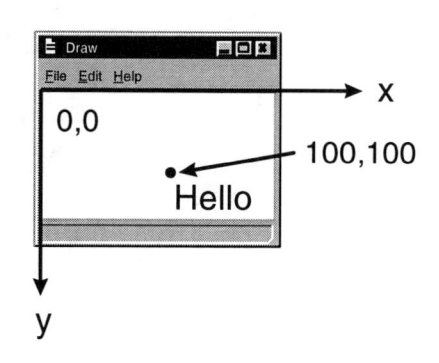

```
case WM_PAINT:
{
  PAINTSTRUCT ps;
  HDC hdc;
  hdc = BeginPaint ( hwnd
         , &ps );
  TextOut ( hdc, 100, 100
         , "Hello", 5 );
  EndPaint ( hwnd, &ps );
}
```

- By default, a window's coordinate system uses pixel units with the origin in the client area's upper left
- This is called the MM_TEXT mapping mode, because it works the same way English-speakers read text (from left-to-right and from top-to-bottom)

Each window has a default coordinate system whose origin is in the upper-left corner of the client area. Also by default, x coordinates grow larger to the right, while y coordinates grow larger downwards.

This default coordinate system is called the MM_TEXT mapping mode. We will discuss other coordinate systems in a later chapter.

This program draws the string "Hello" at coordinates 100, 100. Windows uses the coordinates to position the upper-left corner of the string.

If a program uses coordinates for text or graphics that are larger than the client area width or height, Windows discards the output. In other words, Windows clips the output to the boundaries of the client area.

6-4

GDI Drawing Objects

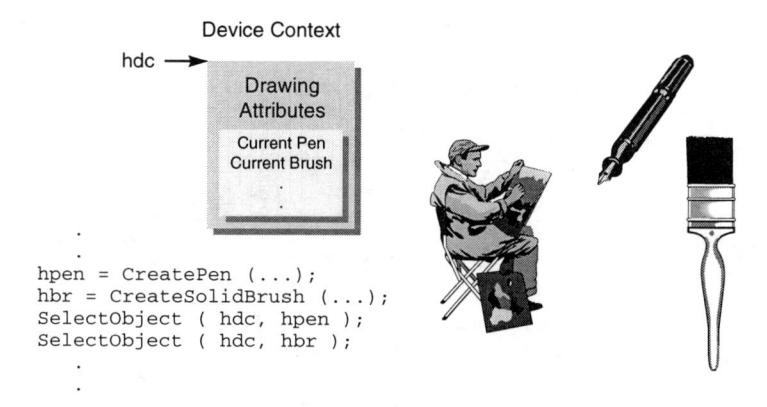

```
hpen = CreatePen (...);
hbr = CreateSolidBrush (...);
SelectObject ( hdc, hpen );
SelectObject ( hdc, hbr );
```

- GDI uses the notion of drawing objects to model the way a human artist works -- GDI lets you create pens, brushes and so on
- A newly-created device context contains default drawing objects, but you can create your own and select them into the device context

To understand how GDI drawing objects work, think about how a human artist draws a picture. An artist might first draw the outline of a figure with a marker pen, and then use a paintbrush to fill in the inside of the figure.

The artist may have several marker pens, each in a different width and color. But most artists only draw with one hand at a time! So to draw with a different pen, the artist must first put down the pen they are holding, and pick up another one.

Similarly, most artists use only one brush at a time, putting down the current brush whenever they decide to select a new one.

GDI works in a similar fashion. At any given instant, a device context can hold one pen object, one brush object, one font object and so on. A program can create as many of the objects of each kind a...

6-5

Drawing Lines

DRAW.CPP

```
case WM_PAINT:
{
    PAINTSTRUCT ps;
    HDC hdc;
    POINT pt;
    hdc = BeginPaint ( hwnd
           , &ps );
    MoveToEx ( hdc, 100, 200
           , &pt );
    LineTo ( hdc, 300, 400 );
    EndPaint ( hwnd, &ps );
}
```

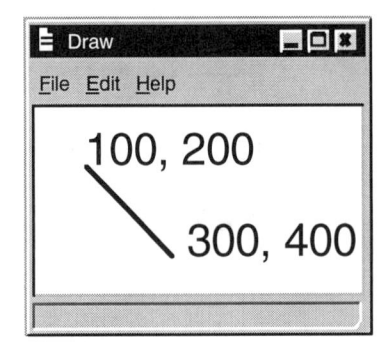

To draw a line, you first set the current position in the device context by calling MoveToEx and then draw the line to the specified end point by calling LineTo.

LineTo draws the line uses the pen that's currently selected into the DC. The pen's attributes include its width, its style and its color. We discuss pens on the next page.

LineTo also sets the current position to the specified endpoint, so if you want to draw two connected lines, you only have to call MoveToEx for the first.

- The LineTo call draws a line from the current position in the device context to the specified endpoint
- The LineTo call uses the currently-selected pen to draw the line

6-6

Creating and Selecting a Pen

```
HPEN hpen, hpenOld;
hpen = CreatePen ( PS_SOLID
       , 1, RGB (0,255,0) );
hpenOld = (HPEN) SelectObject ( hdc
       , hpen );

MoveToEx ( hdc, 100, 200
       , &pt );
LineTo ( hdc, 300, 400 );

SelectObject ( hdc, hpenOld );
DeleteObject ( hpen );
```

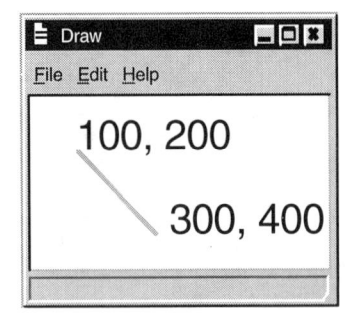

This program first creates a pen object and stores its handle in the hpen variable. The arguments for CreatePen are the pen's style, its width in pixels, and its color. The program then selects the new pen into the device context, displacing the previously-selected pen, whose handle is stored in the hpenOld variable. The program then draws a line using the new pen. To clean up, the program deselects the custom pen and calls DeleteObject to free its memory.

The CreatePen call accepts various styles for the new pen, PS_SOLID, PS_DASHED and so forth. The second argument specifes the pen's width in logical units, which are pixels unless you change the mapping mode. CreatePen has one quirk -- the width argument must be one for all line styles except for PS_SOLID.
To specify colors, GDI us...

- The CreatePen call creates a logical pen in the specified color and width -- to use the pen you must select it into the DC
- A program can create many pens, but only use one at a time
- To prevent memory leaks, you should delete the pen before the program exits -- but you cannot delete a selected pen!

6-7

The Graphical Device Interface

Drawing Rectangles

DRAW.CPP

```
case WM_PAINT:
{
  PAINTSTRUCT ps;
  HDC hdc;
  hdc = BeginPaint ( hwnd
        , &ps );
  Rectangle ( hdc, 100, 200
        , 300, 400 );
  EndPaint ( hwnd, &ps );
}
```

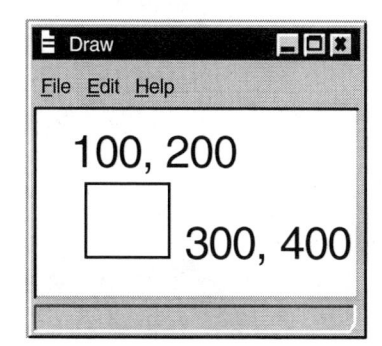

You can use the Rectangle call to draw a box on the screen by supplying the coordinates of the rectangle's upper-left corner and lower-right corner. The Rectangle call neither uses nor changes the current position stored in the device context.

The Rectangle call uses the currently-selected pen to draw the rectangle's outline and uses the currently selected drawing brush to fill the interior. A brush's attributes include the fill color and fill pattern, for example, cross-hatching.

Since this program changes neither the pen or the brush, it will use the default attributes, which are a black, solid pen and a white, solid fill pattern for the brush.

- The Rectangle call uses the currently-selected pen to draw the outline of the rectangle and the currently-selected brush to fill the interior

6-8

Creating and Selecting a Brush

```
HBRUSH hbr, hbrOld;
hpen = CreateSolidBrush (
      , RGB (0,0,255 ) );
hbrOld = (HBRUSH) SelectObject ( hdc
      , hbr );

Rectangle ( hdc, 100, 200, 300, 400 );

SelectObject ( hdc, hbrOld );
DeleteObject ( hbr );
```

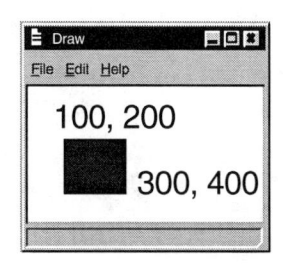

In this example, we create and select a blue solid brush and then draw the same rectangle as on the last page. Since we didn't change the pen, the Rectangle call uses the default black pen. We then must deselect the brush and delete it in the same way we do for all GDI objects.

To fill the interior with a cross-hatching rather than a solid color, call CreateHatchedBrush instead of CreateSolidBrush. To fill the interior with a repeating pattern, call CreatePatternBrush, which requires you to provide a bitmap containing the pattern to repeat.

If you want to draw a transparent rectangle whose interior doesn't obscure what's behind it, you can call GetStockObject to retrieve a handle to a NULL_BRUSH, which you must then select into the DC before drawing the rectangle. Unlike custom bru...

- The CreateSolidBrush call creates a logical brush in the specified color -- to use it, you must select it into the DC
- You can also call CreatePatternBrush or CreateHatchedBrush
- A program can create many brushes, but only use one at a time
- To prevent memory leaks, you should delete the brush before the program exits -- but you cannot delete a selected brush!

6-9

Drawing Text

DRAW.CPP

```
case WM_PAINT:
{
  PAINTSTRUCT ps;
  HDC hdc;
  hdc = BeginPaint ( hwnd
          , &ps );
  TextOut ( hdc, 100, 200
          , "Hello", 5 );
  EndPaint ( hwnd, &ps );
}
```

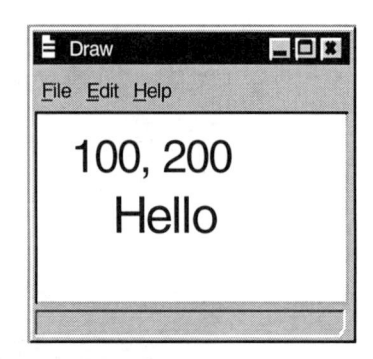

- Windows provides several calls to draw text, including TextOut, ExtTextOut and DrawText
- Each call uses the currently selected font to draw the text
- You can modify text attributes with SetTextColor, SetTextAlign and so on

This program calls TextOut to draw some text using the default font. The arguments for TextOut are the destination DC handle, the x and y coordinates, a pointer to the string, and the string's length.

TextOut is probably the simplest of the text-display calls, but the least powerful. ExtTextOut, for example, lets you pass a rectangle that the call uses to pre-erase and/or clip. Another powerful text-output call is DrawText, which also accepts a rectangle and can even perform word-wrapping.

By default, TextOut interprets the coordinates as the upper-left coordinate of the text, but you can change this by calling SetTextAlign before drawing the text. For example, you might want to draw the text on a baseline -- if so, call SetTextAlign (hdc, TA_BASELINE).

The default text color is black, but you can change it by calling SetTextColor before drawing the text. For exampl...

Creating and Selecting a Font

```
HFONT hfont, hfontOld;
hfont = CreateFont ( 100
        , 0, 0, 0, 0, 0
        , 0, 0, 0, 0, 0, 0
        , "Times New Roman" );

hfontOld = (HFONT)SelectObject (
          hdc
        , hfont );
TextOut ( hdc, 100, 200
        , "Hello", 5 );
SelectObject ( hdc, hfontOld );
DeleteObject ( hfont );
```

- The CreateFont call creates a logical font with the specified attributes -- to use the font, you must first select it
- To prevent memory leaks, you should delete the font before the program exits -- but you cannot delete a selected font!

This program creates a GDI font object, selects it into a device context, draws some text using the font, and then cleans up.

In the CreateFont call, the first argument specifies the font's height in logical units, which are in pixels, if you don't change the mapping mode. Here we create a font with a height of 100 logical units. The font height is sometimes called the "em" height, which is approximately the height of an upper-case "M" character. The second argument of CreateFont is the character width -- since we passed zero, Windows will calculate the normal width of characters, based on the height.

The last argument of CreateFont specifies the font's name string, in this case, "Times New Roman" which is a True Type font provided by Windows. We passed zero for all of the other arguments to accept their defaults, for exa...

Lab Exercise 5: GDI

In this lab, you gain experience creating and selecting fonts, pens and brushes. You will also learn more about text handling under Windows.

To view the lab exercise instructions, press the "Lab Write Up" button. This will display the lab document and let you print it if you wish. When you are finished with the lab, continue to the next page to take a review quiz.

Review Quiz

Before you move on to the next chapter, you should test your comprehension of this chapter by taking the review quiz. The quiz assumes that you have already done the lab exercise.

The quiz will be displayed in a separate window so that you can page through the chapter to help you find the answers. In other words, this is an open book quiz!

After you have answered all of the questions, press the button at the bottom of the quiz window to see how you did. If you didn't score as well as you think you should, you should review the chapter before continuing on.

Chapter Summary

- The graphical device interface (GDI) presents Windows programs with a device-independent interface to graphical output devices, such as a display window or a printer. In other words, you can execute the same output commands to display text and graphics on a printer or in a window.

- Every window must be prepared to redraw its window whenever any part of the window is invalid. Windows pass the window procedure the WM_PAINT message to notify the window procedure that it must repaint its window.

- GDI uses pens, brushes and logical fonts as abstractions of their real-world counterparts. A program can create custom pens, brushes and fonts, but must select them into the device context be they can be used. The program must be sure to delete the drawing objects before the program exits.

Chapter 7: Painting a Window

- ◆ Types of Device Contexts
- ◆ What is a Mapping Mode?
- ◆ Visible and Update Regions
- ◆ The WM_PAINT Message
- ◆ Forcing a WM_PAINT Message

What is the Graphical Device Interface?

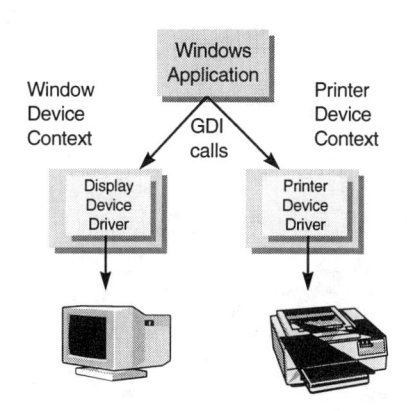

This page is a review from Chapter 6. It is included here to remind you of the basic architecture that Windows programs use to perform graphical output. In this chapter, we will concentrate on the display device.

The key point is that a Windows application must create a device context for an output device, and then can then direct GDI calls to that device context. The device driver converts the generic GDI commands to device-specific output.

- The graphical device interface (GDI) provides Windows programs with a device-independent interface to graphical output devices such as a display window or a printer
- GDI contains commands to draw lines, rectangles, text, bitmaps, metafiles and so on

What is a Device Context?

```
LineTo ( hdc, 10, 10 );
```

Drawing Attributes

Attribute	Used By:	Default Value
current position	lines	(0,0)
font	text	system font
text color	text	black
mapping mode	all	MM_TEXT
pen	lines	BLACK_PEN
brush	rectangles	WHITE_BRUSH

Device Context

hdc → Device Driver Instance

Current Drawing Attributes

Like the last page, this page is a review from Chapter 6, included here to remind you of the essential features of the device context.

The device context acts as a connection to a device driver and also stores a set of drawing attributes, such as color that are used by the GDI commands.

In this chapter, we will take a closer look at the device context for a display window.

- The device context presents an abstraction of an output device and acts as a target for GDI calls
- The device context is the repository for drawing attributes, such as the current position, text color and so on

7-2

Types of Device Contexts

Class Style	Notes
none	Windows of a class with no special style share device contexts from a cache.
CS_OWNDC	Windows allocates each window its own private DC.
CS_CLASSDC	Windows allocates a single DC for all windows based on this class.
CS_PARENTDC	Only for child windows -- when a child asks for a DC, Windows retrieves the DC last used by its parent. Since the DC is already initialized, retrieving the DC is fast, but it does allow a child to inadvertently paint over its parent.

This page lists the most commonly used kinds of window device contexts. Click on each for a brief description. The basic choice concerns how many windows will use the DC – whether the DC comes from a pre-allocated cache or is allocated especially for the window.

You specify the class style when you register a window class. These DC-specific class styles are mutually exclusive -- choose at most one. After registering, when your program requests a DC, Windows examines the class style and returns a handle for the appropriate type of DC.

The two most common styles are none and CS_OWNDC. We will cover those in more detail in the following pages.

When we say that Window's programs don't paint very often, we mean that Windows programs don't spend much time in the WM_PAINT mess...

- A DC is a chunk of memory that Windows allocates from the program's heap
- Since Windows programs don't paint very often, it's memory-efficient to share DCs

Note: Windows programs can also retrieve a window DC to draw on the non-client parts of a window

7-3

DC Memory Allocation (Win32)

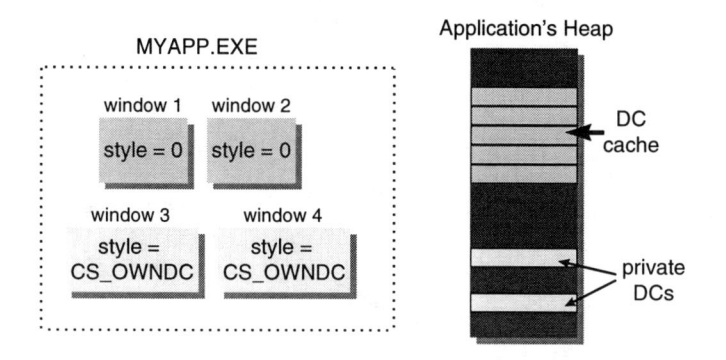

The picture on this page shows a sample Windows application that creates four windows -- two with no special class style, and two with the CS_OWNDC style. The right side of the picture shows what the application's memory heap looks like after each of its windows has painted.

Whenever a Windows program starts up, Windows allocates and initializes a small number of device contexts. This is referred to as the DC cache. Since the DCs in the cache are already allocated by the time a window procedure asks for them, the calls to retrieve them are quite fast. If a program requests more DCs than are preallocated, Windows must expand the cache by allocating additional device contexts, which can be slow. Thus, for best performance, each window should request and release cache DCs within a single message -- that way, the cache will always have an available DC.

In contrast, if a window class...

- If a window class specifies no special class style regarding DCs, all windows of that class in a program share DCs from the DC cache
- Since Windows preallocates and initializes the DC cache, retrieving them is fast
- When a CS_OWNDC window first asks for a DC, Windows must allocate and initialize the private DC for that window

7-4

Using a DC from the Cache

```
wndclass.style = 0;
   .
   .
case WM_PAINT:
  {
    PAINTSTRUCT ps;
    HDC hdc = BeginPaint ( hwnd, &ps );

    // set DC attributes
    // draw the window

    EndPaint ( hwnd, &ps );
  }
  return 0;
```

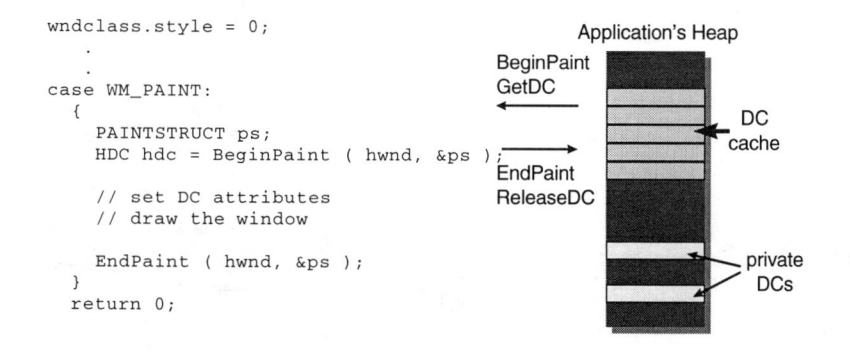

In this code fragment, we register the window class with no special class style, so windows of that class will use DCs from the cache. In the WM_PAINT message, we call BeginPaint, which retrieves a DC from the cache and stores its handle in the hdc variable. After drawing, the program then calls EndPaint, which releases the DC back to the cache – at this point, Windows sets all of the attributes in the DC back to their default values, but doesn't deallocate the DC's memory.

Using DCs from the cache is the proper technique if your program will create many windows, especially if the windows don't need to set a lot of drawing attributes. Each window procedure requests a DC from the cache whenever it needs to draw to the window, and releases it when finished drawing. The window procedure should not hold the device context from one message to the next -- the ru...

- Cache DCs use memory efficiently -- the disadvantage is that EndPaint and ReleaseDC reset the DC's attributes -- the window procedure needs to re-establish any attributes each time it retrieves a DC handle
- Since the cache is shared, each window should retrieve and release a DC within the same message -- or else a memory leak could occur

7-5

Using a Private DC

```
wndclass.style = CS_OWNDC;
    .
    .
static HDC hdc;
    .
    .
case WM_CREATE:
    hdc = GetDC ( hwnd );
    // set DC attributes
    return 0;
case WM_DESTROY:
    ReleaseDC ( hwnd, hdc );
    return 0;
case WM_PAINT:
    {
    PAINTSTRUCT ps;
    BeginPaint ( hwnd, &ps );
    // draw the window
    EndPaint ( hwnd, &ps );
    }
    return 0;
```

Application's Heap

DC cache

BeginPaint
GetDC

EndPaint
ReleaseDC

private DCs

- A private DC is owned by a single window -- the DC's attributes stay set unless that window changes them
- Disadvantage -- the DC occupies memory (800+ bytes) even when the window isn't using it

7-6

In this program, we register with the CS_OWNDC style, which informs Windows that we want each window of the class to have a separately allocated DC, referred to as a private DC. In the WM_CREATE message, we call GetDC. At this point, Windows allocates the memory for the DC and returns its handle. Windows allocates the DC from the program's available storage, called the heap. We store the handle in a static variable so we can use it in other messages.

In WM_DESTROY, we call ReleaseDC to tell windows it's OK to get rid of the DC's storage.

In WM_PAINT, a window still needs to call BeginPaint even though it is using a private DC -- BeginPaint performs some other critical processing that we will discuss later in the chapter. BeginPaint also is smart enough not to retrieve a DC from the cache when the window has the CS_OWNDC class style. ¡˝¡˝Private D...

What is a Mapping Mode?

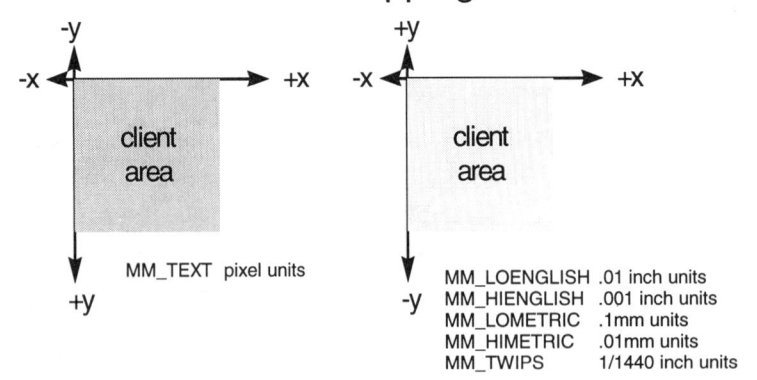

-y
-x ← → +x
client area
MM_TEXT pixel units
+y

+y
-x ← → +x
client area
-y
MM_LOENGLISH .01 inch units
MM_HIENGLISH .001 inch units
MM_LOMETRIC   .1mm units
MM_HIMETRIC   .01mm units
MM_TWIPS   1/1440 inch units

- The mapping mode converts the coordinates a program uses (logical units) into device units and sets the Y-axis orientation
- The default mapping mode is MM_TEXT, where logical units are the same as device units (pixels for a display)
- Note: there are two more mapping modes not shown: MM_ISOTROPIC and MM_ANISOTROPIC

7-7

The mapping mode defines how Windows interprets the coordinates that a program uses in GDI calls. The mapping mode is an attribute stored in the device context -- a window can change it by calling SetMapMode. When you retrieve a fresh DC, Windows sets the mapping mode to MM_TEXT.

The mapping mode controls two things: how Windows interprets the coordinates you pass to GDI calls and the orientation of the Y axis. For private and cached DCs, the coordinate-system origin is always in the client area's upper-left corner.

In the default MM_TEXT mapping mode, Windows interprets all coordinates as device units, which are pixels for the display and printer dots on a printer. Y-coordinate values increase as you move down from the origin. This mapping mode is called MM_TEXT because it model...

Using MM_LOENGLISH Units

```
// draw a 5-inch line

case WM_PAINT:
  {
    PAINTSTRUCT ps;
    POINT pt;
    HDC hdc = BeginPaint ( hwnd, &ps );

    SetMapMode ( hdc, MM_LOENGLISH );
    MoveToEx ( hdc, 100, -300, &pt );
    LineTo ( hdc, 500, 0 );

    EndPaint ( hwnd, &ps );
  }
  return 0;
```

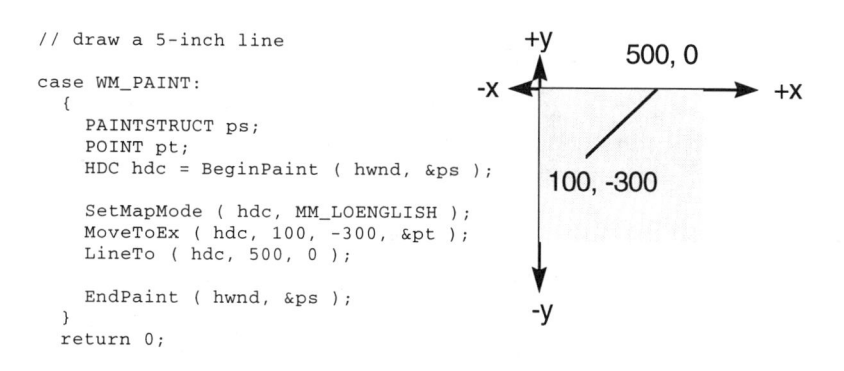

This program sets the mapping mode to MM_LOENGLISH and then draws a 5-inch diagonal line. The line forms the hypotenuse of a right triangle with sides 3 and 4 inches long.

Since we are using MM_LOENGLISH and have not changed the origin, we need to use negative y-coordinates so that the line falls within the client area.

This program uses a cache DC and must reset the mapping mode every WM_PAINT message.

Even though we say that the picture should be the same size and shape on any device, that's not really true for display devices. The problem is that the display device driver doesn't necessarily know how big the actual display is -- it just knows about pixel resolution. So don't be alarmed if the line isn't exactly five inches long on your display -- if the program allowed printing, the line would be exactly five inches on the ...

- When you set the mapping mode to anything else besides MM_TEXT, Windows defines a transform that maps logical coordinates into device units
- Advantage: the drawing's size and shape are the same on any display or printer

7-8

Points and Rectangles

```
#include <windows.h>
    .
    .
    .
POINT pt;

pt.x = 100;
pt.y = 200;

RECT rc, rcClient;

rc.left = 100; rc.top = 300;
rc.right = 300; rc.bottom = 400;

GetClientRect ( hwnd, &rcClient );
```

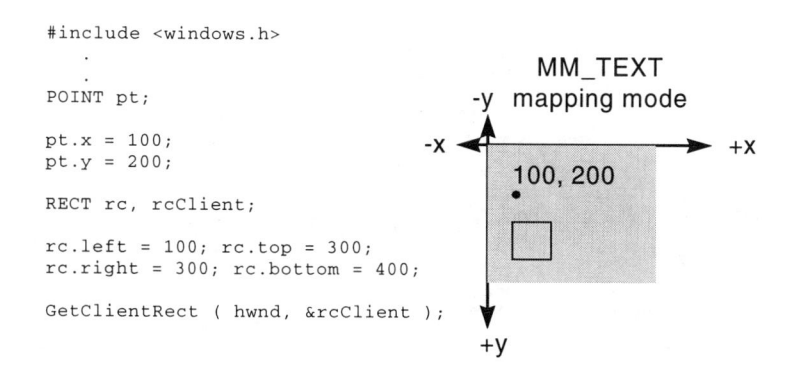

This code fragment demonstrates how to use two of the data types defined by Windows. The types are defined in the WINDEF.H header file, which is included by WINDOWS.H.

The POINT data type describes a coordinate point, x and y. The RECT data type describes a box -- it contains the coordinates of the box's edges.

One use of the RECT data type is to describe a window's client area. GetClientRect returns that rectangle. Since GetClientRect returns the coordinates relative to the client area's upper left corner, the values for left and top are always zero.

- The POINT and RECT data types (defined by WINDOWS.H) are useful in graphics programming -- for example, every client area is a rectangle
- Note: the fields in both types are defined as 16 bits in Win16, 32 bits in Win32

7-9

What is a Region?

```
HRGN hrgn1 = CreateRectRgn ( 100, 100
         , 200, 200 );
HRGN hrgn2 = CreateRectRgn ( 150, 150
         , 250, 250 );
HRGN hgrnDest = CreateRectRgn ( 1, 1
         , 2, 2 );

CombineRgn ( hrgnDest, hrgn1
         , hrgn2, RGN_OR );
  .
  .
  .
DeleteObject ( hgrn1 );
DeleteObject ( hrgn2 );
DeleteObject ( hrgnDest );
```

100, 100
150, 150
200, 200
250, 250

A region is a collection of one or more rectangles, rounded rectangles, ellipses or polygons. A simple region contains only one shape, but you can combine regions to hold multiple shapes.

Windows internally uses regions extensively, as we will see in the next few pages. In addition, Windows programs can use regions to: draw filled shapes, perform clipping, and to perform hit-testing, which lets a program determine if a point falls within the region.

A region is considered to be a GDI object, just like a pen or a brush. Therefore, a Windows program is responsible for allocating and deallocating the region.

In this example, we first create three regions, each containing a simple rectangle. We create the third region with dummy coordinates -- it will act as the output of the CombinRgn call, which requires that all of the region objects that it uses exist beforehand.
ï˜CombineRgn lets you sp...

- A region is a combination of one or more rectangles, ellipses or polygons
- Windows internally uses rectangular regions for managing WM_PAINT messages

7-10

The Visible Region

Window 1:

```
MoveToEx ( hdc, Ax, Ay
         , &pt );
LineTo ( hdc, Bx, By );
```

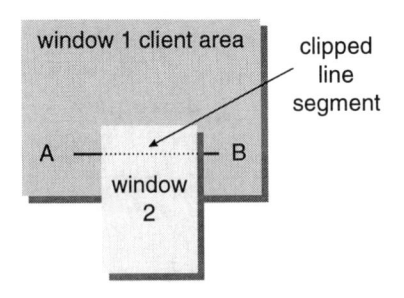

window 1 client area
clipped line segment
A -------- B
window 2

The visible region of a window is the portion of the client area that the user can see. Windows prevents a window procedure from drawing outside its visible region by applying a region as a clip shape.

Clipping is a technique that makes certain kinds of drawing easier. For a real-world analogy, think of a stencil or masking tape -- they let you paint by spraying or brushing paint all over the place -- the stencil or tape prevent some of the paint from "going through". The same is true for clipping in Windows. When Windows applies a clip shape to a device context, all output is filtered through that clip shape -- Windows discards any text or graphics whose coordinates fall outside of the clip shape.

For a window that isn't overlayed by any others, its visible region is a simple rectangle with the coordinate...

- A window's visible region is the portion of the window that isn't obstructed by other non-child windows
- Windows normally restricts a window's output to its visible region using a technique called clipping

7-11

The Update Region

update region for window 1 → window 1 client area

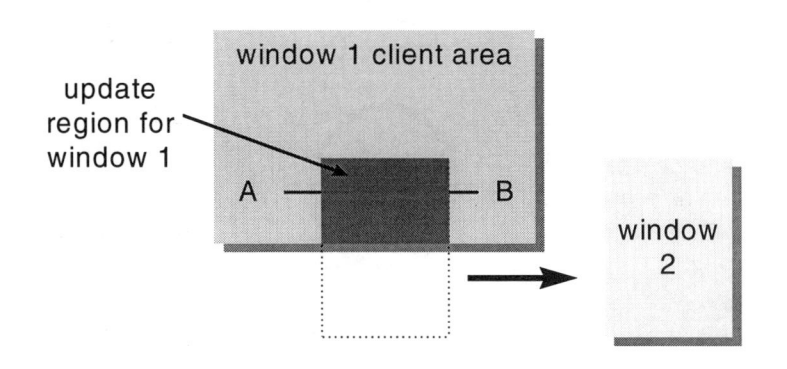

A — B

window 2

- The update region (sometimes called the invalid region) is the portion of the window that must be redrawn
- Invalid windows receive the WM_PAINT message

7-12

In this example, the user has moved window 2 so that it no longer overlays window 1. Window 1 is now invalid. The portion of window 1 that needs to repainted is called the update region, or invalid region.

In this case, the update region is a simple rectangle (the purple area), but it could be a set of rectangles.

There are two ways for a window to become invalid -- the user can manipulate the window or an overlaying window, or a program can call InvalidateRect or InvalidateRgn. In either case, the window procedure for the invalid window receives a WM_PAINT message.

Here, window 2 is not invalid and will not receive a WM_PAINT message. When the user moves a window, Windows actually copies the window's bitmap from its previous location to the new location -- since the bitmap copy is the same as the original, the window is not in...

The WM_PAINT Message

update region for window 1 → window 1 client area

A — B

Message Queue

```
winproc (..)
{
    case WM_PAINT:
        BeginPaint (..);
            .
            .
        EndPaint (..);
}
```

GetMessage (..);
DispatchMessage (..);

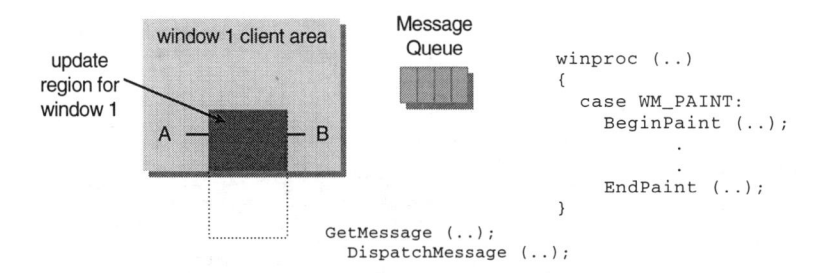

- GetMessage manufactures a WM_PAINT message whenever a window is invalid and there are no other messages in the queue
- BeginPaint does the following:
  - applies a clip to the DC that restricts output to the update region
  - sets the update region to NULL
  - hides the text-entry caret

7-13

WM_PAINT is a strange message -- it doesn't really reside in the message queue. Instead, GetMessage examines the windows owned by the program and sees if they are invalid. If so, GetMessage generates WM_PAINT for that window. That's what we mean by manufacturing a WM_PAINT message -- GetMessage doesn't really pull it from the message queue.

That's also why WM_PAINT is considered to be a low-priority message -- GetMessage manufactures it only if there are no other messages in the queue. For example, if the message queue has a WM_LBUTTONDOWN message in it and a window is invalid, GetMessage will first dequeue the mouse-click message and then manufacture WM_PAINT the next time the program calls GetMessage (assuming no other messages are queued in the meantime.)וֹיֹוֹIn the ...

BeginPaint NULLs the Update Region

Message Queue

GetMessage (...);
DispatchMessage (...);

case WM_PAINT:
return 0;

- A window procedure must call BeginPaint every WM_PAINT message or else GetMessage will manufacture a never-ending stream of WM_PAINT messages
- You must also call EndPaint -- it releases cache DCs and restores the text-entry caret

BeginPaint gets rid of the calling window's invalid region.

If a Window procedure doesn't call BeginPaint, then once a window becomes invalid, it stays invalid -- that causes GetMessage to manufacture a WM_PAINT message whenever the message queue is empty. This obviously can waste a lot of CPU time, which can bog down other programs. That's especially true in Win16, which depends on each Windows program to release the CPU when it has nothing to do.

So all window procedures must call BeginPaint during the WM_PAINT message. And since BeginPaint and EndPaint always work as a tandem, each window procedure must call EndPaint, too. Do not code a window procedure in which the WM_PAINT processing simply returns -- your window will receive a never ending stream of WM_PAINT messages!

Note that if you pass WM_P...

7-14

BeginPaint Clips to the Update Region

Window 1:

```
case WM_PAINT:
  {
    PAINTSTRUCT ps;
    POINT pt;
    HDC hdc = BeginPaint ( hwnd, &ps );

    MoveToEx ( hdc, Ax, Ay, &pt );
    LineTo ( hdc, Bx, By );

    EndPaint ( hwnd, &ps );
  }
```

window 1 client area
update region for window 1
A — B
clipped line segments

- BeginPaint intersects the update and visible regions and sets the result as a clipping region
- In other words, in WM_PAINT, the window refreshes the smallest portion of the window that needs repainting

In the picture on this page, the user has moved a window, Window 2, that previously overlayed Window 1, leaving a portion of Window 1 invalid (the purple rectangle). Before the user moved Window 2, the user could only see part of the line AB -- the middle part of the line was covered by Window 2. Now that Window 1 is invalid, it will receive a WM_PAINT message -- Window 1 must redraw so the user can see the entire line.

Notice that immediately after the user moves Window 2, part of the line is already there -- the two line segments outside of the invalid area (the update region). There's no reason for Window 1 to draw those segments -- Window 1 really only needs to erase the update region and then draw the line segment that falls within the update region. It takes time to draw pixels on a display -- why waste time drawing pixels that are already drawn? However, it might be...

7-15

BeginPaint versus GetDC

BeginPaint

Applies update-region clipping
NULLs the update region
Sends WM_ERASEBKGND
Hides text-entry caret
Retrieves DC handle

GetDC

Retrieves DC handle

- Rule 1: Use BeginPaint/EndPaint during WM_PAINT, GetDC/ReleaseDC in any other message where you wish to draw to the window

- Rule 2: A window procedure must "remember" any output done outside of WM_PAINT -- for example, if the user presses a key, you can echo the key in WM_KEYDOWN, but you should also store the character in a buffer so you can display it during the next WM_PAINT

BeginPaint has many more duties than GetDC -- in fact, you can think of BeginPaint as being a superset of GetDC. And the additional things that BeginPaint do are all related to the WM_PAINT message -- that leads to the First Rule -- use BeginPaint in WM_PAINT, GetDC in any other message.

The second rule is quite important to understand. Most Windows programmers structure their programs so that as much as possible, drawing occurs only from the WM_PAINT message. Then, whenever the program needs to redraw, the program forces a WM_PAINT message as shown on the next page.

However, sometimes it's more efficient to draw in message other than WM_PAINT. Consider a drawing program that draws lines as the user drags the mouse. Such a program would probably draw the lines during the WM_MOUSEMOVE message -- the program could call GetDC to retrieve a window device context. And accordin...

7-16

Forcing a WM_PAINT Message

```
case WM_SYSCOLORCHANGE:
    InvalidateRect ( hwnd, NULL, TRUE );
    return 0;

case WM_PAINT:
    {
        PAINTSTRUCT    ps;

        HDC hdc = BeginPaint ( hwnd, &ps );

        SetTextColor ( hdc, GetSysColor ( COLOR_WINDOWTEXT ) );

        TextOut ( hdc, 100, 100, "Hello", 5 );

        EndPaint ( hwnd, &ps );
    }
    return 0;
```

- Windows requires that each window redraw during WM_PAINT -- from any other message, you can force a repaint by invalidating the window
- In this example, we repaint whenever the user changes the system text color

Since a window must redraw every WM_PAINT message, it makes sense to locate your drawing code in that message case. And instead of repeating the same code in other message cases, you can force a repaint by invalidating all or part of the window. As you saw earlier, whenever a window is invalid, Windows ensures that it receives a WM_PAINT message. Thus, invalidating a window indirectly calls the window's WM_PAINT message case.

Of course, another way to do about the same thing would be to code your drawing routines into a function that you called both from WM_PAINT and other messages. While this technique certainly works, by tradition, most Windows programmers would instead use invalidation.

The example shown on this page draws a text string using the current system Window Text color setting. We retreiv...

7-17

Review Quiz

Before you move on to the next chapter, you should test your comprehension of this chapter by taking the review quiz. The quiz assumes that you have already done the lab exercise.

The quiz will be displayed in a separate window so that you can page through the chapter to help you find the answers. In other words, this is an open book quiz!

After you have answered all of the questions, press the button at the bottom of the quiz window to see how you did. If you didn't score as well as you think you should, you should review the chapter before continuing on.

Chapter Summary

- Windows programs must use a device context to send output to a graphical output device such as a window or a printer. To output to a window, you can use a temporary cached device context, or you can tell windows that you want a separate window DC for each window (the CS_OWNDC style).
- A window receives a WM_PAINT message whenever any portion of the window is invalid.
- The BeginPaint call clips the device context to the invalid region and then validates or clears the invalid region. This prevents any more WM_PAINT messages until the window is again invalid.
- A program can force a repaint by adding a rectangle to the window's invalid region. You can use InvalidateRect for this purpose.

Chapter 8: Classes and Windows

- Class Style Flags
- Creating a Window
- Window Style Flags
- Overlapped, Popup and Child Windows

Window Class Overview

```
WNDCLASS    wndclass;

wndclass.lpszClassName = "MyClass";
     .
     .
     .

RegisterClass ( &wndclass );

HWND hwnd1 = CreateWindow (... "MyClass" ...);
HWND hwnd2 = CreateWindow (... "EDIT" ...);
```

- Before you can create a window, the window's class must be registered
- Windows itself registers several classes at boot time, for example "EDIT", "LISTBOX" and so forth

All windows are members of a window class. The window class establishes characteristics for the group of windows, including style flags, class icon and most importantly, the window procedure for the window class. Each class is known by a string called the class name -- you specify the class name when you create a window.

Classses registered by a program are known as private classes -- only the calling program can use them. Classes registered by Windows are referred to as system classes and are available to all programs.

Here, the program first registers a class named "MyClass" and then creates two windows: a window of the private class and a window of the system "Edit" class. Because "MyClass" is a private class, its window procedure must be provided by this program. The window...

Registering a Class

```
WNDCLASS        wndclass;

wndclass.style              = 0;
wndclass.lpfnWndProc        = WndProc;
wndclass.cbClsExtra         = 0;
wndclass.cbWndExtra         = 0;
wndclass.hInstance          = hInstance;
wndclass.hIcon              = LoadIcon ( 0, IDI_APPLICATION );
wndclass.hCursor            = LoadCursor ( 0, IDC_ARROW );
wndclass.hbrBackground      = (HBRUSH)GetStockObject ( WHITE_BRUSH );
wndclass.lpszMenuName       = NULL;
wndclass.lpszClassName      = "MyClass";

if ( !RegisterClass ( &wndclass ) )
    return 0;
```

- The WNDCLASS structure defines characteristics common to all windows of a class
- RegisterClass returns FALSE if it fails

This page shows an example of registering a private class. Windows of this class have no special class styles, use a window procedure named WndProc, have no extra class or window storage, have a generic icon, use the standard tilted-arrow mouse cursor, draw a white background to the client area and have no menu. The class name is MyClass. We will cover the class styles in more detail in a few pages.

If your program will run on Windows 95 or Windows NT 4.0 or later, you can call RegisterClassEx instead of RegisterClass which lets you assign both large and small icons to the window class. These later versions of Windows display the large icon in the task bar and the small icon in the window's titlebar.

Windows automatically unregisters private classes when the program that registered them exits.

Multiple Windows of a Class

```
WNDCLASS        wndclass;

wndclass.lpszClassName = "MyClass";
    .
    .
    .
RegisterClass ( &wndclass );

HWND hwnd3 = CreateWindow (... "MyClass" . ..);
HWND hwnd4 = CreateWindow (... "MyClass" . ..);
```

```
WndProc ( HWND hwnd, UINT iMsg
        , WPARAM wParam
        , LPARAM lParam )
{
    case WM_LBUTTONDOWN:
        if ( hwnd == hwnd3 )
            do_something();
    .
    .
    .
}
```

- All windows of the same class share the window procedure, class style flags, class icon and so forth
- When Windows calls the window procedure, it passes the window handle as the first argument. This identifies which window received the message

The code on this page registers a window class and then creates two windows of the class. Since both windows are of the same class, they share the same window procedure.

This window procedure checks the incoming window handle and calls a function, depending on the window handle. You probably won't write that kind of code very often, though. Most of the time, the window procedure works the same for each of its windows; for example, pushbuttons always generate the WM_COMMAND message, regardless of the button's window handle.

However, each window of a class generally needs some unique characteristics. For example, buttons on a dialog box usually have different text strings: "OK","Cancel" and the like. This presents a dilemma, since all of the buttons are using the same window proc...

The Class Data Structure

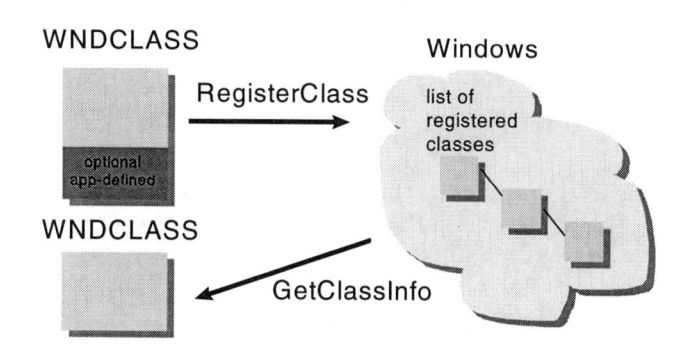

WNDCLASS → RegisterClass → Windows list of registered classes

optional app-defined

WNDCLASS ← GetClassInfo ← Windows

- Windows internally keeps a list of all registered classes -- RegisterClass adds an entry to the list
- Windows automatically deletes (unregisters) application-registered classes when the program exits

Each time you register a class, Windows adds the WNDCLASS structure to its internal registered class list. You can retrieve the WNDCLASS structure by calling GetClassInfo and specifying the class name.

You can also read and write information about the class by calling GetClassLong, GetClassWord, SetClassLong and SetClassWord. For example, to change the mouse-cursor handle for all windows in a class, call SetClassLong passing GCL_HCURSOR and the new handle as arguments.

To be very precise here, Windows actually maintains multiple lists of registered classes -- a list of private classes for each program and a list of system classes registered by Windows itself. When a program registers a private class, Windows adds an entry to the program's private list. Then, when a program uses a class name to create a window, Windows searches the private list, foll...

8-4

Class Style Flags

CS_BYTEALIGNCLIENT	For a faster display, Windows aligns the client area on a byte
CS_BYTEALIGNWINDOW	boundary
CS_CLASSDC	For a faster display, Windows aligns the window on a byte boundary
CS_DBLCLKS	All windows of the class share a common display device context
CS_GLOBALCLASS	The window receives double-click mouse messages
CS_HREDRAW	The class is global
CS_NOCLOSE	The whole window is invalid if the window is sized horizontally
CS_OWNDC	Disables the close command on the system menu
CS_PARENTDC	Each window allocates a private display context
CS_SAVEBITS	The window shares a display device context with its parent
CS_VREDRAW	Windows saves the bitmap image under the window
	The window is invalid if the window is sized vertically

- The class style is a set of 32-bit flags that apply to all windows of a given class -- you bitwise "or" them together to form the class style
- The styles influence the window's behavior and appearance

This page lists the available class style bit flags.

You specify the class style flags when you register the class. Windows stores the class style as a 32-bit value in the internal window-class data structure. You can retreive the class style by calling GetClassLong with the GCL_STYLE command and change the class style flags by calling SetClassLong. Since the class styles are bit-flags, to change one, you normally query the current style, use a C bitwise operator to set, reset or flip a bit, and then call SetClassLong to establish the modified class style flags. For example, to "turn on" the CS_HREDRAW flag:

```
DWORD dwStyle =
GetClassLong ( hwnd,
GCL_STYLE );
dwStyle |= CS_HREDRAW;
SetClassLong ( hwnd,
GCL_STYLE, dwStyle );
```

For more information on CS...

8-5

Creating a Window

```
HWND hwndOverlapped = CreateWindow (
    "MyClass"           // class name
  , "My Window"         // window title
  , WS_OVERLAPPED       // style
  , CW_USEDEFAULT       // initial x
  , CW_USEDEFAULT       // initial y
  , CW_USEDEFAULT       // initial cx
  , CW_USEDEFAULT       // initial cy
  , 0                   // parent
  , 0                   // menu
  , hInstance           // instance handle
  , NULL );             // create
parameters
```

Windows

list of window data structures

CreateWindow

- Windows internally maintains a list of data structures each of which describes a window
- The window procedure receives the create parameters as a field in the CREATESTRUCT, whose pointer is passed as lParam in WM_CREATE

When you create a window, you pass a string containing a class name. If the class has been registered, Windows allocates and initializes an internal data structure that describes the window and then returns the unique window handle. You can think of the window handle as a pointer to the window data structure -- even though that's not literally true -- you use the window handle to manipulate the window, for example, to destroy it.

Internally, Windows links the window data structures to each other. The actual linking scheme that Windows uses is more complicated than the singly-linked list shown in the picture -- the window data structure actually has quite a few fields that reference other windows. For example, each child window references its parent.

Here, we create an overlapped window of the "MyClass" class, assigning "My Windows" as a title, assigning system-supplied size and po...

8-6

The Window Data Structure

	Index
other stuff	
ID	GWL_ID
style	GWL_STYLE
ext. style	GWL_EXTSTYLE
wndproc address	GWL_WNDPROC
hwndParent	
hInstance	GWL_HWNDPARENT
user data	GWL_HINSTANCE
optional app-defined area	GWL_USERDATA

GetWindowLong ←
SetWindowLong →

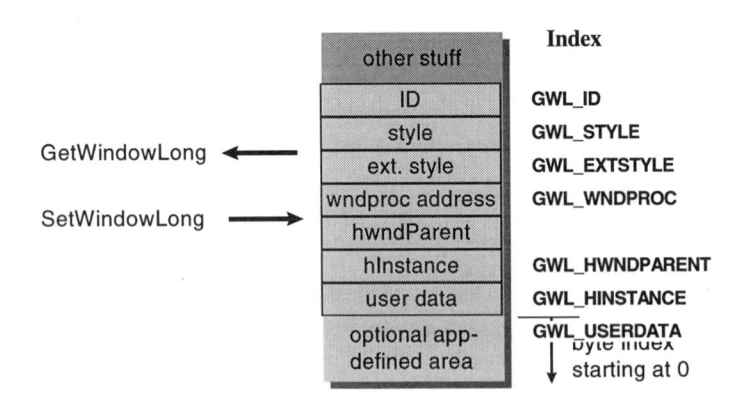

byte index starting at 0

- A program can query or set a window's data structure by calling GetWindowLong and SetWindowLong
- The application-defined area is optional -- you specify its size when you register the class (cbWndExtra)

This picture shows a stylized representation of the window data structure; the actual data structure is undocumented and more complicated and contains pointers to other structures. This stylized version shows the fields of the window data structure that are exposed to programs by calling GetWindowLong and SetWindowLong.

The data structure has two distinct sections: the system area (drawn in pink) and the optional application-defined area (drawn in aqua.) The system-defined area describes everything that Windows knows about the window -- its style, window procedure address and so forth. The application-defined area is optional -- you specify its size when you register the window class. Then when you create a window, Windows allocates this extra storage and tacks it onto the window data structure. Windows itself doesn't do anything to the ap...

8-7

Window Style Flags

Window Style Flags

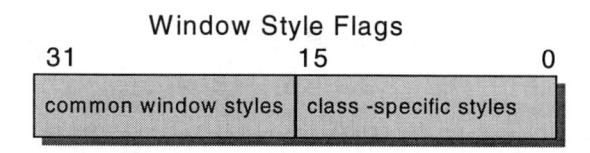

```
31                 15                0
| common window styles | class-specific styles |
```

Extended Window Style Flags (CreateWindowEx)

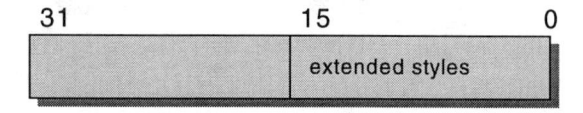

```
31                 15                0
|                   |   extended styles   |
```

- The window style is a set of bit flags that influence a window's behavior and appearance
- The 16 most-significant style flags and the extended styles are used by windows of all classes
- Each window class can define the flags in the bottom 16. For example, the "BUTTON" class defines BS_PUSHBUTTON (0x0000) and BS_CHECKBOX (0x0002)

8-8

Window style flags are similar to class style flags. However, they apply to a single window rather than to a set of windows. To specify the window style flags, create an expression that bitwise "ors" flags together; you then pass the expression as an argument to CreateWindow or CreateWindowEx.

Microsoft added the extended style flags in Windows 3.x. Since CreateWindow has no argument for extended styles, Microsoft also added the CreateWindowEx call that accepts the extra extended window style argument.

The style flags fall into two categories: styles that are possible for windows of any class, referred to as common window styles, and styles that are specific to windows in a particular class. Sixteen of the original style flags and all of the extended style flags are common to windows of all classes. The remaining 16 original style flags are class-specific.
ı˜An example of a common...

Common Window Styles

Window Type
- WS_CHILD
- WS_OVERLAPPED
- WS_POPUP

Border Styles
- WS_BORDER
- WS_DLGFRAME
- WS_THICKFRAME

Clipping Styles
- WS_CLIPCHILDREN
- WS_CLIPSIBLINGS

Window Decorations
- WS_CAPTION
- WS_HSCROLL
- WS_MAXIMIZEBOX
- WS_MINIMIZEBOX
- WS_SYSMENU
- WS_VSCROLL

Appearance Styles
- WS_MAXIMIZE
- WS_MINIMIZE
- WS_DISABLED
- WS_VISIBLE

Dialog Control Styles
- WS_GROUP
- WS_TABSTOP

- These styles apply to all windows, regardless of the window class. They also work in any version of Windows
- You can assign these styles when you call CreateWindow and modify them by calling SetWindowLong (GWL_STYLE)

8-9

This page lists the window style flags common to windows of all classes. The next page shows the extended window style flags. To complete the list, we will cover the class-specific styles as we cover each pre-defined window class in later chapters.

Remember that you form the window style by using a bitwise "or" to combine one or more style flags.

We have grouped the styles into categories such as Window Type and Window Decoration. Click on each category heading for a description of the category.

You may find it a little surprising that there are more than 16 flags listed here, even though the common window style is a 16-bit field in the window data structure. There are a few reasons:

1. WS_OVERLAPPED is defined as zero, so it doesn't...

Extended Window Styles

Styles for All Windows Versions

- WS_EX_ACCEPTFILES
- WS_EX_DLGMODALFRAME
- WS_EX_NOPARENTNOTIFY
- WS_EX_TOPMOST
- WS_EX_TRANSPARENT

Styles for Windows 95, NT 4.0 and Greater

- WS_EX_APPWINDOW
- WS_EX_CLIENTEDGE
- WS_EX_CONTEXTHELP
- WS_EX_CONTROLPARENT
- WS_EX_LEFT
- WS_EX_LEFTSCROLLBAR
- WS_EX_LTRREADING
- WS_EX_MDICHILD
- WS_EX_RIGHT
- WS_EX_RIGHTSCROLLBAR
- WS_EX_RTLREADING
- WS_EX_STATICEDGE
- WS_EX_TOOLWINDOW
- WS_EX_WINDOWEDGE

Microsoft added the extended window style flags in later versions of Windows (after 2.x). To specify the extended flags, you need to call CreateWindowEx instead of CreateWindow.

Some of the styles are ignored in earlier versions of windows. The styles listed on the right side of the page are only available if the program creating the window is running on Windows 95, Windows NT 4.0 or later.

- These styles apply to all windows, regardless of the window class
- You can assign these styles when you call CreateWindowEx and modify them by calling SetWindowLong (GWL_EXSTYLE)

8-10

The Overlapped Window Style

WS_OVERLAPPED

WS_OVERLAPPEDWINDOW

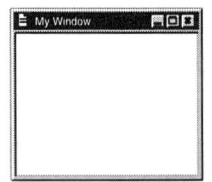

Most programmers use an overlapped window as the application's main window.

Notice that if you specify only WS_OVERLAPPED for the window style, the window has a thin border that doesn't let the user resize the window and also has no system-menu, minimize, maximize and close boxes. To create a "standard" main window that has all of those non-client components, specify WS_OVERLAPPEDWINDOW, which is defined in WINUSER.H as a combination of window styles.

If you want an overlapped window that differs from this "standard" configuration, you can bitwise "or" WS_OVERLAPPED with the components you desire. For example, if you want a window with a sizing border but no other decorations, code:

   WS_OVERLAPPED |
   WS_THICKFRAME|...

- You normally assign the WS_OVERLAPPED style to top-level, main windows -- WS_OVERLAPPED windows always have a titlebar and a border
- You can include window decorations by specifying WS_OVERLAPPEDWINDOW -- this composite flag includes WS_OVERLAPPED | WS_THICKFRAME | WS_SYSMENU | WS_MINIMIZEBOX | WS_MAXIMIZEBOX

8-11

The Popup Window Style

WS_POPUP   WS_POPUPWINDOW

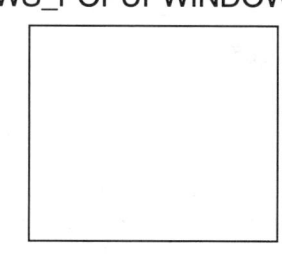

- The WS_POPUP style is intended for dialog boxes, but it's similar to WS_OVERLAPPED (WS_POPUP has no border or titlebar by default)
- The WS_POPUPWINDOW composite style includes WS_POPUP | WS_BORDER | WS_SYSMENU, but no titlebar -- and the system menu is invisible unless there's a titlebar! You can include a titlebar by including WS_CAPTION

8-12

Popup windows are normally used for dialog boxes, but popup windows are actually quite similar to overlapped windows -- the big difference is that overlapped windows always have a titlebar.

The WS_POPUP style by itself results in a window with no titlebar and no border. If you use the WS_POPUPWINDOW composite style, the window will have a border and an invisible system menu -- to see the system menu you must also include the WS_CAPTION style.

Most programmers don't code dialog boxes by hand. Instead, they run a visual editing tool, such as the Microsoft Developer's Studio to create a resource script for the dialog. Such tools typically define the dialog box to have the WS_POPUP and WS_CAPTION styles as well as the DS_MODALFRAME border style. The DS_MODALFRAME is a style specific to the dialog box window class that causes th...

The Child Window Style

WS_POPUPWINDOW

WS_CHILD

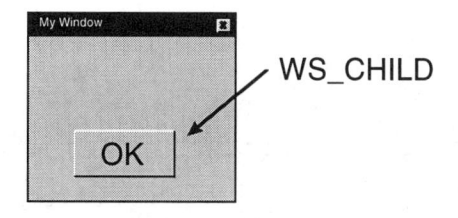

- You can use child windows to subdivide the client area of a parent window. For example, buttons on a dialog box are child windows
- Child windows must have a parent -- they always stay on top of the parent, and are clipped to the parent
- Child windows can have borders, titlebars, and so forth, but no menu

8-13

A child window is any window that has the WS_CHILD style. When you create a child window, you must pass its parent window's handle as an argument to CreateWindow or CreateWindowEx.

Child windows that reside on a dialog box are sometimes called "controls". They include buttons, listboxes, edit boxes and so forth.

You can also create child windows that reside on a main window's client area. For example, a word processor program might open a separate child window for each file that the user is editing.

By default, Windows doesn't draw a border or window decorations on a child window, but you can supply those styles when you create the window. In addition, some window classes, for example buttons, draw their own borders.ı ́ı ́Child window...

Sibling Windows

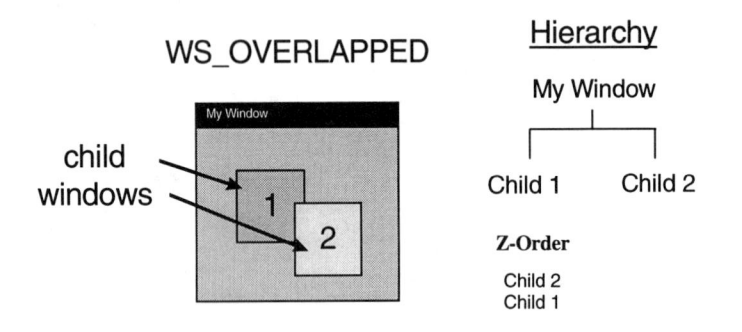

WS_OVERLAPPED

Hierarchy

My Window
├── Child 1
└── Child 2

Z-Order
Child 2
Child 1

On this page, we have a parent window with two child windows, labeled "1" and "2". Since the child windows have the same parent, they are considered to be siblings. In the picture, Child 2 overlays Child 1 -- Child 2 is highest in the Z-order.

The reason the Z-order is called that is because you can think of it as being a third coordinate axis in addition to the x and y-coordinate axes. Image a ray, begininng at the origin, rising outward from the screen -- that's the Z axis. The sibling that is on top of all others is highest in the Z-order; the window at the bottom has the lowest Z ordering.

When you create a window, Windows places it at the top of the Z-order with respect to its siblings. The user changes the Z-order by activating a sibling that's underneath -- as part of activation, Windows moves the window to the top of the Z-order. A program can change a window's Z-order by calling SetWindowPos.

- Child windows that have the same parent are called siblings
- Windows maintains the siblings in a list called the Z-order. The Z-order specifies the siblings' order in the stack of siblings

8-14

The Internal Window Hierarchy

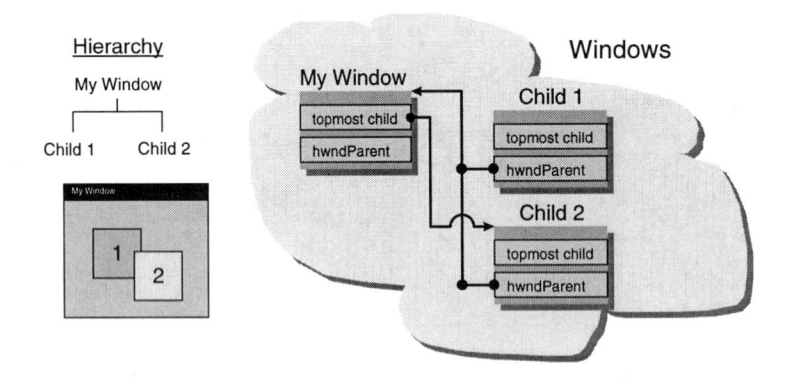

Hierarchy

My Window
├── Child 1
└── Child 2

This page shows how Windows maintains the relationships between windows. Here we have three windows, a parent window and two child windows, which are siblings.

For each window, Windows keeps track of the window's parent (if any), and the window's topmost child (if any). Windows also links the siblings together in the Z-order, even though that isn't shown in the picture.

Windows provides system calls so that you can traverse the hierarchy. Given a child window's handle, you can retrieve its parent's handle by calling GetParent or GetWindowLong (GWL_HWNDPARENT). Given a parent's handle, you can retrieve the topmost child's handle by calling the GetWindow system call, specifying the GW_HWNDFIRST command. You can then retrieve the ha...

- Internally, Windows links the window data structures of parent and child windows
- You can traverse the list by calling GetWindow, GetParent or EnumChildWindows

8-15

Owned Windows

WS_OVERLAPPEDWINDOW
(owner)

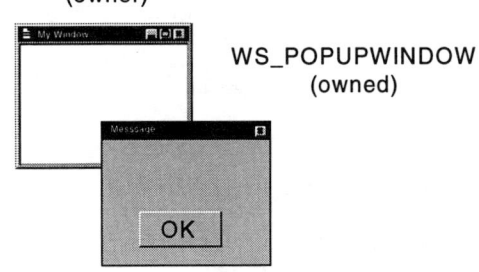

WS_POPUPWINDOW
(owned)

- Even though overlapped and popup windows have no parent (not clipped to another window), you can specify hwndParent in CreateWindow. This window is called the owner
- An owned window cannot "go behind" its owner in the Z-order. In addition, Windows destroys owned windows when the owner is destroyed
- Most dialog boxes are owned by the top-level main application window

When you create a popup or overlapped window, you can pass a window handle in the hwndParent argument -- if you do, that window is considered to be the new window's owner. Windows will not let the owned window go behind its owner, even if the user clicks on the owner window. We often use this technique for secondary windows, since it shows the user that the window somehow belongs to the main window.

If you specify NULL for hwndParent when you create an overlapped or popup window, the new window has no owner. That's what you normally do for a application's main window.

Lab Exercise 6: Window Styles

In this lab, you will gain experience with overlapped, popup and child windows and learn how to query information about a window at runtime.

To view the lab exercise instructions, press the "Lab Write Up" button. This will display the lab document and let you print it if you wish. When you are finished with the lab, continue to the next page to take a review quiz.

Review Quiz

Before you move on to the next chapter, you should test your comprehension of this chapter by taking the review quiz. The quiz assumes that you have already done the lab exercise.

The quiz will be displayed in a separate window so that you can page through the chapter to help you find the answers. In other words, this is an open book quiz!

After you have answered all of the questions, press the button at the bottom of the quiz window to see how you did. If you didn't score as well as you think you should, you should review the chapter before continuing on.

Chapter Summary

- Before you can create a window, its class must be registered. You can register your own private classes or create windows using pre-defined Windows classes.

- Windows maintains a class-data structure for each window class that contains the class's style, window procedure address and so forth.

- When you create a window, Windows internally allocates storage for a window data structure that describes the window. The window data structure contains the window's size, position, style and so forth.

- A window or class style is a 32-bit number made up of bit-flags. The styles influence the window's behavior and appearance. You specify class styles when you register the class -- they apply to allo windows based on the class. You specify window styles when you create the window -- they apply only to the window being created.

Chapter 9: The Mouse

- Mouse Messages

- The WM_LBUTTONDOWN Message

- The WM_MOUSEMOVE Message

- Double-Click Messages

9-0

Mouse Messages

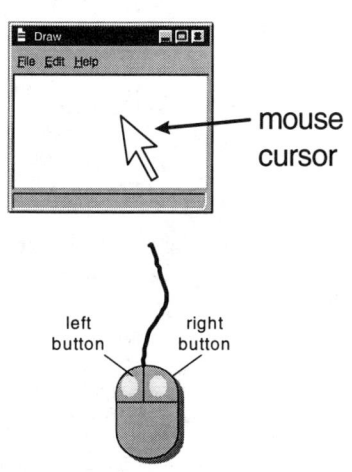

WM_MOUSEMOVE
WM_LBUTTONDOWN
WM_LBUTTONUP
WM_RBUTTONDOWN
WM_RBUTTONUP
WM_MBUTTONDOWN
WM_MBUTTONUP
WM_LBUTTONDBLCLK
WM_RBUTTONDBLCLK
WM_MBUTTONDBLCLK
WM_CONTEXTMENU

- Whenever the user manipulates the mouse, Windows queues one or more messages into a message queue

The mouse is an important user-input device for Windows -- users can click or move the mouse to manipulate windows or the data they display. This page lists the messages that the mouse generates.

The mouse position is represented on the screen by a image referred to as the mouse cursor. The default mouse cursor is a tilted arrow.

Most Windows computers have mice with two buttons. When the user clicks the left mouse button, Windows generates message such as WM_LBUTTONDOWN. When the user clicks the right mouse button, Windows generates messages like WM_RBUTTONDOWN. If the system has a three-button mouse connected, Windows will generate messages like WM_MBUTTONDOWN when the user clicks the middle button. Many programs take no action on the middle mouse button messages, since thre...

9-1

Which Window Receives Messages?

winprocA (...)
{

}

message queue

winprocB (...)
{

}

Window A, Window B, hot spot

Even though there might be many windows on the screen, only one window receives messages when the user manipulates the mouse. To determine which one, Windows looks for the window under the mouse cursor's hot spot, which is a single pixel. For the default tilted-arrow mouse cursor, the hot spot is the arrow's tip. So, in this picture, Windows will route the messages to Window A even though part of the mouse cursor is over Window B, since the hot spot is over Window A.

Each mouse cursor shape defines a single pixel as the hot spot. If you create your own custom mouse cursor in Visual C++, you assign the hot spot when you create the cursor.

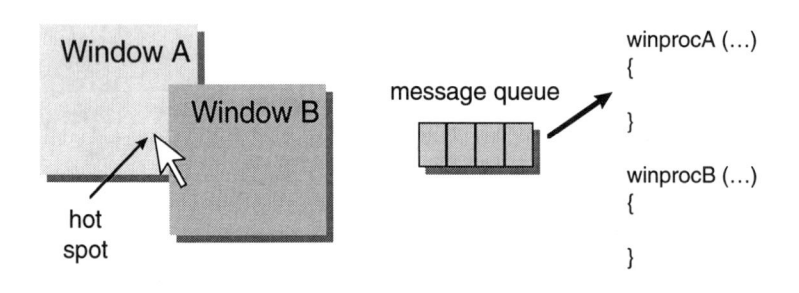

- Normally, Windows routes mouse messages to the window that is underneath the mouse cursor's hot spot
- However, a window can capture the mouse so it can receive all mouse messages (covered later)

9-2

The WM_LBUTTONDOWN Message

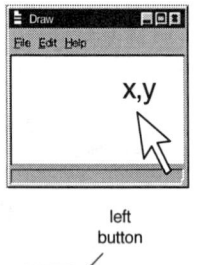

wParam = mouse message flags
cursor.x = LOWORD (lParam)
cursor.y = HIWORD (lParam)

mouse message flags

MK_CONTROL
MK_LBUTTON
MK_MBUTTON
MK_RBUTTON
MK_SHIFT

This is the mouse message that most Window programs act upon. For example, a drawing program could use this message to start a drawing operation or to select a previously-drawn figure. A spreadsheet might use this message to select a spreadsheet cell.

Windows reports the mouse coordinates in pixels, regardless of the mapping mode that the window uses to draw text and graphics. Thus, if a window is using a mapping mode besides MM_TEXT and wishes to draw in response to the mouse click, the program must convert the coordinates using DPtoLP.

The mouse-message flags let you detect if certain keys or other mouse buttons were pressed when the user clicked the mouse. A window might take different action if the user clicks the left button while holding the control or shift keys than it does if the user i...

- Many windows use this message to select or draw text and graphics
- Windows reports the coordinates in pixels, relative to the client area's upper-left corner
- The flags are bit-flags; more than one can be "on" for any mouse message

9-3

The WM_MOUSEMOVE Message

wParam = mouse message flags
cursor.x = LOWORD (lParam)
cursor.y = HIWORD (lParam)

mouse message flags

MK_CONTROL
MK_LBUTTON
MK_MBUTTON
MK_RBUTTON
MK_SHIFT

- The window under the cursor receives WM_MOUSEMOVE messages as the user moves the mouse over the client area
- Many windows use this message to select or draw text and graphics

When the user moves the mouse, it generates a hardware interrupt that is handled by the Windows mouse device driver. The driver then notifies Windows, which generates the WM_MOUSEMOVE message. The window procedure will not necessarily receive this message for each pixel that the mouse moves, especially if the user moves the mouse quickly. That's because the mouse hardware can not generates interrupts fast enough to keep up with quick swipes of the mouse.

You might think that a program's queue could get swamped with mouse-move messages if the program doesn't retrieve them quickly. Fortunately, Windows doesn't let that happen. In fact, Windows will only enqueue at most one mouse-move message into any queue -- if another interrupt comes in, Windows simply updates the coordinates stored in the existing WM_MOUSEMOVE message. While this ensures that the queue doesn't overfl...

Double-Click Messages

```
WNDCLASS    wndclass;

wndclass.style   = CS_DBLCLKS;
wndclass.hCursor = LoadCursor ( NULL, IDC_ARROW );
       .
       .
       .
RegisterClass ( &wndclass );
```

- Windows routes double-click messages only to windows that have registered with the CS_DBLCLKS style
- For a double-click to be sent, the user must click the mouse twice within a certain interval and close to the original location
- The user can configure the double-click interval by running the Control Panel

A double-click message occurs when the user clicks the mouse twice quickly. Windows only passes double click messages to window of classes that register with the CS_DBLCLKS style – all other windows will instead receive just a series of button-up and button-down events.

The reason that Windows requires applications to specifically ask for double-click messages is that processing double clicks can be time consuming. Therefore, Windows only does the work for window classes that require it.

To determine if a double-click message should be generated, Windows examines the message time and position. To be considered a double click, the second click must fall within a small rectangle around the first click and within a certain interval. The user can specify the interval by running the C...

Capturing the Mouse

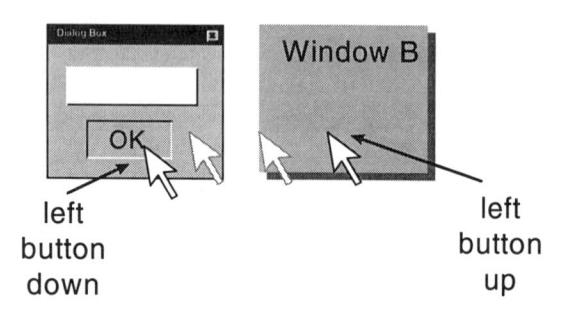

left button down

left button up

- Some windows depend on receiving the "up" message. For example, a pushbutton depresses itself on the down click and un-depresses on the up
- Problem: the user might press the button then move the mouse over another window before releasing it
- Solution: the button can call SetCapture during WM_LBUTTONDOWN and ReleaseCapture during WM_LBUTTONUP

Windows normally routes mouse messages to the window under the mouse cursor's hot spot. So for example, if the user moves the mouse over a window, the window procedure receives WM_MOUSEMOVE only while the mouse cursor is over the client area. As soon as the user moves the mouse over another window, that window will receive the messages instead.

Most of the time, this routing works fine. Sometimes, however, a window may need to receive mouse messages even when the mouse isn't over the window. For example, consider a button, which draws itself as "pushed in" when the user presses the mouse down on it and pops out when the user releases the mouse. Suppose the user presses the button down and then moves the mouse over another window before releasing it. With Window's normal mouse routing, the button wouldn't receive the up-click message and would be unable to pop itself out.ı...

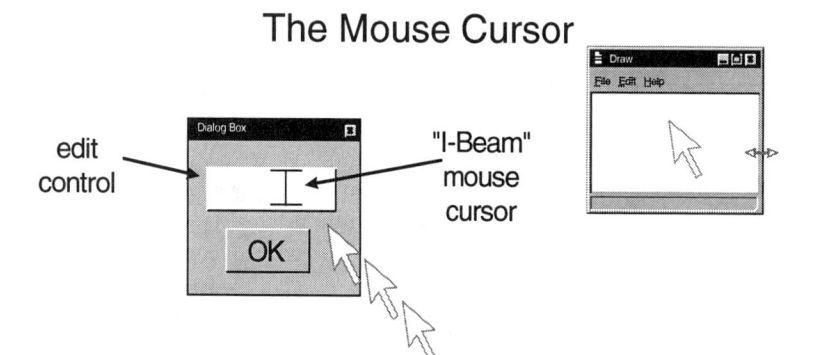

The Mouse Cursor

edit control

"I-Beam" mouse cursor

- You establish the default shape for the mouse cursor by calling LoadCursor when you register a window class
- A window class can also define a custom mouse cursor. For example, edit controls change the mouse cursor to an "I-Beam" shape when the mouse moves over
- In addition, you can change the mouse cursor shape at any time by calling SetCursor -- many programs change the cursor to the hourglass when they are busy

When the user moves the mouse over a window's client area, Windows sets the cursor shape to the shape that was specified when the window's class was registered. When you register, you can specify one of Windows' pre-defined cursors, like the tilted arrow, or you can load a custom cursor from your program's resources -- defining custom cursors is similar to defining icons as covered in Chapter 5. You can create the cursor itself in Visual C++ or other development environment.

When the user moves the mouse over the non-client areas of a window, Windows determines which non-client section the mouse is over and displays an appropriate cursor. For example, when you move the cursor over a vertical sizing border, the cursor changes to a horizontal, double-headed arrow.

In the picture on this page, when the user moves the mo...

Review Quiz

Before you move on to the next chapter, you should test your comprehension of this chapter by taking the review quiz. The quiz assumes that you have already done the lab exercise.

The quiz will be displayed in a separate window so that you can page through the chapter to help you find the answers. In other words, this is an open book quiz!

After you have answered all of the questions, press the button at the bottom of the quiz window to see how you did. If you didn't score as well as you think you should, you should review the chapter before continuing on.

Chapter Summary

- Most Windows programs process messages from the mouse to let the user directly manipulate the text and graphics displayed by the program. Windows generates several types of mouse messages, including WM_LBUTTON1DOWN, WM_LBUTTON1UP and WM_MOUSEMOVE.
- Unless a window has captured the mouse, Windows routes mouse messages to the window underneath the mouse cursor's hot spot.

- The mouse cursor is a small picture that represents the mouse's position. A mouse cursor is actually similar to an icon -- the difference is that cursors have a hot spot.

- You establish the default cursor shape for a window class when you register the class, but you can change the cursor shape at any time by calling SetCursor.

Chapter 10: The Keyboard

- Keyboard Focus
- WM_KEYDOWN and WM_CHAR Messages
- The Caret

Keyboard Messages

WM_KEYDOWN
WM_KEYUP
WM_CHAR
WM_SYSKEYDOWN
WM_SYSKEYUP
WM_SYSCHAR
WM_DEADCHAR
WM_SYSDEADCHAR
WM_HOTKEY

When the user presses a key, Windows passes one or more of the keystroke messages shown on this page to a window procedure. In this chapter, you will learn how Windows determines how to route the keystroke messages.

As you have probably noticed in earlier programs and lab exercises, by default, Windows programs ignore keystrokes. That is, if you pass the messages shown on this page to the default window procedure, nothing happens. So if you want to have your window respond to keystrokes, you must add at least one of the messages shown here to your window procedure.

The two most commonly processed keystroke messages are WM_KEYDOWN and WM_CHAR -- this chapter will concentrate on them and point out the differences between them.

- Whenever the user presses a key, Windows queues one or more messages into a message queue

Which Window Receives Messages?

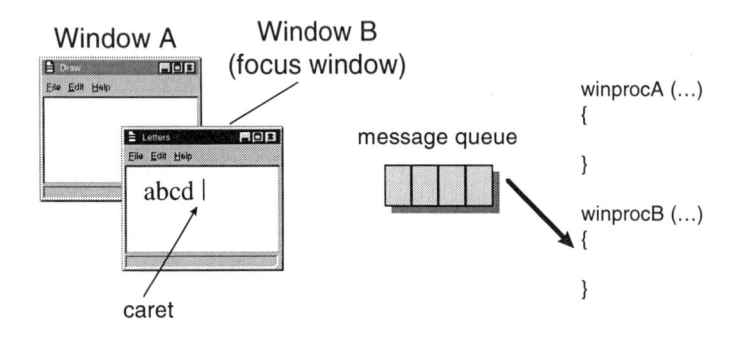

Window A

Window B (focus window)

abcd |

caret

message queue

winprocA (...)
{

}

winprocB (...)
{

}

- Windows routes keystroke messages to the focus window
- At most one window has the focus at any time
- The focus window often displays a caret so the user can see that it has the focus and to indicate where keystrokes will be displayed

10-2

To determine which window should receive the keystroke message, Windows keeps track of which window has the input focus. At any given time, there might be dozens of windows on your desktop, but only one has the focus. Windows then routes the keystroke messages shown on the last page to the focus window's window procedure.

Windows changes the focus whenever the user activates another window. A program can change the focus by calling the SetFocus function, passing the handle of the new focus window. We will do that a lot when we work with dialog boxes. You can query which window has the focus by calling GetFocus.

Whenever a window receives the focus, Windows sends it the WM_SETFOCUS message. Likewise, when a window loses the focus, Windows sends WM_KILLFOCUS.

So the user knows which window has the focus, the fo...

Focus versus Active Window

inactive window

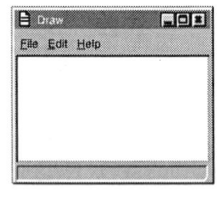

active window

child window with focus

caret

- The active window is always the top-level window at the top of the z-order -- there can be only one active window at any time
- The active window highlights its titlebar
- Either the active window or one of its child windows have the focus

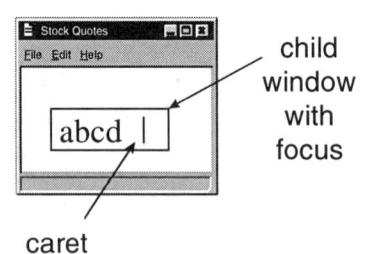

10-3

The notions of active and focus windows are related, but they are not the same. The thing to remember is that the active window is always a top-level window and thus must be either an overlapped or popup window. On the other hand, the focus window could be a child window like the edit control shown on this page.

As another example, consider a dialog box with several edit fields -- each of those is a separate window, but only one accepts keystrokes at any time -- the one with the focus. Furthermore, the edit control with the focus displays a caret so the user knows where keystrokes will be routed.

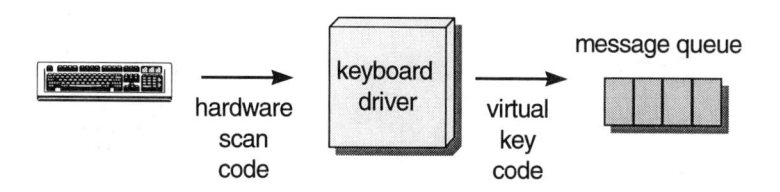

The Keyboard

Virtual Key Codes

hardware scan code → keyboard driver → virtual key code → message queue

On most PCs, the keyboard hardware generates a unique code for each key called the scan code. The scan code really indicates where the key is physically located on the keyboard.

In the bad old days of MS-DOS, the only way programs could process keystrokes was to examine each key's scan code or ASCII code. Some keys had no ASCII codes, for example, the F2 key – those keys had to be handled as scan codes.

The problem with scan codes is that they depend on the keyboard. There's no guarantee that the scan codes will be the same for all platforms on which Windows runs.

To solve this portability problem, the designers of Windows decided that each different type of keyboard needs a device driver that maps the scan codes into hardware-independent codes called virtual key codes. Windows guarantees that th...

- So that Windows programs are independent of the keyboard hardware, the keyboard driver maps the hardware key codes into keyboard-independent virtual key codes (defined in WINUSER.H)
- For example, if the user presses the F2 key on a standard PC keyboard, the driver maps the 0x3C scan code into the VK_F2 virtual key code

10-4

The WM_KEYDOWN Message

key flags:

31 30 29 28 25 24 23	16 15	0
	scan code	repeat count

wParam = virtual key code
lParam = key flags

return: 0 if processed

00..15	repeat count
16..23	scan code
24	extended key
25..28	reserved
29	context code
30	previous key state
31	transition state

Most of the time, Windows generates two messages when a user presses and releases a key – WM_KEYDOWN when the key goes down, and WM_KEYUP when the user releases the key. Most Windows programs only process WM_KEYDOWN, however, because users expect programs to take action when they press a key, not when they release it. In addition, if a user holds down a key, Windows sends a string of WM_KEYDOWN messages, with no intervening WM_KEYUP messages. So if you want your program to process those so-called typematic keystrokes, you need to process WM_KEYDOWN rather than WM_KEYUP.

In this message, wParam contains the virtual key code, which was discussed on the last page. Most programs do a switch-case statement on the virtual key code and process...

- The focus window receives this message when the user presses a key -- the window receives WM_KEYUP when the user lets go
- If the user holds a key down, the keyboard's typematic action causes several consecutive WM_KEYDOWN messages
- Problem: Virtual key codes are not case sensitive

10-5

The WM_CHAR Message

wParam = character code

lParam = key flags

return: 0 if processed

See WM_KEYDOWN for a description of the key flags

- The character code is either an ASCII or UNICODE character - ASCII is the default
- Since the ASCII characters are case sensitive, programs that need to differentiate between upper and lower case keys should process WM_CHAR instead of WM_KEYDOWN

The big difference between this message and WM_KEYDOWN is that this message lets you tell the difference between upper and lower-case characters. There are a couple of other differences, though: for one, this message doesn't have "up" and "down" flavors (it comes in on the key downstroke). For another, while Windows generates WM_KEYDOWN for all keys, Windows only generates WM_CHAR messages for keys that have entries in the ASCII table. The final difference is that this message is actually optional – your window procedure only receives it if you include a special system call in your message loop (covered on the next page).

So for most programs, you'll need to handle both WM_KEYDOWN and WM_CHAR – WM_KEYDOWN for the non-alphanumeric keys and WM_CHAR so you can distinguish between upper and lower-case characters.ı˝ı...

Receiving WM_CHAR

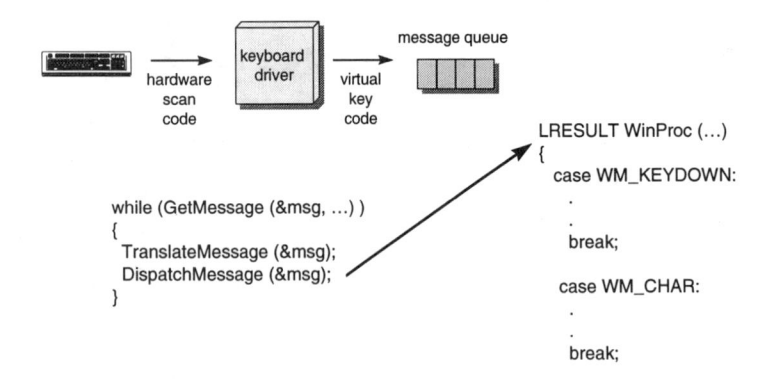

```
while (GetMessage (&msg, ...) )
{
  TranslateMessage (&msg);
  DispatchMessage (&msg);
}
```

```
LRESULT WinProc (...)
{
  case WM_KEYDOWN:
    .
    .
    break;

  case WM_CHAR:
    .
    .
    break;
```

WM_CHAR is an optional message – if you want windows in your application to receive it, you must code the TranslateMessage system call in your program's message loop. TranslateMessage essentially converts WM_KEYDOWN messages that correspond to alphanumeric keys into the WM_CHAR message.

- To receive WM_CHAR, you must code TranslateMessage as part of the message loop in WinMain
- TranslateMessage enqueues the WM_CHAR message with its embedded character code

Sample Keystroke Processing

```
case WM_KEYDOWN
// process non-alphanumeric keys
    switch ( wParam )
    {
        case VK_F2:
           // do something with F2 key
           .
           .
case WM_CHAR:
    {
        char ch = (char)wParam;

        // do something with character
        .
        .
```

- Many Windows programs process both WM_KEYDOWN and WM_CHAR
- You handle WM_KEYDOWN to process non-character keys, such as the function keys and directional keys (such keys have non ASCII codes)
- You handle WM_CHAR to process case-sensitive alpha-numeric keys

The code on this page shows a skeleton of how you might process keystrokes in a typical Windows program. Notice that we handle both WM_KEYDOWN and WM_CHAR – WM_KEYDOWN for the non-alphanumeric keys and WM_CHAR so we can distinguish the case of character keys.

You will write code similar to this in this chapter's lab exercise.

10-8

The Caret

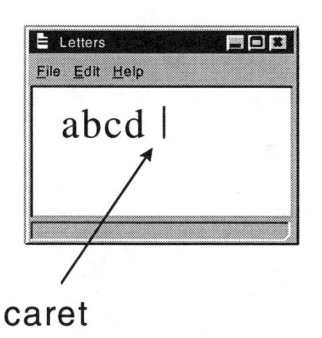

Caret System Calls

CreateCaret
DestroyCaret
ShowCaret
HideCaret
SetCaretPos
GetCaretPos
SetCaretBlinkTime
GetCaretBlinkTime

- Only one program should display a caret at any time, since the caret shows the user which window has the focus
- You can create and show a caret in the WM_SETFOCUS message, and you should destroy it in WM_KILLFOCUS
- Many programs let the user move the caret with the mouse or by pressing a directional key

The caret is sometimes called the text-entry caret or the cursor – but don't confuse it with the mouse cursor. The caret is optional – your window will not display one unless you write code to do so.

The CreateCaret call lets you specify the caret's shape. Common shapes are a vertical line or a reverse-video block. You can also create custom caret shapes by passing a bitmap to CreateCaret.

Many Windows programs let the user move the caret with the keyboard or the mouse. You use the SetCaretPos system call to move the caret. For example, a word-processor lets the user move the caret through a line of text using the left and right arrow keys, and lets the user scroll lines with the up and down arrow keys. In addition, a word processor often positions the caret at the character where the user clicks the mouse. You will do...

10-9

Lab Exercise 8: The Keyboard

In this lab, you will learn how to process keystroke messages and manipulate the caret. You will write a simple window procedure that echos keystrokes to its window and lets the user move the caret through the characters.

To view the lab exercise instructions, press the "Lab Write Up" button. This will display the lab document and let you print it if you wish. When you are finished with the lab, continue to the next page to take a review quiz.

Review Quiz

Before you move on to the next chapter, you should test your comprehension of this chapter by taking the review quiz. The quiz assumes that you have already done the lab exercise.

The quiz will be displayed in a separate window so that you can page through the chapter to help you find the answers. In other words, this is an open book quiz!

After you have answered all of the questions, press the button at the bottom of the quiz window to see how you did. If you didn't score as well as you think you should, you should review the chapter before continuing on.

Chapter Summary

- Even though there might be many windows on the desktop, only one receives messages when the user types keystrokes. The window that receives the messages is called the focus window.

- The focus window typically displays a caret (sometimes called a cursor) to let the user know which window has the focus..

- A window procedure can handle the WM_KEYDOWN message to process non-character keys such as the function keys.

- A window procedure can handle the WM_CHAR message to process alpha-numeric character keys such 'A' to 'Z' and '0' to '9'. The WM_CHAR message lets you tell the difference between upper and lower case characters.

10-12

Chapter 11: Menus

- Creating a Menu
- Popup Menus
- What is an Accelerator?

11-0

What is a Menu?

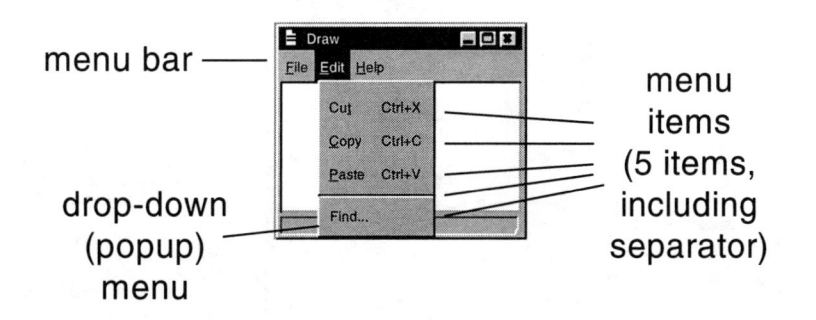

menu bar

drop-down (popup) menu

menu items (5 items, including separator)

- Menus provide a standardized way for user to issue commands to programs -- users don't have to memorize esoteric key sequences
- Users can select menu items using either the keyboard or the mouse
- A Windows program can define accelerator keystrokes so experienced users can bypass menus

Before Windows was popular, most MS-DOS programs required users to memorize dozens of keystrokes to perform common commands, such as opening and saving files. What's worse is that each program had its own set of keystrokes – so if you used both a spreadsheet and a word processor, you had to memorize two ways of opening files!

Obviously, this made it hard for users to learn new programs, so IBM and Microsoft devised a specification called Common User Access that decreed that Windows and OS/2 programs should use menus to show the user the commands to which a program responds. In addition, this specification, called CUA, also designated that common commands, such as opening a file, should have the same menu item text on all programs. That way, a user only needs to learn the menus once. Even though IBM and ...

11-1

Menu Design Guidelines

- Define menu mnemonics (sometimes called menu-item identifiers) so keyboard users can easily select menu items

- Use ellipses (...) to indicate that a menu item leads to a dialog box

- Use cascaded menu items (sparingly) to construct a hierarchy of menu items

- Use the special menu item SEPARATOR to group similar menu items

- At runtime, gray out (disable) menu items that represent unavailable commands

- At runtime, check menu items that represent a current choice (Win32 programs can also use "radio-button" menus)

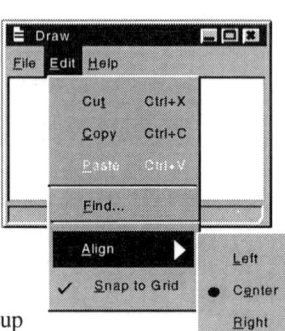

Many of these guidelines are part of the original Common User Access specification.

This program's Edit drop-down menu has eight items – Cut, Copy, Paste, Find, Align, Snap to Grid and two separators. The Paste item is grayed out, indicating that the program will not currently respond to that selection (perhaps there's nothing to paste). You can specify the initial "gray" state of an item when you create a menu, and change it on the fly from within the program.

The Snap to Grid menu item has a check mark next to it that indicates that the Snap to Grid setting is currently "on". Many programs use the check mark on menu items that toggle state – whenever the user selects the menu item, the program adds or removes the check mark. Like the grayed-out menu item attribute, you can specify the initial state when you create or define the menu, and change it at runtime.

The Align menu item is conn...

11-2

Creating a Menu as a Resource

MYAPP.RC

```
#include "resource.h"

MyMenu MENU
{
  POPUP "&Colors"
  {
    MENUITEM "&Red",    IDM_RED
    MENUITEM "&Blue",   IDM_BLUE
    MENUITEM "Blac&k",  IDM_BLACK
  }
}
```

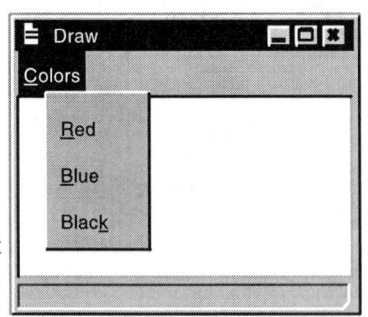

- A menu is a resource, just like an icon

- Most development environments like Visual C++ include a menu designer so you don't have to write the menu resource by hand -- Visual C++ will even write the #defines into the "resource.h" file for the menu item's symbolic names!

11-3

There are two basic ways to create menus – as a resource or by creating the menu at runtime. We will cover both in this chapter, but resource menus are by far the most common, and are much easier for the programmer. And since they are defined in the resource file rather than the source, if you decide to change a menu or translate it to another language, you don't have to recompile your source.

To define a menu, we give the menu a name, in this case "MyMenu", followed by the keyword MENU. Alternatively, we could have given the menu a numeric ID, and defined a symbolic name for the numeric ID in the RESOURCE.H file. We will reference the menu name or ID in WinMain in the source file.

We then start a block, using the left brace character (the text "BEGIN" would work, too). At the end, we close the block with the right brace characte...

The Big Picture

resource.h

```
#define IDM_RED    10
#define IDM_BLUE   11
#define IDM_BLACK  12
```

myapp.cpp

```
#include "resource.h"

wndclass.lpszMenuName = "MyMenu";
    .
    .
  case WM_COMMAND
    .
    .
    case IDM_RED:
```

myapp.rc

```
#include "resource.h"

MyMenu MENU
{
    .
    .
    MENUITEM "&Red",    IDM_RED
    MENUITEM "&Blue",   IDM_BLUE
    MENUITEM "Blac&k",  IDM_BLACK
    .
    .
}
```

- By defining the menu in the separate .RC file, you make it easier to translate it to other national languages
- The source file typically references the menu when it registers a class and while processing the WM_COMMAND message

11-4

This page shows the layout of a typical program that has a menu. We define the menu in the resource file (MYAPP.RC), define the symbolic names for the menu items in a header file (RESOURCE.H) and reference the menu item IDs in the source file (MYAPP.CPP). We include the RESOURCE.H header into both the resource file and the source file so that we can reference the symbolic names from both places.

By the way, there's nothing magic about the name of the header file. Microsoft's Visual C++ automatically assigns the name RESOURCE.H, but you can use any name you wish.

In the source file, we tell Windows to load the menu by specifying the menu's name in the WNDCLASS structure. If we had defined the menu using a numeric ID instead of using a string, we would have used the MAKEINTRESOURCE macro to cast the ID into the string expected by the WNDCLASS structure.
ï˜Also in the source file, we...

Responding to Menu Messages

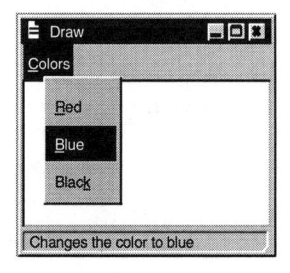

```
#include "resource.h"

LRESULT WndProc (...)
{
  switch ( msg )
  {
    case WM_COMMAND:
      switch ( LOWORD ( wParam ) )
      {
        case IDM_RED
              .
              .
              .
    case WM_MENUSELECT:
              .
              .
```

- The window procedure receives WM_COMMAND when the user clicks a menu item with the mouse or chooses and item with the keyboard
- The window procedure receives WM_MENUSELECT when the user moves the highlight
- The window procedure receives WM_INITMENUPOPUP when the user requests a drop-down or popup menu item

11-5

When the user manipulates a menu, either with the mouse or the keyboard, the window procedure receives a series of messages. It's perfectly OK to ignore these messages and pass them to the default window procedure if you wish. However, you probably should respond to at least WM_COMMAND, which indicates that the user wants you to execute the command that the menu represents.

To process WM_COMMAND, the window procedure can find the menu-item ID in the least significant 16 bits of wParam. Like always, we can use the LOWORD macro to extract the ID from the 32-bit message parameter.

Most programmers then do a nested switch-case statement with cases for each of the menu items, using the symbolic names for the menu items (they are defined in RESOURCE.H). In each sub-case, the window proce...

Graying or Checking a Menu Item

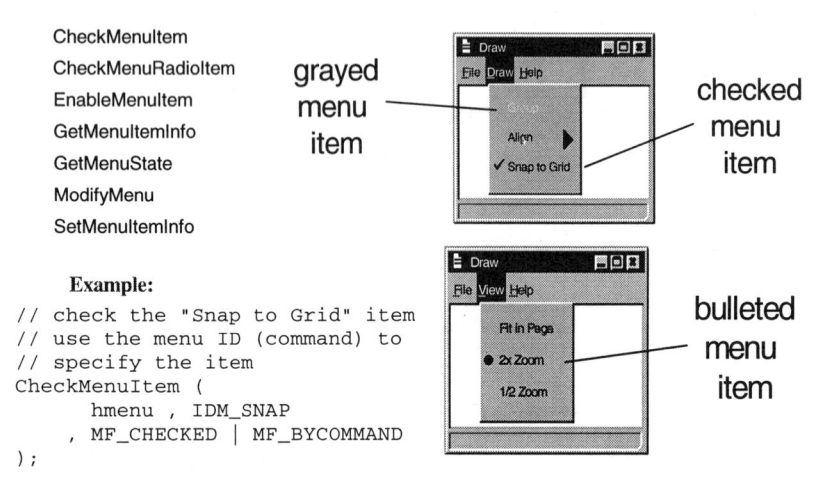

CheckMenuItem
CheckMenuRadioItem
EnableMenuItem
GetMenuItemInfo
GetMenuState
ModifyMenu
SetMenuItemInfo

grayed menu item

checked menu item

bulleted menu item

Example:
```
// check the "Snap to Grid" item
// use the menu ID (command) to
// specify the item
CheckMenuItem (
     hmenu , IDM_SNAP
   , MF_CHECKED | MF_BYCOMMAND
);
```

- You can define the initial menu state in the menu resource script and change it at runtime using these system calls

This page lists the system calls that let you manipulate a menu from your program. Click on each for a short description.

To manipulate a menu, you need to retrieve the menu's handle. The next page in the workshop describes how to obtain menu handles.

The three system calls that are most commonly used are EnableMenuItem, CheckMenuItem and CheckMenuRadioItem. You can use EnableMenuItem to gray-out or re-enable a menu item. You can use CheckMenuItem to place or remove a check mark from a menu item. You can use CheckMenuRadioItem to establish a bulleted menu item.

In all three of these calls, you need to specify which menu item to affect. The calls let you do that in two ways: by specifying the menu item's ID, or by specifying the menu item's position within its menu. You tell the system call whic...

11-6

Changing a Menu at Runtime

AppendMenu
CreateMenu
DestroyMenu
DrawMenuBar
GetMenu
GetSubMenu
GetSystemMenu
InsertMenu
InsertMenuItem
LoadMenu
ModifyMenu
SetMenu

This sample works the same as the sample on Page 11-5, but creates its menu at runtime instead of by loading as a resource.

- To modify a submenu, first call GetSubMenu to retrieve the submenu's handle
- After modifying the menu, call DrawMenuBar to update the menu

This page lists more system calls that let you manipulate menus. Click on each for a short description.

On the last page, you learned how to change a menu item's flags, for example graying-out an item or checking it. But that's not all you can do to a menu – this page shows system calls that let you perform major surgery on your menus. In fact, you can use the system calls on this page to build an entire menu from scratch at runtime, without creating a menu resource. While this technique is more difficult than using a menu resource, it is more flexible, since you can decide what the menu should look like at runtime. See the sample program on this page, which uses CreateMenu and AppendMenu to build a menu at runtime.

To use these calls, you need to understand the concept of menu handles. A menu hand...

11-7

Cascaded Menus

```
MyMenu   MENU
{
     .
     .
  POPUP      "&Draw"
  {
    MENUITEM    "&Group",   IDM_GROUP
    POPUP       "&Align"
    {
      MENUITEM "&Left",     IDM_LEFT
      MENUITEM "C&enter",   IDM_CENTER
      MENUITEM "&Right",    IDM_RIGHT
    }
    MENUITEM    "&Snap to Grid", IDM_SNAP, CHECKED
  }
     .
     .
}
```

cascaded menu item

On this page, the picture shows a window that has a cascaded menu to let the user choose some sort of alignment. Defining a cascaded menu is easy – simply nest a POPUP within another POPUP. Windows will automatically draw the arrow on the cascaded menu item and display the cascade when the user moves the highlight to that menu item.

Cascaded menu items generate messages in exactly the same way as non-cascaded menu items. Thus, you just need to handle the WM_COMMAND message as shown on page 11-5.

- Cascaded (sometimes called hierarchical or child menus) let you organize menus by groups
- Though they let you design more compact top-level drop-down menus, they annoy some users, so use them sparingly

11-8

Floating Popup Menus

```
case WM_CONTEXTMENU:
  {
    // display popup menu
    BOOL fSuccess = TrackPopupMenu (
          hmenuPopup
        , TPM_LEFTALIGN | TPM_RIGHTBUTTON
        , LOWORD ( lParam )
        , HIWORD ( lParam )
        , 0
        , hwnd
        , NULL );

  }
  return 0;
```

Floating popup menus are becoming more and more popular – they let a program display a list of commands right where the action will take place. For example, in the picture on this page, the user has highlighted a figure in the Draw program, and then clicked the right mouse button on it. The Draw program displays a popup menu that shows the actions that you can take in the current situation – here the menu lets the user cut or copy the selection to the clipboard.

Most programs display a popup in response to the right mouse button – the proper message to handle is WM_CONTEXTMENU. Windows generates this message when the right mouse button is released. WM_CONTEXTMENU differs from WM_RBUTTONUP in that it passes the mouse-click coordinates in screen units rather than client units – that's handy, because the TrackPo...

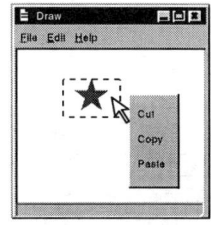

- You can display a popup menu (sometimes called a context menu) to let the user take action on an element displayed in the client area
- Most programs display the popup menu at the coordinates where the user clicks the right mouse button by responding to the WM_CONTEXTMENU message
- Popup menus generate the same messages as "normal" menus so you can use the same sort of code in the window procedure

11-9

What is an Accelerator?

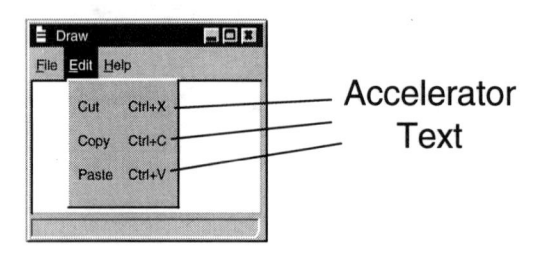

Accelerator keys are much appreciated by people that hate the mouse – they let such people issue commands to programs without having to lift their fingers from the keyboard. Of course, they must still learn the keys, which is why you should document the keys in the corresponding menu item. For example, the picture on this page shows the accelerators for Cut, Copy and Paste.

Please note that just putting the text in the menu item doesn't define the accelerator – you will have to define another resource as shown in the next few pages.

- Menus show new users the commands to which your program responds -- however, menus can be tedious
- Your program can define accelerator keys to let experienced users bypass the menus
- You should show the accelerators in the corresponding menu-item text so users can learn the accelerators

It's important to understand the difference between accelerators and menu keyboard mnemonics (underlined characters in menu text). Keyboard mnemonics also let keyboard users invoke the menu, but they require multiple keystrokes – the user must press and release the Alt key to start menu selection, followed by the mnemonic fo...

11-10

How Does an Accelerator Table Work?

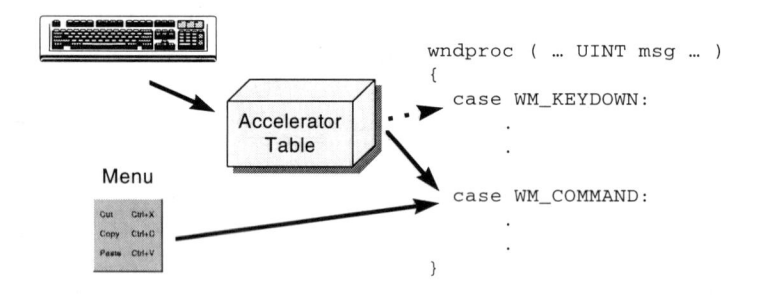

An accelerator is really nothing more than a message translator – it changes keystrokes into WM_COMMAND messages. That's nice, since menus also generate WM_COMMAND – once you have the code in place to handle menu selection, you don't have to change your window procedure when you add accelerators.

```
wndproc ( ... UINT msg ... )
{
    case WM_KEYDOWN:
        .
        .
    case WM_COMMAND:
        .
        .
}
```

- An accelerator table is a set of keystrokes and matching WM_COMMAND ID values
- In other words, an accelerator table translates keystroke messages into menu messages

11-11

Defining an Accelerator

```
MyAccel ACCELERATORS
{
  "X",     IDM_CUT,    CONTROL, VIRTKEY
  "C",     IDM_COPY,   CONTROL, VIRTKEY
  "V",     IDM_PASTE,  CONTROL, VIRTKEY
}

MyMenu   MENU
{
  POPUP    "&Edit"
  {
    MENUITEM    "Cu&t\tCtrl+X",    IDM_CUT
    MENUITEM    "&Copy\tCtrl+C",   IDM_COPY
    MENUITEM    "&Paste\tCtrl+V",  IDM_PASTE
  }
}
```

See Responding to Menu Messages to view the full source.

- An accelerator table is a resource -- most development environments like Visual C++ let you define the accelerators without writing a script by hand
- Use "\t" in the menu-item text to insert a tab character so that accelerator text lines up in the menu

Each entry in an accelerator table lists a key, the ID to which Windows will translate, and then some options. In this case, all of our accelerators require the user to press the Control key. We also used the VIRTKEY option – that tells Windows that the keystroke value, for example, "X", is a virtual-key constant, which for characters, is the same as the upper-case ASCII value. The advantage of using VIRTKEY is that the translation ignores the case of the key: it doesn't matter if the user has the Caps Lock on or not.

Other options include "SHIFT" and "ALT" – if you include one of these, then the accelerator only translates if that key is down when the user presses the character key. You can specify more than one qualifier key, separating with commas – if you do, then the user must hold down each of the qualifier keys as well as the character key. For example, if you listed CONTROL, ALT, SHIFT for the "Y" key, the user would have to press all four keys simultaneously to generate t...

11-12

Loading an Accelerator Table

```
// load the accelerator table
  HACCEL   haccel = LoadAccelerators ( hInstance, "MyAccel" );

// enter the event loop -- remain in loop until window closes
  while ( GetMessage ( &msg, NULL, 0, 0 ) != FALSE )
  {
    // translate accelerator keys
    if ( !TranslateAccelerator ( hwnd, haccel, &msg ) )
    {
      TranslateMessage ( &msg );
      DispatchMessage  ( &msg );
    }
  }
```

- In WinMain, you load the accelerator table and retrieve its handle by calling LoadAccelerators
- Your message loop must call TranslateAccelerator, which translates the WM_KEYDOWN message (if necessary) and automatically sends WM_COMMAND

Even though you don't have to modify your window procedure if you add accelerators, you will have to modify your source code. There are two things you need to do, both in WinMain: first, you must load the accelerator table and second, you must modify your message loop so that it calls TranslateAccelerator after calling GetMessage.

To load the accelerator, specify the current instance handle (passed as an argument to WinMain) followed by the name or ID of the accelerator table. As you saw with menus, you can assign the accelerator table either a string name or a numeric ID. If you assign a string name, as shown here, you pass the name as the second argument. If you assigned a numeric ID, then you must use the MAKEINTRESOURCE macro to convert the numeric ID to a string type, and pass the result as the second argument of L...

11-13

Lab Exercise 9: Menus

In this lab, you will learn how to create a menu and accelerator table as a resource and how to respond to menu messages. The program draws a series of random lines -- the menus let the user start and stop the drawing and configure what the lines look like. Press the "Run Lab Solution" button to see what your completed program should look like -- click the right mouse button on the client area to see the floating popup menu.

To view the lab exercise instructions, press the "Lab Write Up" button. This will display the lab document and let you print it if you wish. When you are finished with the lab, continue to the next page to take a review quiz.

Review Quiz

Before you move on to the next chapter, you should test your comprehension of this chapter by taking the review quiz. The quiz assumes that you have already done the lab exercise.

The quiz will be displayed in a separate window so that you can page through the chapter to help you find the answers. In other words, this is an open book quiz!

After you have answered all of the questions, press the button at the bottom of the quiz window to see how you did. If you didn't score as well as you think you should, you should review the chapter before continuing on.

Chapter Summary

- Menus provide visible documentation for the commands that a program accepts. In addition, Microsoft defines many standard menu items for common commands, such as file and clipboard operations.

- Normally, programs load menus from a resource. That makes it easy to modify the menu without needing to recompile the source file. It also makes it easier to translate the menu text to another national language.

- When the user manipulates a menu, the menu passes the window procedure with several messages. The most important message is WM_COMMAND, which the menu generates when the user chooses a menu item.
- Accelerators are keystrokes that let advanced users bypass a program's menus. Like menus, programs typically load accelerators from a resource. Accelerators translate keystroke messages into the same WM_COMMAND message that menus generate.

11-16

Chapter 12: Strings, Status and Tool Bars

- What is a String Table?
- Defining and Loading Strings
- What is a Status Bar?
- Creating a Status Bar
- What is a Tool Bar?
- Creating a Tool Bar

12-0

Displaying Text Strings

MYAPP.CPP

```
MessageBox ( ... "Hello" ... );
        or
MessageBox ( ... "Guten Tag" ... );
```

- Many programs hard-code text strings in the source file. This can lead to problems:
  - If you fix a typo, you must recompile
  - If you wish to translate the text to a different national language, you must recompile

In the program shown on this page, the developer has hard-coded the English "Hello" string into a message box. Then, apparently, the developer needed to convert the program to German language. Since the program has embedded text strings, someone must tediously search the program for all of the strings and translate them. That's especially difficult if the translator is not a programmer – how does a non-programmer know which strings are safe to translate, and which are not?

Luckily, as you will see in this chapter, Windows makes it fairly easy to pull the translatable strings from the source file and put them all in one place – the resource file

12-1

What is a String Table?

MYAPP.CPP

```
char sz[80];

LoadString ( ... IDS_STRING1
           , sz ... );

MessageBox ( ... sz ... );
```

MYAPP.RC

```
STRINGTABLE
{
    IDS_STRING1, "Hello"
}
```

- Instead of defining strings in the source file, you can define them in a STRINGTABLE resource
- If you then change a string, you just recompile the resources, not the source

So instead of defining strings in the source file, Windows developers can store all of the translatable strings in a string table resource and then load the strings by calling the Windows LoadString system call. While this is a bit harder than just hard-coding the strings, it pays dividends when the time comes to translate the strings to another national language. Since the strings are all defined in one place – the string table – the person who translates the strings can ignore all other text strings and just translate the ones in the string table.

Of course, the translator will also need to translate menu and dialog-item text – these strings are also located in the resource file. They are a bit harder to translate, though, since menu and dialog-item strings are not nicely organized into a table.

Notice that if you use string tables religiously, you won't even need to recompile your program if you translate the text!

12-2

Defining a String Table

MYAPP.RC

```
#include "resource.h"

STRINGTABLE DISCARDABLE
{
    IDS_STRING1,    "String 1 has\n a new line"
    IDS_STRING2,    "Hello"
}
```

- Each string should have a unique ID, typically defined in a header file
- The maximum length of a string is 4097 bytes
- Development environments like Visual C++ have tools to help you create string tables

To define a string, you assign the string an ID and then list the string's text. The maximum length of the string is 4097 bytes. If you wish, you can put new-line characters in the string.

Each string in a string table needs a unique identifier. Here, we have defined the symbolic names for the strings in the RESOURCE.H file. Note also that we've used the prefix "IDS_" (it stands for ID of a String) on all of the string IDs – that's not required, but it reminds you that the ID is for a string rather than a menu item or some other resource.

12-3

Loading a String

MYAPP.CPP

```
#include "resource.h"

const int MAXLEN=255;

char sz[MAXLEN];

int cb = LoadString ( hInstance, ID_STRING1, sz
                    , MAXLEN );

if ( cb == 0 )
    my_err_handler ( "Unable to load string" );
```

To load a string from the resources, the program calls LoadString, specifying the current instance handle, the string's ID, a pointer to the memory that will hold the string and the size of the memory buffer. LoadString returns the string's length. If the return value is zero, then LoadString failed, probably due to an unknown string ID.

Unfortunately, there's no easy way to determine a string's length without before loading it. See the Microsoft Knowledge base article Q20011 for a technique you can use (the Knowledge base is available on the Microsoft Developer Library CD-ROM or from http://www.microsoft.com/kb

- If the string is larger than the buffer, LoadString truncates and null-terminates the string to fit

---

What is a Status Bar?

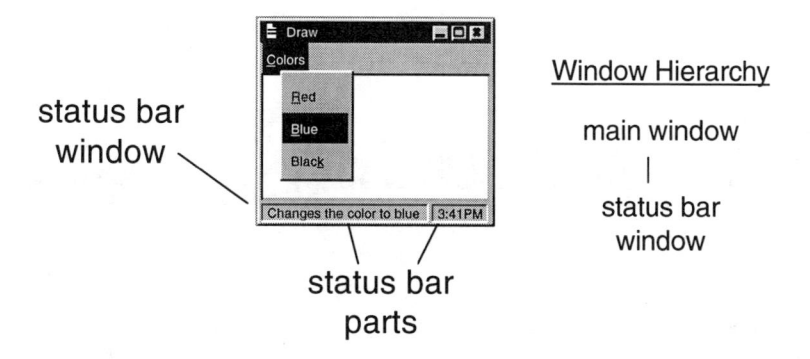

Window Hierarchy

main window
|
status bar window

status bar window

status bar parts

A status bar is a child window that overlays part of a window's client area, typically at the bottom.

A status bar can have one or more parts, or sections. You can have up to 255 parts and you can control the width of each part and set the text that each part displays. This status bar has two parts.

Many programs use a status bar to display menu-item information – that is, the program updates the status bar text as the user moves the highlight through a menu. Other uses include showing the time and date, page number, the state of the insert key and so on. This status bar uses its leftmost part to display menu information and the rightmost part to display the current time.

A status bar is one of the so-called common controls – these are window classes that are contained in the COMCT...

- A window can use a status bar to provide menu information, print progress, current page number and so forth
- A status bar can contain one or more parts, each with a different text string

Creating a Status Bar Window

```
const int IDW_STATUS = 10;

HWND hwndStatus = CreateStatusWindow (
    WS_CHILD | WS_VISIBLE   // style
    , NULL                  // initial text
    , hwnd                  // parent window
    , IDW_STATUS );         // window ID
```

Optional Styles:

    CCS_TOP

    CCS_BOTTOM

    SBARS_SIZEGRIP

- By default, a status bar has only one part and sizes and positions itself at the bottom of its parent's client area
- The parent must pass WM_SIZE messages to the status bar window so it can resize itself

There are two ways to create a status bar window – you can call CreateWindowEx or call CreateStatusWindow as shown here. CreateStatusWindow is a little easier, since it provides defaults for some of the CreateWindowEx arguments.

Programs typically create the status bar window in the WM_CREATE case of the main window procedure and specify the main window's handle as the parent. You must assign a window ID to the status bar – here we use the constant IDW_STATUS.

Status bar windows must have the WS_CHILD style and can also have the optional styles listed here. Click on each optional style for a description. The default style of CCS_BOTTOM causes the status bar to reside at the bottom of the client area.

In this sample, we create the status window with no text – that's because we will later send a message to the status window with the text string. A...

Multiple Status Bar Parts

```
RECT rc;
GetClientRect ( hwnd, &rc );

INT ai[2];    // two parts

// initialize with right-side
// coordinate of each part
// -1 means right edge of
// status bar

ai[0] = rc.right / 2;
ai[1] = -1;

SendMessage ( hwndStatus, SB_SETPARTS, 2, (LPARAM)ai );
```

Part 0   Part 1   ← cxClient →

- To split the status bar window into parts, send SB_SETPARTS and specify the coordinates of each part's right edge. You must re-send this message every time the parent's client area's width changes
- You can have a maximum of 255 parts!

By default, a status bar has a single part. To create multiple parts, you need to send the SB_SETPARTS message and pass the part count and the address of an array that describes each part.

In the array, you must allocate an integer for each part and initialize the integer to contain the coordinates of the part's right edge, in pixels. Here we set the first part's right edge to be one half of the status bar's width and specify -1 for the second part – that causes the status bar to set that part's right edge to the right edge of the status bar itself.

Note that at this point, we have not yet assigned text to the parts – we'll see how to do that in a moment.

Setting Status Bar Window Text

```
SendMessage ( hwndStatus
    , SB_SETTEXT
    , 0                    // part number
    , (LPARAM)"Text 0" );
SendMessage ( hwndStatus
    , SB_SETTEXT
    , 1                    // part number
    , (LPARAM)"Text 1" );
```

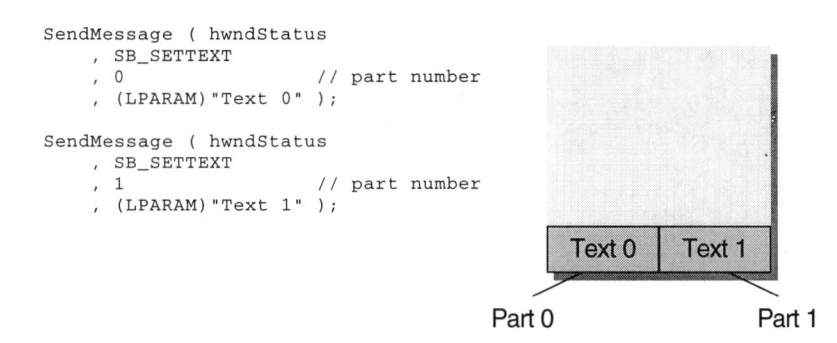

Part 0 — Text 0 | Text 1 — Part 1

It's quite easy to set the text for each part: simply send SB_SETTEXT once for each part, passing the part number and a pointer to the text for the part. As the page notes, to make translating to another language easier, you should load the text strings from a string table, rather than hard-coding them as English like the sample code does.

If the text string is too large to fit in the part's width, the status bar window clips the text.

- To set each part's text, send SB_SETTEXT and specify the part number (starts at zero) and the text
- You probably should load the text strings from a string table!

12-8

What is a Tool Bar?

tool bar buttons

tool bar window

Window Hierarchy

main window
├── toolbar window
└── status bar window

A toolbar is another common control. Toolbar windows normally reside at the top of the client area and contain one or more buttons, each of which typically corresponds to a menu item. When the user presses the toolbar button, the program takes the same action as it would if the user had selected the command from the menu. Thus, toolbars give users quick access to commands.

Like a status bar, a toolbar is a child window that overlays part of the client area.

Some programs create toolbars that contain things other than buttons, such as combo boxes or list boxes. The toolbar window class doesn't directly support this – it only draws buttons. However, it's not all that hard to put other controls on toolbars – see the Microsoft Systems Journal August 1994 issue for an article that shows how to do it.ı˙¨˙˙In additio...

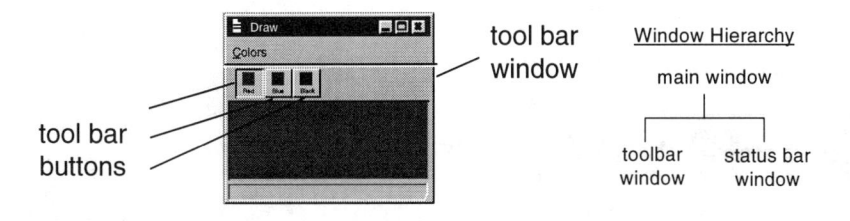

- A window can display a toolbar window to give users quick access to frequently used menu commands - the toolbar generates WM_COMMAND (same as menus) when the user clicks a button - you should assign each button the same command ID as the corresponding menu item
- A toolbar window contains bitmap buttons with optional text

12-9

Creating a Tool Bar Window

```
// create empty toolbar

HWND hwndToolbar;

hwndToolbar = CreateToolbarEx ( hwnd
    , WS_CHILD              // style
    , IDW_TOOLS             // toolbar window ID
    , 3                     // image count
    , hInstance
    , IDB_TOOLS             // bitmap ID
    , NULL, 0, 0, 0, 0      // no buttons yet
    , sizeof (TBBUTTON));   // button struct size
```

Optional Styles:

CCS_ADJUSTABLE	TBSTYLE_ALTDRAG
CCS_TOP	TBSTYLE_TOOLTIPS
CCS_BOTTOM	TBSTYLE_WRAPABLE

- By default, a toolbar window sizes and positions itself at the top its parent's client area - parent must pass WM_SIZE messages to the toolbar
- It's a good idea to create the toolbar empty, because you cannot adjust the button size (and other attributes) unless the toolbar is empty

12-10

As you saw with status bars, there's two ways to create tool bar windows. One, as shown here, is to call CreateToolbarEx. Or, you could call CreateWindowEx, specifying TOOLBARCLASSNAME as the class name (no quotes). CreateToolbarEx is a bit easier to use, since it supplies reasonable defaults for many of the CreateWindowEx arguments.

To create a toolbar window, you need to specify the toolbar's parent window, its style, ID, count of images, the resource ID of the bitmap that contains the toolbar images and some optional information about the buttons' size. Here we have created a toolbar window with no buttons, so we can ignore the button-size arguments and pass zero or null. We will add the buttons in a moment. The last argument of CreateToolbarEx specifies the size of a structure that we will use to add the buttons – this argument exists for compatibility with previous and future versions of Windows ...

Tool Bar Button Images

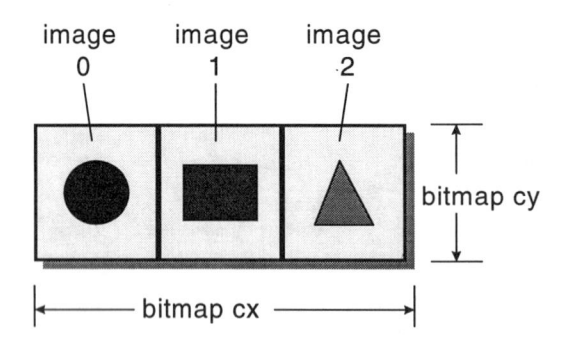

- When you create the toolbar, you can specify a single bitmap that contains multiple images. Each image must have the same width and height - by default, the tool bar assumes each component image's size is 16 x 15 pixels
- When you add a button to the toolbar, you specify the image index - that tells the toolbar which image to draw for the button

12-11

You may have noticed on the last page that when you create the toolbar window, you specify the resource ID of a bitmap that holds images that the toolbar buttons display. You might have wondered why that you specified only one bitmap, even though a toolbar might have several buttons. The reason is, the single bitmap holds multiple distinct images, typically, a separate image for each button.

Each image in the bitmap has an associated index, starting at zero. When you add each button to the toolbar, you need to specify the image index. So in this example, when we add the button that displays a triangle shape, we would specify an index of 2.

All of the component images must be the same size. That means that the entire bitmap must be wider than it is tall: in fact, the width must be N * CX, where N is the number of buttons (assuming each has ...

Tool Bar Button Text

```
// add index 0 string
SendMessage ( hwndToolbar
    , TB_ADDSTRING
    , 0 , "Circle" );

// add index 1 string
SendMessage ( hwndToolbar
    , TB_ADDSTRING
    , 0, "Square" );

// add index 2 string
SendMessage ( hwndToolbar
    , TB_ADDSTRING
    , 0 , "Triangle" );
```

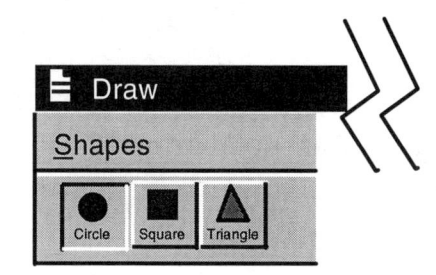

- The toolbar will optionally display a text string in each button
- Each time you send TB_ADDSTRING, the toolbar stores the string and increments an internal index (zero based)
- You specify a string index when you add each button to associate the string with the button

If you wish, each toolbar button will display a text string along with the image. Toolbar button text makes the buttons easier to decipher, but it also makes your program language specific. If you decide to use toolbar text, you should load the strings from a string table resource to make it easier to translate your program to a different national language.

To cause the buttons to display text, you first need to send TB_ADDSTRING to tell the toolbar about the strings. There are two ways to use TB_ADDSTRING – you can either pass the address of a string, or you can pass a stringtable ID. If you pass zero for wParam, like we did here, then lParam is the address of a string. Alternatively, you could pass an instance handle for wParam and then pass a stringtable ID for lParam – that causes TB_ADDSTRING to load the string from the stringtable.

TB_ADDSTRING does not associate a string with a button – all it does is add the...

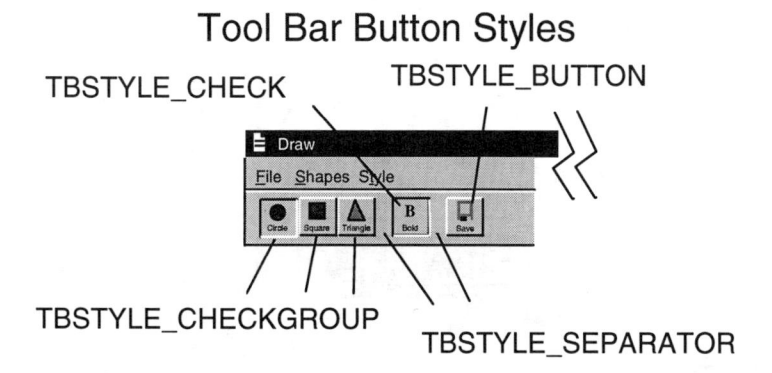

12-12

Tool Bar Button Styles

TBSTYLE_CHECK   TBSTYLE_BUTTON

TBSTYLE_CHECKGROUP   TBSTYLE_SEPARATOR

- You assign each button a style when you add it to the toolbar. The most common style is TBSTYLE_BUTTON
- A button with the TBSTYLE_SEPARATOR style cannot be selected - it also marks the end of any group of buttons
- Consecutive buttons with TBSTYLE_CHECKGROUP act like a bulleted menu item group
- Buttons with TBSTYLE_CHECK act as an on/off toggle

Button styles let you configure how a button reacts when the user clicks on the button. Probably the most common style is TBSTYLE_BUTTON, like the "Save" button in the picture. When the user clicks on a button of this style, the button appears to "press in" when the user clicks on it and then "presses out" when the user releases the mouse button. Buttons with this style act like menu items – when the user selects them, they simply pass a command to the owner window.

In contrast, buttons with the TBSTYLE_CHECK act like an on/off toggle. When the user clicks on such a button, the button "presses in" and stays "pressed in" until the user clicks on the button again. These style of buttons act like a checked menu item – they have an "on" and a "off" state. And like checked menu items, they generate a message whenever the user clicks them, regardless if they are "...

12-13

Tool Bar Button States

TBSTATE_CHECKED	A button with TBSTYLE_CHECKED is currently pressed
TBSTATE_ENABLED	A button is enabled
TBSTATE_HIDDEN	A button cannot be seen
TBSTATE_INDETERMINATE	A button is grayed out
TBSTATE_PRESSED	A button is currently being pressed
TBSTATE_WRAPPED	The button following this button wraps to a new line

The button states are bit flags that indicate the current attributes of a toolbar button. Since they are bit flags, more than one can be "on" at a time.

You can specify the initial state when you add each button and then send messages to modify the state at runtime. Notice that the state can also change due to the user's actions. For example, if the user "presses in" a TBSTYLE_CHECK button, it will adopt the TBSTATE_CHECKED state.

One reason you might need to change the state under program control is to keep your toolbar and menu synchronized. For example, if you have both a checkable menu item and a corresponding TBSTYLE_CHECK toolbar button, if the user selects the menu item, you need to send TB_CHECKBUTTON so that the toolbar button "presses in" to match the menu item's checkmark.

- You can set a button's initial state when you add it to the toolbar, query it by sending TB_GETSTATE, and change it by sending TB_SETSTATE
- You can send TB_CHECKBUTTON, TB_ISBUTTONCHECKED and so on to get or set the button's state

12-14

Adding Buttons to a Tool Bar

```
TBBUTTON atbb[3];    // three buttons

atbb[0].iBitmap = 0;    // image index
atbb[0].idCommand = IDM_RED;
atbb[0].fsState = TBSTATE_ENABLED;
atbb[0].fsStyle = TBSTYLE_CHECKGROUP;
atbb[0].dwData = 0;
atbb[0].iString = 0;    // string index
    .
    .
    .
SendMessage ( hwndToolbar, TB_ADDBUTTONS
    , 3                  // 3 buttons
    , (LPARAM)atbb );    // button array
```

Finally, we can now talk about adding buttons to the toolbar – we've covered image indexes, button styles, button states and button text indexes. Once you understand all of these topics, adding the buttons is actually pretty easy.

You send TB_ADDBUTTON to append one or more buttons to a toolbar. In wParam, you specify the count of buttons, and in lParam, you pass the address of an array that describes the buttons.

The array consists of TBBUTTON structures, one for each button. Let's take a look at the structure fields. The first field is the iBitmap field, in which you specify an image index as discussed on page 12-11.

The second field is the idCommand field – here you tell the toolbar the ID to pass as wParam in the WM_COMMAND message when the user clicks the butt...

- This message appends all of the buttons described by the array to the toolbar
- You can send TB_INSERTBUTTON to insert a new button between existing buttons

12-15

Enabling Tool Tips

```
case WM_NOTIFY:
  {
    switch (((LPNMHDR) lParam)->code)
    {
      case TTN_NEEDTEXT:
      {
        TOOLTIPTEXT *pttt = (TOOLTIPTEXT *) lParam;
        pttt->hinst = 0;

        switch ( pttt->hdr.idFrom )
        {
          case IDM_BLUE:
            pttt->lpszText = "Blue (Ctrl+B)";
            break;
          .
          .
          .
```

> Tool tips are small windows that we often use with toolbars. You can define them to display a string for each toolbar button that describes the button, listing any associated accelerator text, if desired. When the user hovers the mouse over the button, the toolbar automatically creates and displays the tool tip window and then destroys the window when the user moves the mouse.
>
> Since the tool tip window displays text, you should define the text in a stringtable to make translating to other languages easier.
>
> Whenever the user hovers the mouse over a toolbar with the TBSTYLE_TOOLTIPS style, the toolbar window sends WM_NOTIFY to its owner asking for the tool tip text for that button. The owner window should respond to the message by returning the appropriate text string for each button.
>
> The WM_NOTIFY message is a little bit weird. It is a generi...

- Tool tips are popup windows that the toolbar displays if the user lingers the mouse over a button
- To enable tool tips, create the toolbar with the TBSYTLE_TOOLTIPS style and provide a text string in response to the TTN_NEEDTEXT notification. You really should load the text from a string table!

12-16

Lab Exercise 10: Status and Tool Bars

In this lab, you will learn how to create a menu and accelerator table as a resource and how to respond to menu messages. The program draws a series of random lines -- the menus let the user start and stop the drawing and configure what the lines look like. Press the "Run Lab Solution" button to see what your completed program should look like -- click the right mouse button on the client area to see the floating popup menu.

To view the lab exercise instructions, press the "Lab Write Up" button. This will display the lab document and let you print it if you wish. When you are finished with the lab, continue to the next page to take a review quiz.

12-17

Review Quiz

Before you move on to the next chapter, you should test your comprehension of this chapter by taking the review quiz. The quiz assumes that you have already done the lab exercise.

The quiz will be displayed in a separate window so that you can page through the chapter to help you find the answers. In other words, this is an open book quiz!

After you have answered all of the questions, press the button at the bottom of the quiz window to see how you did. If you didn't score as well as you think you should, you should review the chapter before continuing on.

Chapter Summary

- Instead of hard-coding text strings in your source file, you can define the strings in a string table resource and then load them when you need them. That makes translating the strings to another language easier, since they are all defined in one place.

- A status bar is a child window that displays application-specific information to the user, such as the current page number, the date and time and so forth. You can also use a status bar to display information about the currently selected menu item.

- A tool bar is a window that contains buttons that let the user send commands to a program. It essentially provides short cuts to commonly used menu commands.

Chapter 13: Introduction to Dialog Boxes

- Message Boxes
- Modal Dialog Boxes
- Writing a Dialog Function
- Pushbutton Controls

What is a Dialog Box?

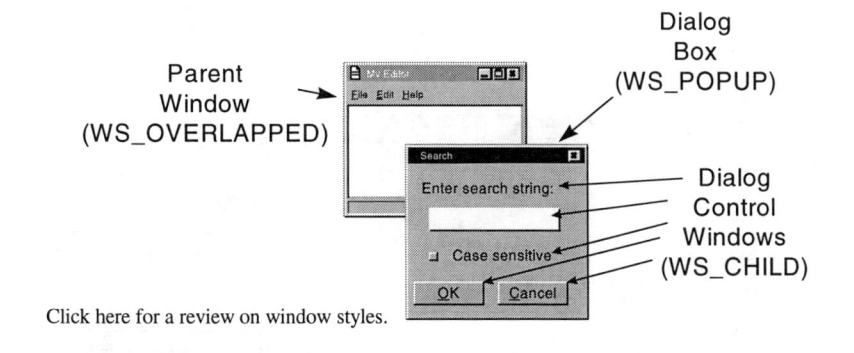

Parent Window (WS_OVERLAPPED)

Dialog Box (WS_POPUP)

Dialog Control Windows (WS_CHILD)

Click here for a review on window styles.

- A dialog box is a WS_POPUP window that contains child windows called dialog controls
- This dialog box contains a static text control, an edit box control, a check-box control and two pushbutton controls

A dialog is a popup window that contains child windows, called controls, that let the user enter text, choose options and so forth. The dialog shown on this page contains five controls: a static text window, an edit control, a check box control and two pushbuttons. Each control is a separate window, and each has an application-defined window ID and a unique window handle.

Programs normally display dialog boxes in response to the user selecting a menu item on the main window.

Most dialogs have a parent window (sometimes called the owner). In this case it's the "My Editor" window. As we'll see in a moment, Windows maintains a relationship between the dialog and its parent.

Most dialogs have one or more pushbuttons that the user presses to dismiss the ...

Types of Dialog Boxes

Message Box

- Displays a title, text string, one or more pushbuttons and an optional icon
- Very easy to program, but not very flexible
- Modal: while visible, Windows prevents parent window from receiving user input

Modal Dialog Box

- Program must supply a dialog function
- More flexible than a message box
- Modal: while visible, Windows prevents parent window from receiving user input

Modeless Dialog Box

- Program must supply a dialog function
- Windows doesn't disable the parent window

This page lists the types of dialog boxes supported by Windows. We will cover each in more detail later, but here's a quick overview of each.

You've probably seen message boxes – programs often display them in situations like "File not found", or "Do you really want to do what you just asked". They are very easy to program, but are rather limited. They prevent the user from interacting with the parent window until the message box is dismissed. In other words, the user has to get rid of the message box before they can go back to the parent window.

Modal dialogs are probably the most common type – the search dialog on the previous page may well have been modal. Like message boxes, modal dialogs impose order on the user in that the user cannot interact with the parent window until they dismiss the dialog. They are a bit more involved to program than message boxes, but are much more flexible.ı˝ı˝Modeles...

Message Boxes

```
int MessageBox ( HWND hwndParent
               , LPSTR lpText
               , LPSTR lpTitle
               , UINT uType )
```

Example:

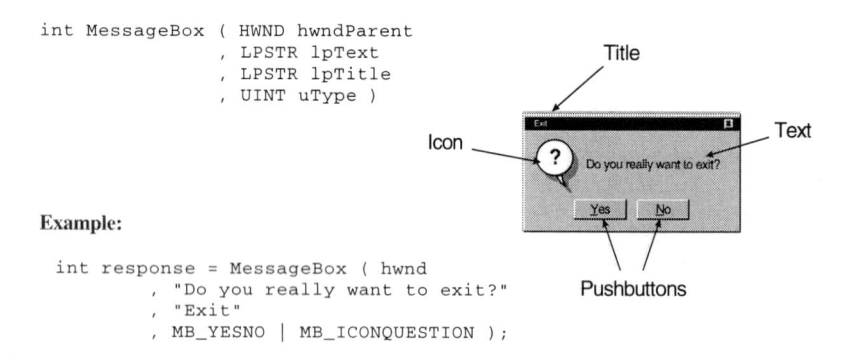

```
int response = MessageBox ( hwnd
               , "Do you really want to exit?"
               , "Exit"
               , MB_YESNO | MB_ICONQUESTION );
```

- Message boxes are always modal - the user cannot interact with the parent window until they dismiss the message box

This page shows a typical message box with an icon, a text string, a title and two pushbuttons. As you will see in the next pages, you can customize a message box's appearance, but not very radically.

It's easy to display a message box, though – simply call MessageBox and specify the parent window, the text, the title and a flags parameter that we will cover on the next page. The MessageBox call doesn't return until the user dismisses the box by clicking one of the pushbuttons. When they do, MessageBox returns a response code that indicates which button the user pressed. That lets your program make a decision based on which button the user pressed.

Message Box Styles

Button Styles

    MB_ABORTRETRYIGNORE
    MB_OK
    MB_OKCANCEL
    MB_RETRYCANCEL
    MB_YESNO
    MB_YESNOCANCEL

    MB_DEFBUTTON1
    MB_DEFBUTTON2
    MB_DEFBUTTON3

Icon Styles

    MB_ICONEXCLAMATION
    MB_ICONINFORMATION
    MB_ICONQUESTION
    MB_ICONSTOP

Modality Styles

    MB_APPLMODAL
    MB_SYSTEMMODAL
    MB_TASKMODAL

This page shows the possible values for the uType parameter shown on the previous page. Click on each style for a short description.

To combine the styles, use the C "or" operator. However, some styles cannot be combined – for example, you can choose only one button style and one icon style.

- You can combine any button, icon and modality style, but only one of each category

---

Message Box Responses

From WINUSER.H:

```
#define IDOK       1
#define IDCANCEL   2
#define IDABORT    3
#define IDRETRY    4
#define IDIGNORE   5
#define IDYES      6
#define IDNO       7
```

These are the possible response integers that MessageBox returns. They each correspond to a button on the message box. Even though we show them here, the actual values aren't really important.

- These symbols are defined by the Windows header files
- Each symbol corresponds to a button on a message box

What is a Modal Dialog?

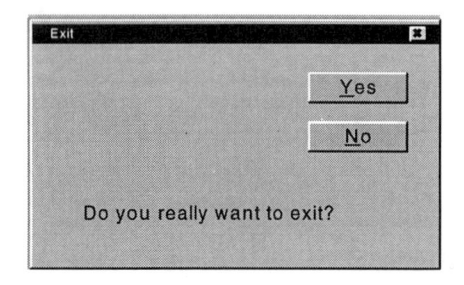

Now let's take a look at modal dialogs, which are similar to message boxes. The big difference is that you can design their appearance. For example, in this case, we'd like to display a text string but have the buttons in the dialog's upper-right corner. This is very similar to a message box, but with a message box, you can't specify the button's coordinates. With a modal dialog, you have complete control over the dialog child windows' size and position.

Normally, you create modal dialogs from a resource script, much like we saw with menus. And also like menus, you can use Visual C++ or other tool to create and edit the dialog visually. The tool will then generate the dialog script for you.

Modal dialog boxes are a bit harder to program than message boxes. The call to display a modal dialog isn't really any more difficult than MessageBox, but you must write a dialog function for mo...

- Modal dialog boxes disable their parent window from receiving user input - they are like message boxes, but are more flexible
- You must write a dialog function that responds to messages from the dialog controls
- You define the dialog's appearance in a resource script (like a menu). Most Windows development environments like Visual C++ include tools that let you design dialogs

---

The Dialog Resource Script

MYAPP.RC

```
#include <windows.h>
#include "resource.h"

DLG_EXIT DIALOG DISCARDABLE  0, 0, 187, 9
STYLE DS_MODALFRAME | WS_POPUP |
    WS_CAPTION | WS_SYSMENU
CAPTION "Exit"
FONT 8, "MS Sans Serif"
{
    DEFPUSHBUTTON    "&Yes",IDYES,130,7,50,14
    PUSHBUTTON       "&No",IDNO,130,24,50,14
    LTEXT            "Do you really want to exit?",
                     IDC_STATIC,27,50,78,8
}
```

This is the dialog script that was generated by Microsoft's Visual C++ dialog editor tool for our sample dialog. By default, Visual C++ stores the dialog script in the resource file – the same file where your menu script resides. And like with menus, Visual C++ writes any dialog symbolic identifiers into a header file named RESOURCE.H.

While it's true that you probably won't need to write a dialog script by hand, it is important that you have a general understanding of the script. It's especially important that you can recognize the symbolic IDs contained in the script – if you design the dialog on Tuesday but don't write the supporting code until Wednesday, you can look here if you forget the IDs.

The first line of the dialog script defines the dialog ID, in this case DLG_EXIT. Each dialog should have a unique ID. Like with menus, you can...

- You probably won't ever need to write a dialog script yourself, since Windows development tools like Visual C++ include a dialog editor
- The dialog itself has a unique ID, usually defined in RESOURCE.H
- Each dialog control has a unique ID, usually defined in RESOURCE.H

Introduction to Dialog Boxes

Pushbutton Controls

```
#include "resource.h"

BOOL DialogFunction (...)
{
  switch ( msg )
  {
    case WM_COMMAND:
      switch ( LOWORD ( wParam ) )
      {
        case IDYES:
             .
             .
        case IDNO:
             .
             .
```

pushbutton control, ID = IDYES

pushbutton control, ID = IDNO

- When the user clicks a pushbutton, it transmits a WM_COMMAND message to the dialog function

13-8

Pushbuttons are a very common dialog control – in fact, it's quite rare to see a dialog that has no buttons. Their programming is similar to menus – each button on a dialog should have a unique identifier – when the user clicks the button, the button generates a WM_COMMAND message with the ID in the least-significant 16 bits of wParam.

There is a difference from menus, however – menus transmit the WM_COMMAND message to the main window procedure – pushbuttons transmit the message to the dialog function that controls the dialog on which they reside. That means that you must, in general, write a separate dialog function for every dialog that you have in your program.

In this example, we have two pushbuttons on the dialog – one with ID of IDYES and the other with IDNO. In the dialog function, we have written a WM_COMMAND case, in which we switch on the butto...

Displaying a Modal Dialog

Main Window Procedure
```
WndProc (...)
{
  int response;

  response = DialogBoxParam (
      hInstance
    , MAKEINTRESOURCE(DLG_EDIT)
    , hwnd
    , EditDialogProc
    , 0 )
// response now == xxxxx
}
```

Dialog Function
```
BOOL EditDialogProc (...)
{
         .
         .
    case WM_INITDIALOG:
         .
         .
    case WM_COMMAND:
         .
         .
         EndDialog ( hwndDlg, xxxxx );
         .
         .
```

- DialogBoxParam doesn't return until the dialog box is dismissed by the dialog function
- Typically, the dialog function dismisses the dialog by calling EndDialog when the user presses pushes a button control
- EndDialog hides and destroys the dialog - Windows passes the second argument of EndDialog back to calling program, which has been blocked in DialogBoxParam

13-9

This page shows how the dialog function and the main window procedure interact. We generally display a dialog in response to a menu item – the code shown here in the main window procedure is from the main window's WM_COMMAND case.

To display a dialog, we call DialogBoxParam. The arguments to DialogBoxParam are: the instance handle that specifies where the dialog box resource resides, the dialog's ID or name, which matches the dialog script, the parent of the dialog, the address of the dialog function, and an application-defined argument, which we'll discuss in a moment.

In the dialog function, we show the two most common messages, WM_INITDIALOG, which is similar to WM_CREATE in a window procedure, and WM_COMMAND, which is the message generated by push...

The Dialog Box Function

```
BOOL CALLBACK ExitDialogProc ( HWND hwndDlg, UINT iMsg
                             , WPARAM wParam, LPARAM lParam )
{
    switch ( iMsg )
    {
        case WM_COMMAND:
            switch ( LOWORD (wParam) )
            {
                case IDYES:
                    EndDialog ( hwnd, IDYES );
                    return TRUE;
                    .
                    .
                    .
            }
            return FALSE;

        default:
            return FALSE;
    }
}
```

- The dialog box function initializes controls and then responds to notification messages from the controls
- You should return TRUE in a message case if you processed the message, FALSE otherwise (WM_INITDIALOG is an exception)

13-10

Here we see part of a the dialog function for our sample dialog – when the user presses the Yes button, the dialog function dismisses the dialog box and passes IDYES as the second argument of EndDialog. We don't show the code for the No button, but it's very similar (click the Full Sample Source button to see it). The difference is that we return IDNO if the user presses the No button.

A dialog function is similar to a window procedure, but there are a few differences. The most important is the return value of the dialog function itself, which is a boolean, instead of an LRESULT. The rule of thumb is that you return TRUE from a case if you process the message, FALSE if you didn't. That's why we return FALSE in the default case of the switch statement. This is different from a window procedure, where we call the default window procedure in the default case of the main switch statement.

The Dialog BoxParam System Call

From WINUSER.H:

```
int DialogBoxParam ( HINSTANCE hInstance
                   , LPCSTR lpTemplateName
                   , HWND hWndParent
                   , DLGPROC lpDialogFunc
                   , LPARAM dwInitParam );
```

Other Modal Dialog Box System Calls

DialogBox

DialogBoxIndirect

DialogBoxIndirectParam

- The last argument of DialogBoxParam is application-defined, Windows passes it as lParam in the dialog function's WM_INITDIALOG message
- Many programs use this last argument to pass a 32-bit value (could be a pointer) to the dialog function

13-11

The last argument of DialogBoxParam is especially interesting, because it lets the calling program pass an application-defined value to the dialog procedure. The dialog procedure receives the pointer in the WM_INITDIALOG message. This can be very handy, as you will see in later chapters.

The "indirect" calls listed on this page are not commonly used because they are much harder to program. They require you to build a memory-based array that describes the dialog controls instead of loading the dialog from a resource. They are nice, though, for programs that need to build dialog boxes dynamically instead of statically defining them in the resource file.

Lab Exercise 11: An About Dialog

In this lab, you will learn how to create a simple dialog that the user can display by choosing About from the Help menu.

Press the "Run Lab Solution" button to see what your completed program should look like -- click the right mouse button on the client area to see the floating popup menu.

To view the lab exercise instructions, press the "Lab Write Up" button. This will display the lab document and let you print it if you wish. When you are finished with the lab, continue to the next page to take a review quiz.

Review Quiz

Before you move on to the next chapter, you should test your comprehension of this chapter by taking the review quiz. The quiz assumes that you have already done the lab exercise.

The quiz will be displayed in a separate window so that you can page through the chapter to help you find the answers. In other words, this is an open book quiz!

After you have answered all of the questions, press the button at the bottom of the quiz window to see how you did. If you didn't score as well as you think you should, you should review the chapter before continuing on.

Chapter Summary

- There are two basic kinds of dialogs -- modal dialogs that disable their parent window, and modeless dialogs that don't. Message boxes are a special kind of modal dialog box.

- Message boxes are very easy to display, but cannot be customized easily.

- Before you can display a modal dialog box, you must write a dialog function that responds to messages from the dialog controls.

13-14

Chapter 14: Simple Dialog Box Controls

- ♦ Check Boxes
- ♦ Edit Controls
- ♦ Radio Buttons
- ♦ List Boxes

14-0

Introduction to Dialog Box Controls

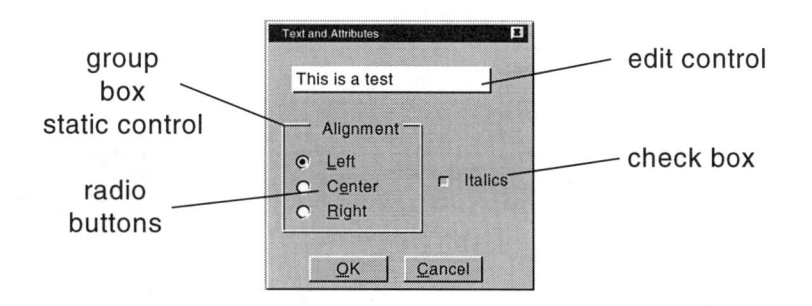

group box
static control

radio buttons

edit control

check box

- We will cover several dialog controls in this chapter - enough so that you can learn any others on your own
- All dialog controls have styles, notifications and respond to a set of messages

In the last chapter and lab exercise, you learned how to create a simple dialog with pushbuttons and static controls – that was great for displaying data. In this chapter, you will learn how to add controls to a dialog that let the user enter or choose data.

For example, the dialog shown on this page has an edit control that lets the user enter text, a group of radio buttons, from which the user can select a choice, and a check box control that lets the user choose a on-off option.

The programming for all dialog controls is similar:

- They all have one or more styles that let you customize their behavior and appearance.

- They all generate WM_COMMAND messages, passing a notification code in the high-word of wParam that indicates the message's cau...

14-1

Messages and Dialog Controls

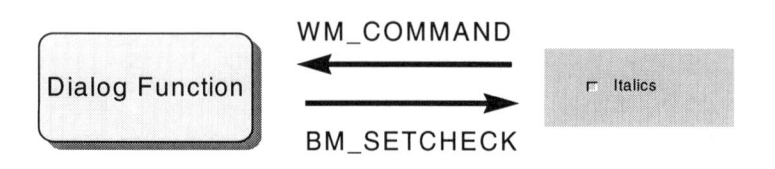

WM_COMMAND ← Dialog Function → BM_SETCHECK ☐ Italics

A program interacts with dialog controls using messages. The way that you learn a new dialog control is to study the messages it transmits and the messages it expects to receive.

In the example on this page, we have a check box control. When the user clicks on the checkbox, it passes WM_COMMAND to the dialog function. The dialog function can choose to respond to the message or to ignore it.

The dialog function can also send messages to the checkbox. For example, when this dialog first comes up, you probably want the Italics checkbox to reflect the current italic state of the text it represents. To do so, the dialog function, during its initialization, can send the BM_SETCHECK message to the checkbox to turn the check-mark off or on.

There is a convention that makes this easier to learn and remember. Each message that a control recognizes has a pr...

- Dialog controls send the WM_COMMAND message to notify their parent (usually the dialog function) of significant events, such as mouse clicks
- The dialog function can send messages to the control window to manipulate it. For example, you can send the BM_CHECK message to a checkbox to turn it off or on

14-2

The WM_COMMAND Message

Message Queue

MSG
hwnd
message = WM_COMMAND
wParam = control ID and notification code
lParam = control window handle

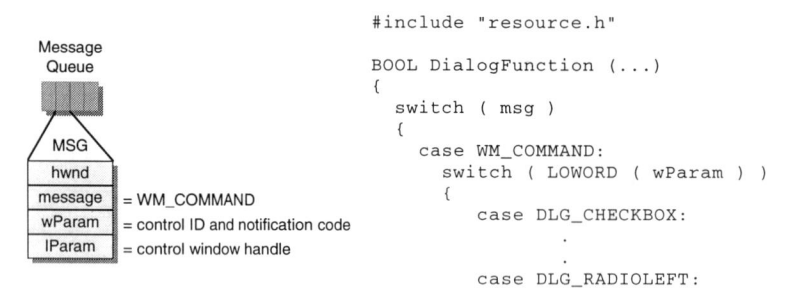

```
#include "resource.h"

BOOL DialogFunction (...)
{
   switch ( msg )
   {
     case WM_COMMAND:
       switch ( LOWORD ( wParam ) )
       {
          case DLG_CHECKBOX:
             .
             .
          case DLG_RADIOLEFT:
             .
             .
```

When the user interacts with a dialog control, the control sends WM_COMMAND to its parent, which is usually a dialog procedure. In that message, wParam has two 16-bit fields packed into it: the least significant 16 bits contain the control's ID and the most significant 16 bits contain the notification code. Since all dialog controls generate WM_COMMAND, the only way to distinguish messages from controls is to examine the ID. On a given dialog, each control thus needs a unique ID.

The code shown on this page is pretty typical. It performs a switch on the control ID and then has a case for each dialog control.

Although this code doesn't examine the notification code, that code can be quite useful if a given dialog control can generate many different kinds of events. For example, a edit control sends WM_COMMA...

- You should assign each dialog control a unique ID -- the WM_COMMAND message contains the ID in the low word of wParam
- Each dialog control window class defines its own notification codes (passed in high word of wParam). For example, the edit control class defines EN_CHANGE and EN_SETFOCUS

14-3

What is a Checkbox?

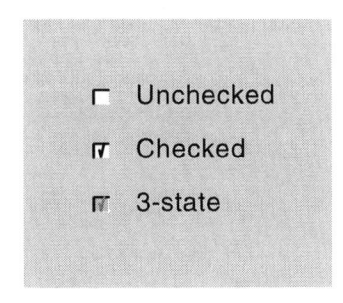

[ ] Unchecked
[x] Checked
[x] 3-state

Styles

BS_CHECKBOX
BS_AUTOCHECKBOX
BS_3STATE
BS_AUTO3STATE

Notification codes

BN_CLICKED

This page shows three checkboxes, each in a different state. The first is in the unchecked state, the second is checked, and the third is in the indeterminate state.

This page also lists the styles and notification codes for the checkbox class.

The most common style is the BS_AUTOCHECKBOX style. With this style, if the user clicks on the checkbox, Windows automatically adds or removes the check mark. If you use the BS_CHECKBOX style, then your dialog function must send the BM_SETCHECK message whenever the user clicks on the checkbox to tell the checkbox window to draw or remove the check mark.

The three-state style is useful if you have a "mixed value" condition. For example, if the user highlights some text, only some of which is italicized, and then displays a dialog box containing an "Italics" checkbox, you could set the ...

- Checkbox controls are actually a style of the BUTTON class. They are useful to give the user an on/off choice
- Click on the styles and notifications for a brief description of each

14-4

Button Messages

BM_CLICK
BM_GETCHECK
BM_GETIMAGE
BM_GETSTATE
BM_SETCHECK
BM_SETIMAGE
BM_SETSTATE
BM_SETSTYLE

Example: Setting a check box check state

```
HWND hwndCheckbox = GetDlgItem ( hwndDlg
                          , DLG_CHECK);

SendMessage ( hwndCheckbox, BM_SETCHECK
            , (WPARAM)BST_CHECKED, 0 );
```

All of the button message names begin with the BM_ prefix. Please don't confuse them with the BN_ notification code you saw on the last page -- these are messages you send to buttons, a notification comes from a button.

You don't really need to send some of these messages very often, since Windows provides system calls that do the same thing and are easier to use. We will cover those in a moment.

The example code turns a check mark on. We first call GetDlgItem to retrieve the check box's window handle, given its ID, then send BM_SETCHECK. wParam for this message contains the button's new state – in this case, we specify BST_CHECKED to turn the check mark on. lParam isn't used in this message.

- You can send these messages to checkboxes, radio buttons and pushbuttons
- Click on each for a brief description

14-5

Programming Check Boxes

These functions actually send button messages "under the covers". They are a bit easier to use than sending the messages directly, since you don't have to supply the check box window handle. In other words, these functions internally call GetDlgItem, so you can supply just a window ID.

```
BOOL CheckDlgButton ( HWND hDlg, int nIDButton
                    , UINT uCheck );

UINT IsDlgButtonChecked ( HWND hDlg, int nIDButton );
```

- You can check or uncheck a check box from a program by sending the BM_SETCHECK message or by calling CheckDlgButton
- You can retrieve a check box's check state by sending BM_GETCHECK or by calling IsDlgButtonChecked

14-6

Passing Data to a Dialog Box Function

The information on this page really applies to all dialog controls, not just check boxes. The idea is that dialog boxes expose your program's data to the user – at least the subset of the data that you want the user to see. In this case, the program has boolean variable it uses to determine whether or not to italicize its text and uses a check box to visually represent the italics attribute.

The fItalic variable is defined in the main window procedure, but the dialog function needs to have access to the variable, too. How can we do this? One way would be to make the fItalic variable global, but that's not a good way to structure a program, since it tightly couples the dialog function with the global variable, which makes it hard to re-use the dialog function for similar dialogs.

Instead, we can pass the address of the fItalic variable to the dialog function in the l...

```
mainwinproc (...)
{
static BOOL      fItalic;
    .
    .                       dialogfunction (...)
    .                       {
response = DialogBoxParam (  static BOOL  *pfItalic;
    ... &fItalic );             .
    .                           .
    .                           .
    .                       case WM_INITDIALOG:
                                pfItalic = (BOOL *) lParam;
                                .
                                .
                                .
```

- Dialog controls generally correspond to a chunk of data that you want the user to be able to view or modify
- The calling program can pass the data's address to the dialog function - since the dialog function receives a pointer, it can both read and write the data

14-7

The Dialog Contract

```
mainwinproc (...)
{
static BOOL        fItalic;
    .
    .
    .
response = DialogBoxParam (
    ... &fItalic );

if ( response == IDOK )
    redrawtext ( fItalic );
    .
    .
    .
```

```
dialogfunction (...)
{
static BOOL    *pfItalic;
    .
    .
    .
case IDOK:
    UINT u;
    u = IsDlgButtonChecked(...);
    if ( u == BST_UNCHECKED )
        *pfItalic = FALSE;
    else
        *pfItalic = TRUE;
    EndDialog ( hwndDlg, IDOK );
    .
    .
    .
```

- The main window should pass the address of the data it wants the dialog to modify
- The dialog should modify the data only if the user OKs the dialog
- The dialog should return the ID of button that dismissed the dialog back to the main window

14-8

We call this the dialog contract because it imposes a specific interaction between the main window procedure and the dialog function. To the main window procedure, the dialog function is a black box --- the main window procedure should not be concerned with the inner workings of the dialog. Similarly, the dialog function should be concerned only with the dialog – it should contain no application logic, just code to manipulate the dialog user interface. If you use this contract, then it makes it easy to write fairly generic dialog functions that you can re-use for other dialogs. It will also make your mainline code more maintainable, since it doesn't have to change if you change the dialog's user interface.

Here are the rules for the contract:

1. The main window should pass the address of the data it wants the dialog to expose. Since we pass the address, the dialog potentially can modify the data.ı´ı´2. Th...

Checkbox Sample Program

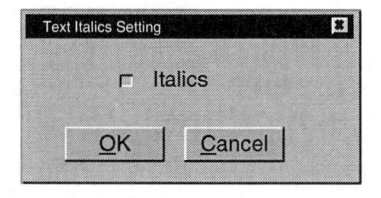

This sample displays a text string in its client area. The user can choose either italicized or normal text by displaying the dialog shown on this page and clicking on the checkbox.

This program uses the dialog contract discussed in the last two pages, that is:

1. The dialog function's WM_INITDIALOG case sets the checkbox state.

2. The dialog function's WM_COMMAND case updates the caller's fItalic variable only if the user OKs the dialog box.

3. The main window examines the return from DialogBoxParam.

- This program displays text in its client area - the user can choose whether or not the text is displayed in an italic font via the dialog
- The user invokes the dialog by choosing from a menu

14-9

What is a Single Line Edit Control?

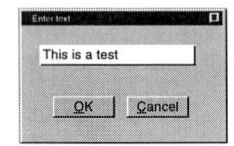

Styles	Notification codes
ES_AUTOHSCROLL	EN_CHANGE
ES_AUTOVSCROLL	EN_ERRSPACE
ES_CENTER	EN_HSCROLL
ES_LEFT	EN_KILLFOCUS
ES_LOWERCASE	EN_MAXTEXT
ES_MULTILINE	EN_SETFOCUS
ES_NOHIDESEL	EN_UPDATE
ES_NUMBER	EN_VSCROLL
ES_OEMCONVERT	
ES_PASSWORD	
ES_READONLY	
ES_RIGHT	
ES_UPPERCASE	
ES_WANTRETURN	

Edit controls come in two basic styles – single line and multiline. You specify the style when you create the edit control in your dialog box editor. The dialog shown on this page has a single-line edit control. Multiline edit controls have the ES_MULTILINE style, and as you might expect, let the user enter more than one line of text.

In addition to letting the user enter text, edit controls also let the user edit the text using the keyboard or mouse. Edit controls also support the system clipboard so that users can cut, copy or paste text to or from an edit control without any extra code in the dialog function.

Unlike checkboxes, edit controls have more than one notification code. Remember that all notifications are passed as WM_COMMAND messages – the high word of wParam contains one of the codes shown on this page. Click on the "Extracing the Notification Code" button to see a program fragment that...

- Single line edit controls are windows of the EDIT class - they let the user enter text and edit it using the keyboard or mouse
- Click on the styles, notifications and control messages for a brief description of each

14-10

Edit Control Messages

EM_CANUNDO	EM_GETRECT	EM_SCROLLCARET
EM_CHARFROMPOS	EM_GETSEL	EM_SETHANDLE
EM_EMPTYUNDOBUFFER	EM_GETTHUMB	EM_SETLIMITTEXT
EM_FMTLINES	EM_GETWORDBREAKPROC	EM_SETMARGINS
EM_GETFIRSTVISIBLELINE	EM_LIMITTEXT	EM_SETMODIFY
EM_GETHANDLE	EM_LINEFROMCHAR	EM_SETPASSWORDCHAR
EM_GETLIMITTEXT	EM_LINEINDEX	EM_SETREADONLY
EM_GETLINE	EM_LINELENGTH	EM_SETRECT
EM_GETLINECOUNT	EM_LINESCROLL	EM_SETRECTNP
EM_GETMARGINS	EM_POSFROMCHAR	EM_SETSEL
EM_GETMODIFY	EM_REPLACESEL	EM_SETTABSTOPS
EM_GETPASSWORDCHAR	EM_SCROLL	EM_SETWORDBREAKPROC
		EM_UNDO

These are the messages that you can send to edit controls to change their behavior and appearance.

All of the edit control message names begin with the EM_ prefix. Please don't confuse these with the EN_ notification codes shown on the last page – these are messages you send to edit controls, while notifications come from edit controls.

Windows has system calls that you can use instead of sending some of these messages. In fact, simple programs can get by without sending any of the messages shown here. We will cover those calls on the next page.

- You can send many of these messages to both single and multiline edit controls
- Click on each for a brief description

14-11

Reading and Writing Edit Controls

From WINUSER.H:

```
BOOL SetDlgItemInt ( HWND hDlg, int nIDDlgItem, UINT uValue
                   , BOOL bSigned );

BOOL SetDlgItemText ( HWND hDlg, int nIDDlgItem
                    , LPCSTR lpString );

UINT GetDlgItemText ( HWND hDlg, int nIDDlgItem
                    , LPSTR lpString, int nMaxCount );

UINT GetDlgItemInt ( HWND hDlg, int nIDDlgItem
                   , BOOL *lpTranslated, BOOL bSigned );
```

- Though edit controls, like all dialog controls, respond to messages, Windows provides system calls that read and write text by sending the messages "under the covers"

You can issue these system calls instead of sending some of the messages shown on the last page. They are easier to use, since they figure out the edit control's window handle, given the edit control's ID and the window handle of the dialog box. These functions internally call GetDlgItem, followed by SendMessage.

SetDlgItemInt and GetDlgItemInt do one more thing: they convert a string to an integer or the other way around. After all, edit controls display text, so if you want to display a numeric value, you must convert it to a string first – SetDlgItemInt does that conversion for you. GetDlgItemInt reads the string from the edit control and then converts the string (if possible) to an integer.

14-12

Single Line Edit Control Sample

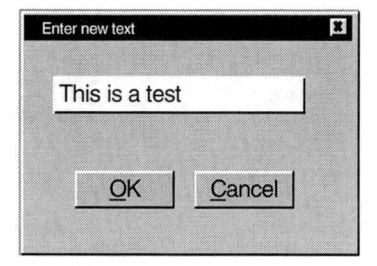

- This program displays text in its client area - the user can edit the displayed text using the dialog
- The user invokes the dialog by choosing from a menu

This sample program displays a string centered in its client area. The user can enter the text for the string by displaying the dialog shown on this page, which has one single-line edit control and two pushbuttons.

When you look at the sample's source code, please notice that it adheres to the dialog-contract style of programming.

The main window procedure defines a character string variable that holds the current text string. When the user requests the dialog box from the menu, the program calls DialogBoxParam, passing the address of the string. Upon return from DialogBoxParam, the window procedure repaints the client area if the user OKed the dialog.

The dialog function ignores all of the notifications from the edit control and simply reads the text out of the edit control when the user presses the O...

14-13

What is a Radio Button?

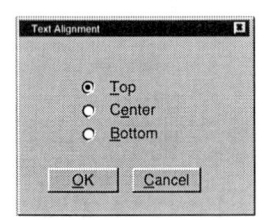

Styles

BS_AUTORADIOBUTTON
BS_RADIOBUTTON

Notification codes

BN_CLICKED

For radio button messages, see Button Messages

- Radio buttons are another BUTTON class style - they are similar to checkboxes, but we use them to present the user with a set of mutually-exclusive choices
- Click on the styles and notifications for a brief description of each

Radio buttons are similar to checkboxes in that they are styles of the BUTTON class and have an "on" or "off" state. The main difference is how you use them. Radio buttons are always in groups – they provide the user with a one-out-of-many selection. In contrast, you could use a set of checkboxes to let the user choose many-out-of-many.

This dialog box contains three radio buttons organized into a group. Whenever the user selects one of the radio buttons, they de-select the one that was previously selected. You normally use the automatic style of radio buttons so that the system takes care of the de-selection.

When the user clicks a radio button, it transmits WM_COMMAND with the BN_CLICKED notification code. The dialog procedure can respond to this notifcation.

Radio buttons are a bit more challenging to program than checkboxes. That's because...

Programming Radio Buttons

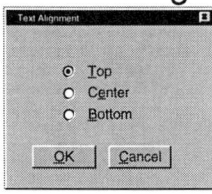

```
                          dialogfunction (...)
                          {
                          static int *pnAlign;
                          static int tempAlign;

                          case WM_INITDIALOG:
                              pnAlign = (int *) lParam;
                              .
                              .
mainwinproc (...)         .
{
static int nAlign = DT_TOP;
    .                     case DLG_BOTTOM:
    .                         tempAlign = DT_BOTTOM;
    .                         break;
response = DialogBoxParam (
    ... &nAlign );        case IDOK:
    .                         *pnAlign = tempAlign;
    .                         EndDialog ( hwndDlg, IDOK );
    .                         .
                              .
                              .
```

- The dialog function can use a local variable to track the currently selected radio button. Then if the user OKs the dialog, the dialog function can copy the local variable to the caller's variable

In this sample, the caller passes the address of an alignment variable, which the dialog function stores away in the WM_INITDIALOG case. To fulfill the dialog contract, the dialog function must update the caller's variable if the user OKs the dialog. The question is, when the user presses OK, how does the dialog figure out which radio button is selected?

We could have the dialog function send a BM_GETCHECK message to each button to see which one is selected. That technique works perfectly well; however, here we present an alternate technique.

The dialog defines a local variable, tempAlign, that we use to track the currently selected radio button. Whenever the user clicks a radio button, the button sends the WM_COMMAND message, passing the radio button's ID, for example DL...

Simple Dialog Box Controls 115

Radio Button Sample

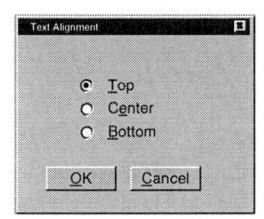

This sample uses the alignment dialog that we've discussed in the previous two pages The program draws a string in its client area and lets the user choose the text's vertical alignment by selecting one of the radio buttons and then pressing OK.

Things to look at in the sample source:

1. The program adheres to the dialog contract, passing a pointer in DialogBoxParam and expecting a button ID response.

2. Notice the rather complex code in WM_INITDIALOG. The dialog function is passed the current alignment value, and from it, must figure out which radio button to select by calling CheckDlgButton.

3. In the dialog's WM_COMMAND case, we need sub-cases for each pushbutton and a separate case for each radio button. In the radio button cases, we simply assign the local tempAlign variable. Then wh...

- This program displays text in its client area - the user can choose the text's horizontal alignment using the dialog
- The user invokes the dialog by choosing from a menu

14-16

What is a Listbox?

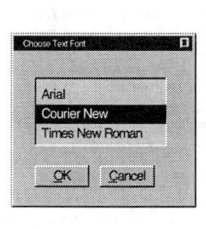

Styles	Notification codes
LBS_DISABLENOSCROLL	LBN_DBLCLK
LBS_EXTENDEDSEL	LBN_ERRSPACE
LBS_HASSTRINGS	LBN_KILLFOCUS
LBS_MULTICOLUMN	LBN_SELCANCEL
LBS_MULTIPLESEL	LBN_SELCHANGE
LBS_NODATA	LBN_SETFOCUS
LBS_NOINTEGRALHEIGHT	
LBS_NOREDRAW	
LBS_NOSEL	
LBS_NOTIFY	
LBS_OWNERDRAWFIXED	
LBS_OWNERDRAWVARIABLE	
LBS_SORT	
LBS_STANDARD	
LBS_USETABSTOPS	
LBS_WANTKEYBOARDINPUT	

The dialog on this page has a listbox that lets the user select a font name string. The page also lists the listbox styles and notification codes.

Listboxes and radio buttons both let the user select one-out-of-many. So how do you decide which to use in a dialog box?

The answer depends on two factors: how many choices do you have, and how dynamic are the choices? Clearly, radio buttons don't work well if you have a lot of choices: Microsoft's Windows User Interface Guidelines recommend a maximum of seven. Radio buttons also are difficult if the number of choices might be different from one time to the next – it's difficult to add and delete dialog control windows on the fly. So listboxes are called for in those situations.

Listboxes have other capabilities, too. See the styl...

- A listbox is a window of the LISTBOX class - you can use a listbox to present the user with a set of choices
- Listboxes are similar to radio buttons, but they are better if you have many choices or the choices are dynamic

14-17

Listbox Control Messages

LB_ADDFILE	LB_GETITEMRECT	LB_SELITEMRANGE
LB_ADDSTRING	LB_GETLOCALE	LB_SELITEMRANGEEX
LB_DELETESTRING	LB_GETSEL	LB_SETANCHORINDEX
LB_DIR	LB_GETSELCOUNT	LB_SETCARETINDEX
LB_FINDSTRING	LB_GETSELITEMS	LB_SETCOLUMNWIDTH
LB_FINDSTRINGEXACT	LB_GETTEXT	LB_SETCOUNT
LB_GETANCHORINDEX	LB_GETTEXTLEN	LB_SETCURSEL
LB_GETCARETINDEX	LB_GETTOPINDEX	LB_SETHORIZONTALEXTENT
LB_GETCOUNT	LB_INITSTORAGE	LB_SETITEMDATA
LB_GETCURSEL	LB_INSERTSTRING	LB_SETITEMHEIGHT
LB_GETHORIZONTALEXTENT	LB_ITEMFROMPOINT	LB_SETLOCALE
LB_GETITEMDATA	LB_RESETCONTENT	LB_SETSEL
LB_GETITEMHEIGHT	LB_SELECTSTRING	LB_SETTABSTOPS
		LB_SETTOPINDEX

This page lists the messages you can send to listboxes to change their behavior and appearance. We will cover some of the more interesting listbox messages in more detail in the next few pages.

- Click on the messages for a brief description of each

Programming Listboxes: Adding Entries

```
dialogfunction (...)
{
static char *pszFont; // caller's string

static  char *apszFontNames[] = { "Arial", "Times New Roman",
                                  "Courier New" };

case WM_INITDIALOG:
    pszFont = (char *)lParam;

    HWND    hwndList = GetDlgItem ( hwndDlg
                                , DLG_FONTLIST );

    for ( int i = 0; i < 3; i++ )
        SendMessage ( hwndList, LB_ADDSTRING, 0
                    , (LPARAM)apszFontNames[i] );

    int nSel = (int)SendMessage ( hwndList, LB_SELECTSTRING
                                , 0, (LPARAM)pszFont );
    .
    .
    .
```

This code shows how to add items to a listbox by sending the LB_ADDSTRING message. We define a static array of strings and then send LB_ADDSTRING in a loop, once for each array entry. If the listbox has the LBS_SORT or LBS_STANDARD styles, it will sort the entries as you add them, so they won't necessarily appear in the same order in which they are in the array.

We then pre-select the entry that corresponds to the calling program's current choice by sending the LB_SELECTSTRING message. This message finds the string in the listbox, sets the selection highlight to the string, and scrolls the listbox if necessary to ensure that the string is visible.

One way to improve this code would be to load the strings from a string table instead of hard-coding them as shown in the sample.

- You add entries to a listbox by sending the LB_ADDSTRING message

Programming Listboxes: Retrieving Text

```
dialogfunction (...)
{
case IDOK:
    {
      // retrieve the index of the currently
      // selected string
        HWND    hwndList = GetDlgItem ( hwndDlg
                , DLG_FONTLIST );

        int nCurSel = (int)SendMessage ( hwndList
                , LB_GETCURSEL, 0, 0 );

      // retrieve the text of the currently
      // selected item and store the text in the
      // caller's string
        SendMessage ( hwndList, LB_GETTEXT
                , nCurSel
                , (LPARAM)pszFont );
      .
      .
      .
```

When the user OKs a dialog box containing a listbox, to fulfill its contract, the dialog must return the current selection from the listbox back to the caller. Here, we first send LB_GETCURSEL to retrieve the zero-based index of the current item, and then retrieve its text by sending LB_GETTEXT. When we send LB_GETTEXT, we specify the selected item's index, and the address of the main window's string. This fulfills the dialog contract.

- You can retrieve the currently-highlighted item's text by sending LB_GETCURSEL followed by LB_GETTEXT

14-20

Listbox Item Data

```
case WM_INITDIALOG:
    int nIndex;

    nIndex = (int)SendMessage ( hwndList
            , LB_ADDSTRING, 0
            , (LPARAM)"Red" );
    SendMessage ( hwndList, LB_SETITEMDATA
            , nIndex
            , (LPARAM)RGB (255, 0, 0 ) );
      .
      .
      .
case IDOK:
    int nCurSel = (int)SendMessage ( hwndList
            , LB_GETCURSEL, 0, 0 );
    RGB rgb = (RGB)SendMessage ( hwndList
            , LB_GETITEMDATA
            , nCurSel, 0 );
```

This is a very useful listbox technique – it lets you show the user a list of human-readable strings, but lets the program work with binary data. In the dialog shown here, we present the user with a list of color names, but the program actually manipulates the binary RGB values that represent a color.

Here's how it works: we first add a string to the listbox using LB_ADDSTRING, which returns the new item's index. We then assign the string a 32-bit value by sending LB_SETITEMDATA, passing the item index and the 32-bit number, in this case, an RGB value. The 32-bit number can be whatever you want: a simple 32-bit number, a pointer to a structure, a database key value, or even a pointer to a function.

Then when the user OKs the dialog, we query the currently selected item's index, just as before. But now, we're not re...

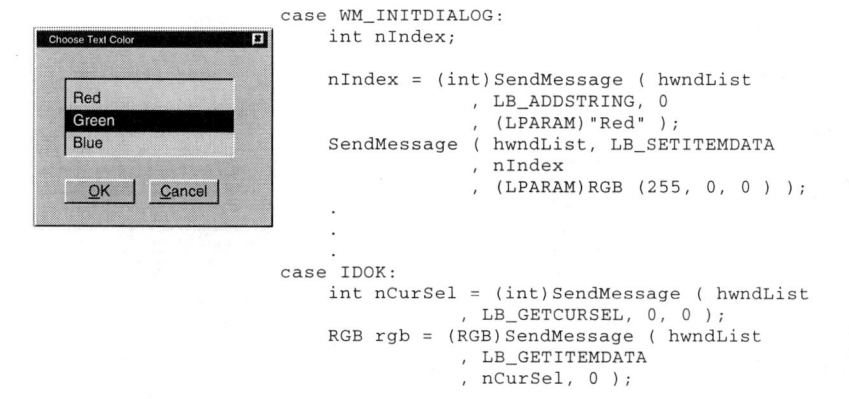

- Listboxes display text strings, but often you are really interested in a numeric value. You can use the listbox "item data" to associate a number with a listbox entry

14-21

Listbox Sample

This sample program displays a string in the client area and lets the user choose the string's font name by displaying a dialog box with a listbox.

In the WM_INITDIALOG case, we add the font names to the listbox. Then in the IDOK case, we extract the currently selected string from the listbox and return it to the caller to fulfill the dialog contract.

You should also check out the code in the DLG_FONTLIST subcase in the dialog function's WM_COMMAND case. We receive this notification when the user interacts with the listbox. The only interaction we're interested in is when the user double-clicks the listbox – we want to dismiss the dialog in that case. In fact, we want a double-click to act the same way as the user OKing the dialog box – so rather than repeating the code that's already in the IDOK case, we send the dialog function a WM_COMMAND message, specifying the OK button's ID...

- This program lets the user choose a font name for the program's displayed text
- The user invokes the dialog by choosing from a menu

14-22

Combining Several Controls on a Dialog

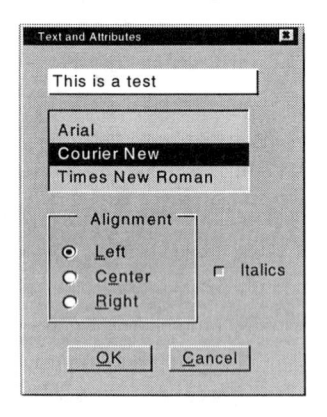

```
typedef struct
{
    char    sz[MAXLEN];
    BOOL    fItalic;
    int     nAlign;
    char    szFont[MAXFONTNAME];
} TEXTATTRS;
```

All of the samples up until this point have had a single dialog control on the dialog box (the group of radio buttons act like a single control). But in real-world programming, you often need more complex dialogs. For example, this dialog has an edit field where the user can enter a string, a listbox where the user can choose a font, a group of radio buttons that let the user select text alignment, and a checkbox that lets the user choose whether the text is italicized or not.

The question is: how do you program such a dialog and still adhere to the dialog-contract style of programming?

The best way is to define a structure that defines a field for each dialog control (or group of radio buttons). Then the main window procedure can allocate such a structure, initialize it with the current values, and then pass the address of the structure to th...

- If you need to obtain several items from the user in a single dialog, you can define a structure with a field for each dialog control
- The caller passes the address of the structure when it displays the dialog - the dialog function updates the structure if the user OKs the dialog

14-23

Lab Exercise 12: Dialog Controls

In this lab, you will write a program that displays a "Spirograph" image. You will create a dialog that lets the user enter the parameters for the image.

Press the "Run Lab Solution" button to see what your completed program should look like -- click the right mouse button on the client area to see the floating popup menu.

To view the lab exercise instructions, press the "Lab Write Up" button. This will display the lab document and let you print it if you wish. When you are finished with the lab, continue to the next page to take a review quiz.

Review Quiz

Before you move on to the next chapter, you should test your comprehension of this chapter by taking the review quiz. The quiz assumes that you have already done the lab exercise.

The quiz will be displayed in a separate window so that you can page through the chapter to help you find the answers. In other words, this is an open book quiz!

After you have answered all of the questions, press the button at the bottom of the quiz window to see how you did. If you didn't score as well as you think you should, you should review the chapter before continuing on.

Chapter Summary

- Checkboxes are a style of the BUTTON class that let you present the user with an on/off choice
- Radio buttons are a style of the BUTTON class that let you present the user with a list of mutually exclusive choices
- Edit controls let the user enter one or more lines of text
- Listboxes let you present the user with a list of choices, even if the number of choices is large or changes dynamically
- All dialog controls provide a set of styles, respond to a set of messages, and generate a set of notifications
- By using the "contract style" of dialog programming, you can de-couple your user-interface code from your application's logic, thus making it easier to adapt your program to a new user interface

14-26

Chapter 15: Common Controls

- List View Control

- Tree View Control

Introduction to Common Controls

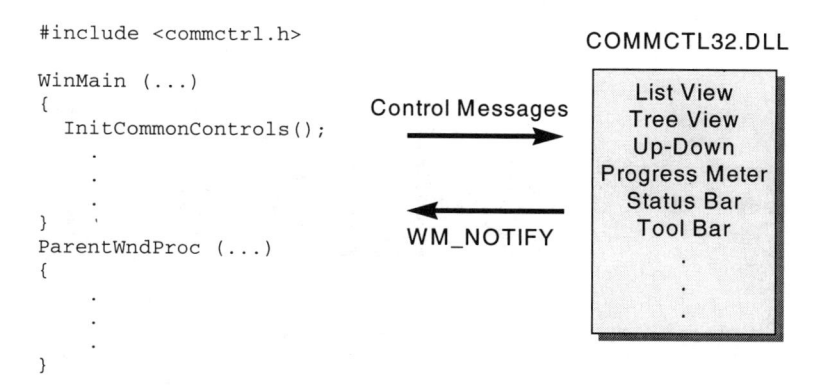

```
#include <commctrl.h>

WinMain (...)
{
   InitCommonControls();
   .
   .
   .
}
ParentWndProc (...)
{
   .
   .
   .
}
```

Control Messages →

← WM_NOTIFY

COMMCTL32.DLL

List View
Tree View
Up-Down
Progress Meter
Status Bar
Tool Bar
.
.
.

Windows now ships with a set of so-called common controls, which are simply window classes contained in a special dynamic link library (DLL) that wasn't included with the first few versions of Windows. There is really nothing special about these controls, except that they all have a similar programming interface and that you must call InitCommonControls before you create one of them.

This chapter covers the ListView and TreeView controls. We covered the progress meter, status bar and tool bar controls in earlier chapters.

All of the common controls generate the WM_NOTIFY message when the user interacts with them. That makes the common controls a bit different from the standard dialog controls, like listboxes, which generate WM_COMMAND instead.

- Common controls are a set of window classes that are useful as dialog box controls and as child windows
- An application that wishes to use the common controls must #include <commctrl.h> and call InitCommonControls, and then link to COMCTL32.LIB

The WM_NOTIFY Message

lParam →

```
HWND hwndFrom
UINT idFrom
UINT code
```
} NMHDR Common to all WM_NOTIFY messages

} Control-specific structure

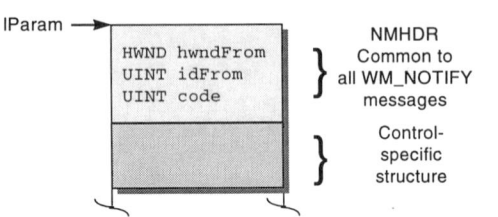

Common code values
NM_CLICK
NM_DBLCLK
NM_KILLFOCUS
NM_OUTOFMEMORY
NM_RCLICK
NM_RDBLCLK
NM_RETURN
NM_SETFOCUS

From COMMCTRL.H:

```
typedef struct
{
    HWND  hwndFrom;
    UINT  idFrom;
    UINT  code;
} NMHDR;
```

- When common controls need to inform their parent window of an event, they send the WM_NOTIFY message
- In WM_NOTIFY, lParam points a NMHDR structure that's the same for all common controls. Each type of common control can append fields

All common controls send WM_NOTIFY to inform their parent of a significant event. Since they all use the same message, how can the parent determine which control sent the event, and why? In addition, how can each common control "customize" this message so that it can convey information specific to that control?

Microsoft solved these problems by defining a structure, pointed to by lParam, that acts as a header for all WM_NOTIFY information. Each control can append control-specific fields to the structure.

The NMHDR structure contains three fields: the handle of window that generated the message, that window's ID, and a code that indicates why the control sent the message. Most programs do a switch-case statement on the window ID to determine which control sent the message, and then do a nested switch-case on the code so they can respond to ...

15-2

Introduction to Image Lists

```
int cxIcon = GetSystemMetrics ( SM_CXICON );
int cyIcon = GetSystemMetrics ( SM_CYICON );

HIMAGELIST himg;
himg = ImageList_Create (
    cxIcon
    , cyIcon
    , ILC_MASK, 3, 0 );

HICON hiconBike = LoadIcon ( hInst
    , MAKEINTRESOURCE ( IDI_BIKE ) );
    .
    .
    .
nIndexBike = ImageList_AddIcon ( himg, hiconBike );
    .
    .
    .
```

- Many common controls display one or more images - and use an image list object to manage the images
- An image list is a collection of equal-sized bitmaps or icons - each time you add an image to a list, the list returns you an index that identifies the image

Many of the common controls display pictures, including the list view and tree view controls that we cover in this chapter. All of the common controls use image list objects to store the pictures that they display. You can also use image lists to help you manage images even if you're not using any common controls.

An image list essentially is a wide bitmap, divided into equal-sized, rectangular sections. All of the images in the list must be the same size, but you can create multiple image lists if you need to manage images of different sizes. Each time you add an image to an image list, the list ensures there's enough room for the new image, re-allocating itself if necessary. Each image in the list has a unique, zero-based index that refers to the image. The list assigns the index in the order in which you add images. In this example, the bicyclist image has index 0, the jogge...

15-3

What is a List View Control?

Icon View

Small Icon View

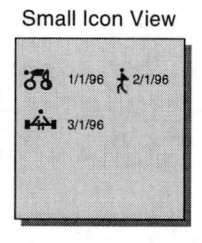

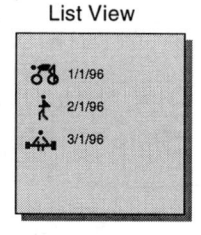

List View

Report View

Activity	Duration	Comments
1/1/96	1:00	Great ride!
2/1/96	4:00	Ran a marathon
3/1/96	0:30	Bench press session

- List view controls are useful for displaying lists of items - they are similar to a listbox, but far more flexible
- Each item consists of an optional image, a label, and optional columnar data

A list view control is like a listbox, in that it displays a list of items. But a list view is more powerful, since each item can have a picture. In addition, list views supports four different view styles, each of which change the presentation of the list.

In icon view, each item has an image with a label below it. If the parent window responds to the appropriate notifications, the user can drag an item to any position in the list view window.

Small icon view is the same as icon view, except that the icons are smaller (big surprise).

List view is similar to small icon view, except that the user cannot move the items to any arbitrary position – they always are ordered in a list.

Finally, report view, sometimes called details view, displays multiple columns. By default, each column has a header. Many programs respond to notifications so that when th...

15-4

List View Styles and Notifications

Styles

LVS_ALIGNLEFT
LVS_ALIGNTOP
LVS_AUTOARRANGE
LVS_EDITLABELS
LVS_ICON
LVS_LIST
LVS_NOCOLUMNHEADER
LVS_NOLABELWRAP
LVS_NOSCROLL
LVS_NOSORTHEADER
LVS_OWNERDRAWFIXED
LVS_REPORT
LVS_SHAREIMAGELISTS
LVS_SHOWSELALWAYS
LVS_SINGLESEL
LVS_SMALLICON
LVS_SORTASCENDING
LVS_SORTDESCENDING

Notification codes

LVN_BEGINDRAG
LVN_BEGINLABELEDIT
LVN_BEGINRDRAG
LVN_COLUMNCLICK
LVN_DELETEALLITEMS
LVN_DELETEITEM
LVN_ENDLABELEDIT
LVN_GETDISPINFO
LVN_INSERTITEM
LVN_ITEMCHANGED
LVN_ITEMCHANGING
LVN_KEYDOWN
LVN_SETDISPINFO

This page lists the styles you can assign to a list-view control and the possible values for the "code" field in the WM_NOTIFY message NMHDR structure. Click on each for a brief description and refer to your Windows programming documentation for more details.

- The list view sends notifications as WM_NOTIFY messages

15-5

List View Notifications

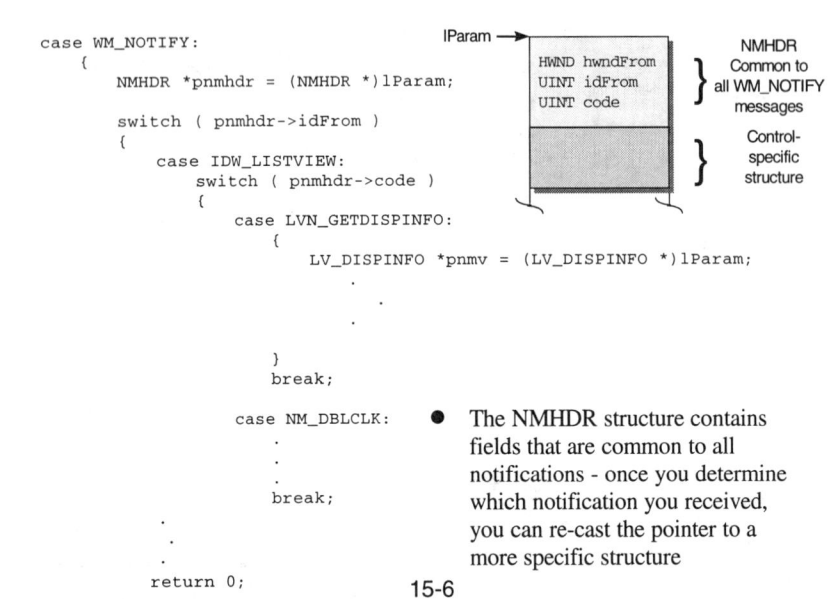

```
case WM_NOTIFY:
    {
    NMHDR *pnmhdr = (NMHDR *)lParam;

    switch ( pnmhdr->idFrom )
    {
        case IDW_LISTVIEW:
            switch ( pnmhdr->code )
            {
                case LVN_GETDISPINFO:
                    {
                    LV_DISPINFO *pnmv = (LV_DISPINFO *)lParam;
                    .
                    .
                    .
                    }
                    break;

                case NM_DBLCLK:
                    .
                    .
                    .
                    break;
                .
                .
                .
            return 0;
```

lParam →

```
HWND hwndFrom    } NMHDR
UINT idFrom        Common to
UINT code          all WM_NOTIFY
                   messages

                 } Control-
                   specific
                   structure
```

- The NMHDR structure contains fields that are common to all notifications - once you determine which notification you received, you can re-cast the pointer to a more specific structure

15-6

When the user interacts with a list view control, it sends WM_NOTIFY, passing the notification codes listed on the last page. The program fragment on this page shows how you might respond to this message.

When we receive WM_NOTIFY, we first cast lParam to a pointer to the generic NMHDR structure. We then examine the idFrom field, which indicates which control sent the message. Here we look for the ID of a list view control. If we had multiple list view controls or other common controls, each would have a unique ID.

We then examine the notification code, which indicates the reason for the message. Here, we are looking for the LVN_GETDISPINFO notification, which indicates that the list view needs our help in displaying an item.

Once we have determined the notification code, we can cast the generic NMHDR structur...

List View Control Message Macros

ListView_Arrange
ListView_CreateDragImage
ListView_DeleteAllItems
ListView_DeleteColumn
ListView_DeleteItem
ListView_EditLabel
ListView_EnsureVisible
ListView_FindItem
ListView_GetBkColor
ListView_GetCallbackMask
ListView_GetColumn
ListView_GetColumnWidth
ListView_GetCountPerPage
ListView_GetEditControl
ListView_GetImageList
ListView_GetISearchString
ListView_GetItem
ListView_GetItemCount
ListView_GetItemPosition
ListView_GetItemRect
ListView_GetItemSpacing
ListView_GetItemState
ListView_GetItemText
ListView_GetNextItem
ListView_GetOrigin

ListView_GetSelectedCount
ListView_GetStringWidth
ListView_GetTextBkColor
ListView_GetTextColor
ListView_GetTopIndex
ListView_GetViewRect
ListView_HitTest
ListView_InsertColumn
ListView_InsertItem
ListView_RedrawItems
ListView_Scroll
ListView_SetBkColor
ListView_SetCallbackMask
ListView_SetColumn
ListView_SetColumnWidth
ListView_SetImageList
ListView_SetItem
ListView_SetItemCount
ListView_SetItemPosition
ListView_SetItemPosition32
ListView_SetItemState
ListView_SetItemText
ListView_SetTextBkColor
ListView_SetTextColor
ListView_SortItems
ListView_Update

This page lists the macros that you can use to manipulate a list view control. We will cover some of the more useful macros in more detail in the next few pages.

Each of these macros is defined in COMMCTRL.H and each of them simply sends a message to a list view control. The advantage of using the macros is that they are easier than sending the messages yourself. That's because the macros aren't limited to the generic wParam and lParam arguments that SendMessage uses -- the macros essentially take care of packaging the macro arguments into wParam and lParam and then sending the message.

15-7

Creating a List View Window

```
hwndList = CreateWindowEx ( 0, WC_LISTVIEW, "listview"
                , WS_VISIBLE | WS_CHILD | LVS_REPORT
                , 0, 0, 0, 0, hwnd
                , (HMENU)IDW_LISTVIEW
                , hInst, NULL );
    .
    .                                       himageNormal
    .
himgNormal = ImageList_Create (...);
himgSmall  = ImageList_Create (...);        himageSmall
    .
    .
ListView_SetImageList ( hwndList, himgNormal, LVSIL_NORMAL );
ListView_SetImageList ( hwndList, himgSmall,  LVSIL_SMALL );
```

- This shows creating a list view as a child window, but you can also create them in dialog scripts
- If you want to, you can switch views "on the fly"
- You don't necessarily have to create both large and small image lists - for example, if your list is always in report view, you don't need to create an image list for large images

The program shown on this page is taken from the WM_CREATE section of a sample program that you will see in a moment. This program uses a list view as a child window on a client area, rather than as a dialog control.

We create the list view as a child window, initially in report view. We set the initial size and position to zero since we will resize the listview whenever the main window's size changes, so that the list view occupies the main window's entire client area.

We continue by creating two image lists: one for normal-sized images, one for small images. We need to create both, since this program will let the user choose the view style on the fly. The list view uses the normal-sized images when it's in icon view, and uses the small-sized images for all of the rest of the views.

This program supports all view styles, but if you write a prog...

15-8

Adding Items to a List Control

```
LV_ITEM       lvi;

lvi.mask = LVIF_TEXT | LVIF_IMAGE;
lvi.iItem = 0;                          // first item
lvi.iSubItem = 0;                       // not adding subitem
lvi.pszText = "1/1/96";                 // item label
lvi.iImage = nIndexBike;                // image index

ListView_InsertItem ( hwndList, &lvi );
```

- To add an item, specify the new item's index in the list, its label and its image index

To add an item, fill in the LV_ITEM structure and then use the ListView_InsertItem macro, which sends the LVM_INSERTITEM message. The mask field in the structure is a set of bit-flags that you use to indicate which of the fields in the LV_ITEM structure you initialized. In this case, we want to specify a label and an icon for the item, so we use the LVIF_TEXT and LVIF_IMAGE flags and fill in pszText with the label, and iImage with the image index. The list view will ignore the rest of the fields except for iItem and iSubItem, which we'll discuss next.

The iItem and iSubItem fields identify the new item. The iItem field is a zero-based index that indicates where the item should be placed in the list control. In this case, we specify zero since this is the first item we are adding. The iSubItem field must be zero – on the next page we will see that it refers to a column nu...

15-9

Configuring Columns

```
LV_COLUMN    lvc;

lvc.mask = LVCF_SUBITEM | LVCF_TEXT | LVCF_FMT;
lvc.fmt = LVCFMT_LEFT;

lvc.pszText = "Activity";
lvc.iSubItem = 0;   // column 0

ListView_InsertColumn ( hwndList
                      , 0, &lvc );

lvc.pszText = "Duration";
lvc.iSubItem = 1;

ListView_InsertColumn ( hwndList
                      , 1, &lvc );
    .
    .
    .
```

- In report view, the list view displays rows of data, each with one or more columns
- Before you can display list view in report view, you must configure the columns by specifying the column index, header text and text alignment

Report view is a little more challenging than the other views, because you have tell the list view control about the columns and then add the columnar data for each item. On this page, we'll discuss how to configure the columns. The next page will cover how to add columnar data.

In this example, the report view will have three columns, one labeled Activity, one labeled Duration and one labeled Comments. Each column has a zero-based column index.

To add a column, we use the ListView_InsertColumn macro, passing a pointer to a LV_COLUMN structure.

Let's start with the left-most column, which is column zero.

In the LV_COLUMN structure, we fill in the mask field to indicate that we will specify a subitem number, the column heading text and the column heading format. We specify the column heading format to be left-aligned, we specify th...

15-10

Adding Columnar Data

```
LV_ITEM      lvi;
    .
    .
lvi.iItem    = 0;              row 0
lvi.pszText = "1/1/96";        row 1

ListView_InsertItem (...);     row 2

ListView_SetItemText ( hwndList
                     , 0            // row number
                     , 1            // column number
                     , "1:00" );    // field text

ListView_SetItemText ( hwndList
                     , 0            // row number
                     , 2            // column number
                     , "Great ride!" ); // field text
```

- Column 0 displays the item's small image and its label - you add the data for column zero as shown previously for non-columnar data
- To insert data for subsequent columns, you specify the item index (row number), the column index and the text

As you saw on page 15-9, when you add an item to a list control, you specify the item's icon and label. A report view displays the icon and label in column zero. After adding the item, you then need to specify the text for the other columns. And that's what we'll cover here.

We start by adding our first item, which will occupy row zero. This establishes the item's icon and label which are displayed in column zero.

To set the text for column 1, the Duration column, we issue ListView_SetItemText, specifying the row number of zero since this is the first item, the column number, and the text.

We then do the same for the next column, this time specifying column 2 to and the text for the Comments column.

We then need to repeat these steps for any other items

15-11

Changing the List View Style

From COMMCTRL.H:

```
#define LVS_ICON        0x0000
#define LVS_REPORT      0x0001
#define LVS_SMALLICON   0x0002
#define LVS_LIST        0x0003
#define LVS_TYPEMASK    0x0003
```

```
31                               1   0
┌─────────────────────────────┬──────┐
│                             │ view │
│                             │ style│
└─────────────────────────────┴──────┘
        Window style flags
```

Example: change to small icon view

```
LONG lStyle = GetWindowLong ( hwndList, GWL_STYLE );

lStyle &= ~LVS_TYPEMASK;
lStyle |= LVS_SMALLICON;

SetWindowLong ( hwndList, GWL_STYLE, lStyle );
```

- You can change the view "on the fly" by changing the list view's style flags by doing a read/modify/write operation

There is no list-view macro or message to change the view style – instead, you must changes the control's window style flags. Changing the view is a bit complicated because you probably don't want to change any of the other windows style flags other than the view flags. That means that you must execute a read-modify-write sequence to change the view style. To make this a little more maintainable and self-documenting, COMMCTRL.H defines the LVS_TYPEMASK constant that you can use to isolate the style flags.

So to change the style flags, we first read the current window style flags with GetWindowLong, mask out the view style bits, "or" in the style that we want, and then re-set the window style by calling SetWindowLong.

15-12

List View Sample Program

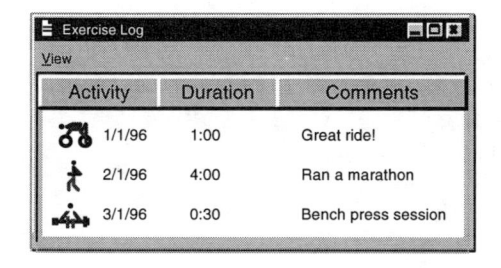

This sample program displays a list view control that occupies the entire client area of the main window. It starts out in report view, but you can change to any of the other list-control views by choosing from the menu. When you run the program, you should try changing the view and you should also try double-clicking on an item – the program will display a message box with that item's attributes.

Then take a look at the sample source code and click on the speaker button for further explanation.

- This program displays a list of exercise activities. You can change the view by choosing from the menu

15-13

What is a Tree View Control?

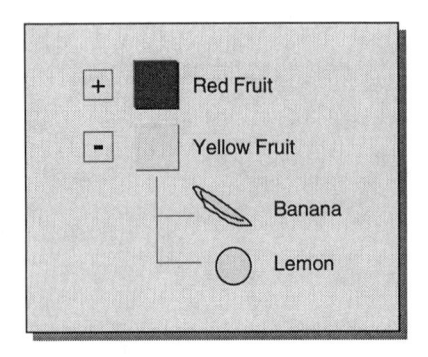

[Diagram showing a tree view with:
- [+] Red Fruit
- [-] Yellow Fruit
  - Banana
  - Lemon]

- A tree view control displays lists of hierarchical data
- Each item consists of an optional image, a label, an optional parent item, and optional child items

A tree view control is similar to a list view in that it displays a list of data. There are two big differences, however. First, a list view control allows different views, but a tree view only has one. Second, a tree view lets you define a parent-child relationship between items, thus allowing you to create a hierarchical list. The hierarchy can have any number of levels, and each level in the hierarchy can have zero or more child entries. When you add an item to a tree view, you must specify the new item's relationship to existing items.

Each item displays an image and a label.

The user can expand or collapse a parent item by clicking on the "+" or "-" box or by double-clicking on the parent item. You can also expand or collapse an item under program control.

Tree views also let you customize their display. For example, you can choose whether the tree view display...

15-14

Tree View Styles and Notifications

Styles	Notification codes
TVS_DISABLEDRAGDROP	TVN_BEGINDRAG
TVS_EDITLABELS	TVN_BEGINLABELEDIT
TVS_HASBUTTONS	TVN_BEGINRDRAG
TVS_HASLINES	TVN_DELETEITEM
TVS_LINESATROOT	TVN_ENDLABELEDIT
TVS_SHOWSELALWAYS	TVN_GETDISPINFO
	TVN_ITEMEXPANDED
	TVN_ITEMEXPANDING
	TVN_SELCHANGED
	TVN_SELCHANGING
	TVN_SETDISPINFO

This page lists the styles you can assign to a tree-view control and the possible values for the "code" field in the WM_NOTIFY message structure.

15-15

Tree View Notifications

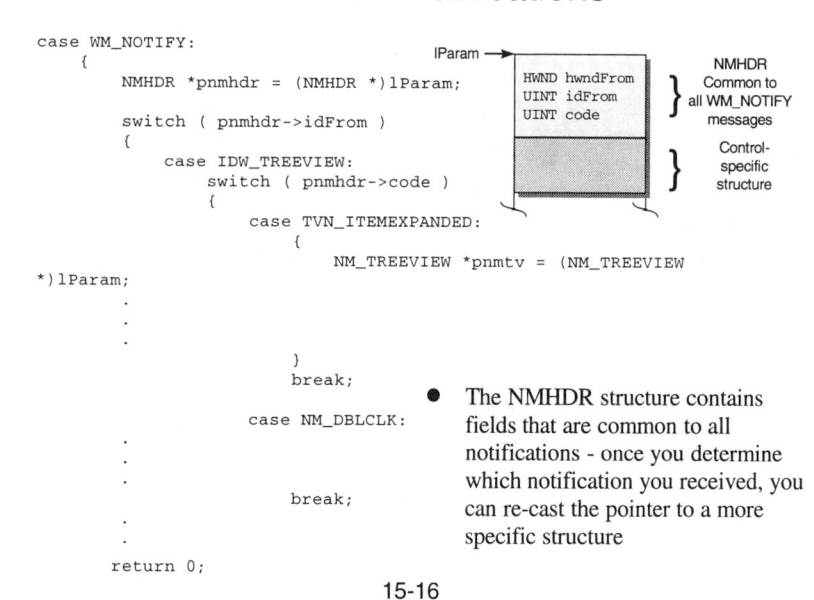

```
case WM_NOTIFY:
    {
        NMHDR *pnmhdr = (NMHDR *)lParam;

        switch ( pnmhdr->idFrom )
        {
            case IDW_TREEVIEW:
                switch ( pnmhdr->code )
                {
                    case TVN_ITEMEXPANDED:
                    {
                        NM_TREEVIEW *pnmtv = (NM_TREEVIEW *)lParam;
                        .
                        .
                        .
                    }
                    break;

                    case NM_DBLCLK:
                        .
                        .
                        .
                    break;
                    .
                    .
                    .
        return 0;
```

```
         IParam →  ┌─────────────────┐  ⎫ NMHDR
                   │ HWND hwndFrom   │  ⎬ Common to
                   │ UINT idFrom     │  ⎭ all WM_NOTIFY
                   │ UINT code       │    messages
                   ├─────────────────┤  ⎫
                   │                 │  ⎬ Control-
                   │                 │  ⎭ specific
                   │                 │    structure
                   └─────────────────┘
```

- The NMHDR structure contains fields that are common to all notifications - once you determine which notification you received, you can re-cast the pointer to a more specific structure

When the user interacts with a tree view control, it sends WM_NOTIFY, passing the notification codes listed on the last page. The program fragment on this page shows how you might respond to this message.

When we receive WM_NOTIFY, we first cast lParam to a pointer to the generic NMHDR structure. We then examine the idFrom field, which indicates which control sent the message. Here we look for the ID of a tree view control. If we had multiple tree view controls or other common controls, each would have a unique ID.

We then examine the notification code, which indicates the reason for the message. Here, we are looking for the TVN_ITEMEXPANDED notification, which indicates that a parent item expanded or collapsed.

Once we have determined the notification code, we can cast the generic NMHDR structur...

15-16

Tree View Message Macros

TreeView_CreateDragImage
TreeView_DeleteAllItems
TreeView_DeleteItem
TreeView_EditLabel
TreeView_EndEditLabelNow
TreeView_EnsureVisible
TreeView_Expand
TreeView_GetChild
TreeView_GetCount
TreeView_GetDropHilight
TreeView_GetEditControl
TreeView_GetFirstVisible
TreeView_GetISearchString
TreeView_GetImageList
TreeView_GetIndent
TreeView_GetItem
TreeView_GetItemRect
TreeView_GetNextItem

TreeView_GetNextSibling
TreeView_GetNextVisible
TreeView_GetParent
TreeView_GetPrevSibling
TreeView_GetPrevVisible
TreeView_GetRoot
TreeView_GetSelection
TreeView_GetVisibleCount
TreeView_HitTest
TreeView_InsertItem
TreeView_Select
TreeView_SelectDropTarget
TreeView_SelectItem
TreeView_SelectSetFirstVisible
TreeView_SetImageList
TreeView_SetIndent
TreeView_SetItem
TreeView_SortChildren
TreeView_SortChildrenCB

This page lists the macros that you can use to manipulate a tree view control. We will cover some of the more useful macros in more detail in the next few pages.

Each of these macros is defined in COMMCTRL.H and each of them simply sends a message to the tree view. The advantage of using the macros is that they are easier than sending the messages yourself. That's because the macros aren't limited to the generic wParam and lParam arguments that SendMessage uses -- the macros essentially take care of packaging the macro arguments into wParam and lParam and then sending the message.

15-17

Tree View States and Images

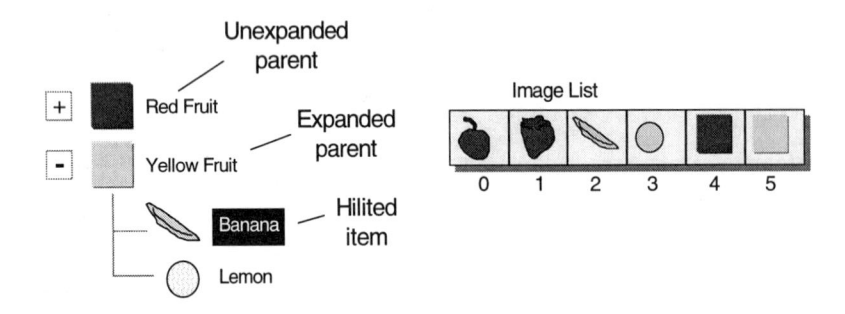

On this page, the tree view is organized into a fruit hierarchy – red fruits and yellow fruits. Each parent item has two children – cherries and strawberries are red fruits, and bananas and lemons are yellow fruits. The red fruit parent is currently collapsed, while the yellow fruit parent is expanded. The Banana item is the currently highlighted item in the tree view.

Unlike list-view controls, you don't need two separate image lists for small or normal-sized images. You only need to decide which size images that your tree view will display. To support this tree view, we need an image list with the six images shown here.

Some programs display a different image for selected and non-selected items. For example, the Windows Explorer displays an open-folder image when a folder is selected and a closed-folder image otherwise. The Explorer essentially is a tree-view control in the left-most pane and a list-vie...

- When you insert an item into a tree view, you specify two images - the image displayed when the item is selected, and the image displayed when it isn't. If you wish, the images can be the same
- If you want to display a different image for expanded and non-expanded parent items, you must handle the TVN_ITEMEXPANDED notification and use TreeView_SetItem to change the image

15-18

Creating a Tree View Window

```
hwndTree = CreateWindowEx ( 0, WC_TREEVIEW, "treeview"
            , WS_VISIBLE | WS_CHILD | TVS_HASLINES |
              TVS_HASBUTTONS | TVS_LINESATROOT
            , 0, 0, 0, 0, hwnd
            , (HMENU)IDW_TREEVIEW
            , hInst, NULL );
    .
    .
himgNormal = ImageList_Create (...);
    .
    .
int nIndexRed = ImageList_AddIcon (...);
    .
    .
TreeView_SetImageList ( hwndTree, himgNormal, TVSIL_NORMAL );
```

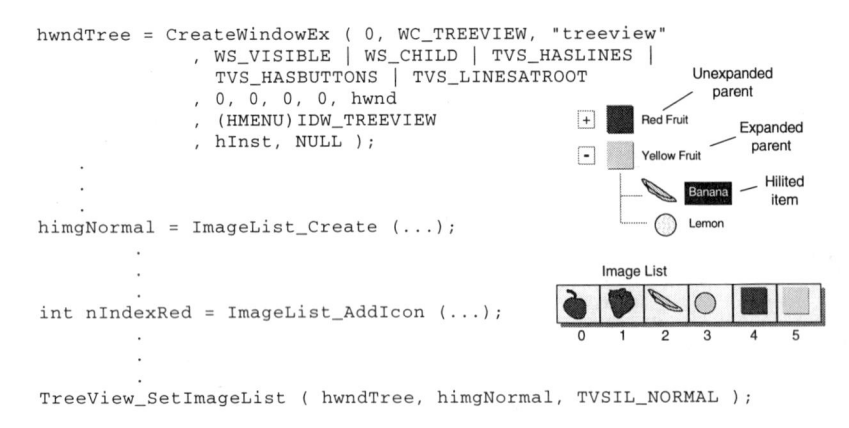

The program shown on this page is taken from the WM_CREATE section of a sample program that you will see in a moment. This program uses a tree view as a child window on a client area, instead of as a dialog control.

We create the tree view as a child window, specifying the TVS_HASLINES, TVS_HASBUTTONS and TVS_LINESATROOT styles. These styles make the tree view look like the one shown on the previous page.

We continue by creating an image list and adding the six images shown here.

We then attach the image list to the tree view control by calling TreeView_SetImageList and specifying the tree view control handle, the image list handle, and a flag that indicates the image size.

- This shows creating a tree view as a child window, but you can also create them in dialog scripts

15-19

# Common Controls

Adding Items to a Tree View

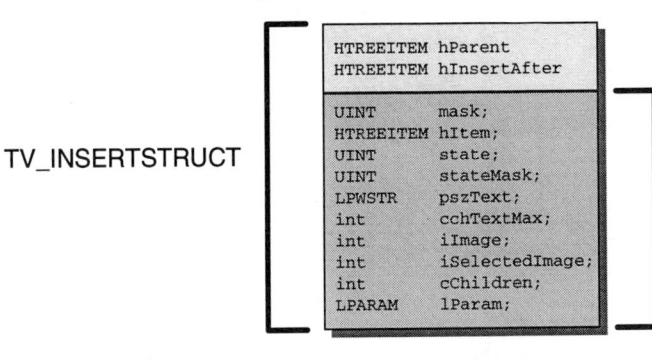

```
TV_INSERTSTRUCT
    HTREEITEM hParent
    HTREEITEM hInsertAfter
    UINT      mask;          ┐
    HTREEITEM hItem;         │
    UINT      state;         │
    UINT      stateMask;     │
    LPWSTR    pszText;       ├─ TV_ITEM
    int       cchTextMax;    │
    int       iImage;        │
    int       iSelectedImage;│
    int       cChildren;     │
    LPARAM    lParam;        ┘
```

Inserting items into a tree view is a little trickier than adding to a list view, since you need to tell the tree view control about the new item's parent. So to insert an item, you fill in two structures, one of which is embedded inside of the other. The first field of the combined structure lets you specify the new item's parent. The second field lets you stipulate where the new item should be added in relation to other items with the same parent (siblings).

The rest of the structure fields describe the new item – we will cover them in more detail on the next page.

- To add an item, you fill in a TV_INSERTSTRUCT that specifies where to add the new item
- This structure contains an embedded TV_ITEM structure that describes the new item
- When you add the item, the tree view returns an item handle that you can use in subsequent calls (for example as the parent of another item)

15-20

Adding an Item at the Root

[+] Red Fruit

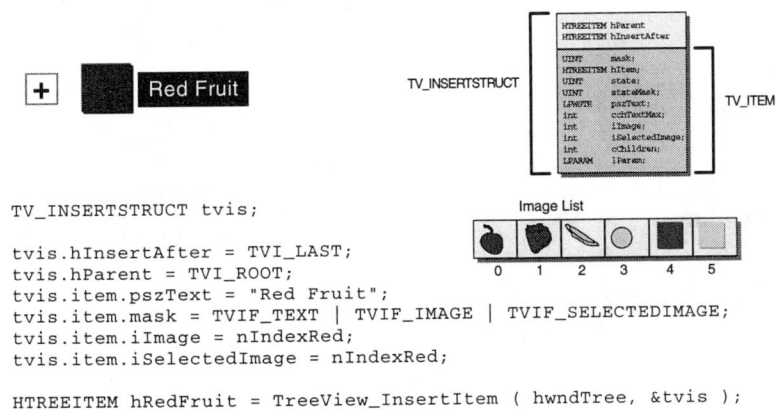

Image List: 0 1 2 3 4 5

```
TV_INSERTSTRUCT tvis;

tvis.hInsertAfter = TVI_LAST;
tvis.hParent = TVI_ROOT;
tvis.item.pszText = "Red Fruit";
tvis.item.mask = TVIF_TEXT | TVIF_IMAGE | TVIF_SELECTEDIMAGE;
tvis.item.iImage = nIndexRed;
tvis.item.iSelectedImage = nIndexRed;

HTREEITEM hRedFruit = TreeView_InsertItem ( hwndTree, &tvis );
```

This page shows example code that adds a "Red Fruit" item at root level in a tree view control. We fill in the first two fields of the TV_INSERTSTRUCT structure to indicate that we want the new item to have no parent, and that it should be inserted after any siblings.

In the TV_ITEM embedded structure, we set the mask to indicate that the pszText, iImage and iSelectedImage fields are relevant and then fill in those fields in the structure. We specify the item's label, its image index when not selected, and its selected image.

Note that we specify the same image index in both fields – that's because we want to use the same image for selected and non-selected states.

We then use the TreeView_InsertItem macro to insert the item. This macro returns new item's handle. ...

- To add an item with no parent, specify TVI_ROOT as the parent item handle
- Here we specified the same image for the selected and non-selected states

15-21

Adding a Child Item

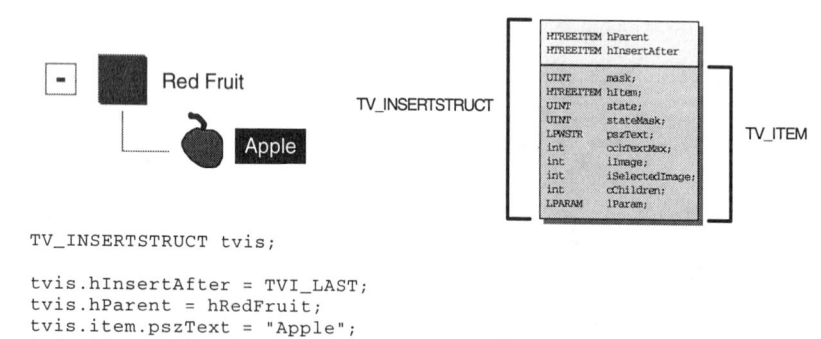

Red Fruit
Apple

TV_INSERTSTRUCT

```
HTREEITEM   hParent
HTREEITEM   hInsertAfter
UINT        mask;
HTREEITEM   hItem;
UINT        state;
UINT        stateMask;
LPWSTR      pszText;
int         cchTextMax;
int         iImage;
int         iSelectedImage;
int         cChildren;
LPARAM      lParam;
```

TV_ITEM

Now let's add a child using the "Red Fruit" item we added on the last page as the parent.

Now when we fill in the structure, we specify the Red Fruit item's handle in the hParent field. The rest of the fields work pretty much the same as on the last page.

```
TV_INSERTSTRUCT tvis;

tvis.hInsertAfter = TVI_LAST;
tvis.hParent = hRedFruit;
tvis.item.pszText = "Apple";
tvis.item.mask = TVIF_TEXT | TVIF_IMAGE | TVIF_SELECTEDIMAGE;
tvis.item.iImage = nIndexApple;
tvis.item.iSelectedImage = nIndexApple;

HTREEITEM hApple = TreeView_InsertItem ( hwndTree, &tvis );
```

- To add a child item, specify an existing item handle as the parent item handle

15-22

Tree View Sample Program

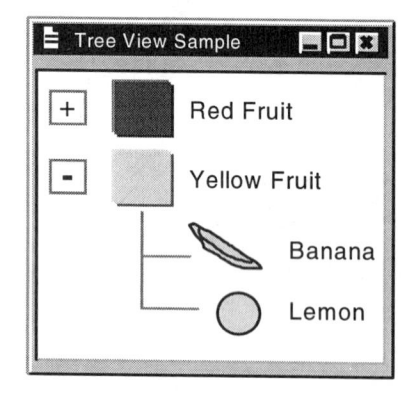

Tree View Sample
+ Red Fruit
- Yellow Fruit
    Banana
    Lemon

This sample program displays a hierarchical list of red and yellow fruits. You can expand or collapse the list by clicking on the "+" or "-" boxes. About the only other thing the program does is to respond to double-clicks on an item – the program displays the item's text in a message box.

After running the program, open the sample source and click on the speaker button for more explanation.

- This program displays a hierarchy of fruits - you can expand or contract the lists

15-23

Lab Exercise 13: List View Controls

In this lab, you will write a program that displays a list of "students" and their scores on a test. You will use a report-view list view control to display the information.

Press the "Run Lab Solution" button to see what your completed program should look like -- click the right mouse button on the client area to see the floating popup menu.

To view the lab exercise instructions, press the "Lab Write Up" button. This will display the lab document and let you print it if you wish. When you are finished with the lab, continue to the next page to take a review quiz.

Review Quiz

Before you move on to the next chapter, you should test your comprehension of this chapter by taking the review quiz. The quiz assumes that you have already done the lab exercise.

The quiz will be displayed in a separate window so that you can page through the chapter to help you find the answers. In other words, this is an open book quiz!

After you have answered all of the questions, press the button at the bottom of the quiz window to see how you did. If you didn't score as well as you think you should, you should review the chapter before continuing on.

Chapter Summary

- Windows provides a set of window classes called common controls. Developers can create instances of the common controls in dialog boxes or as children of a main window

- The list view control lets you present the user with lists of data and let you show the list in icon view, small-icon view, list view or report view

- The tree view control lets you display lists of hierachical data, for example the file structure of a disk

Chapter 16: Keystrokes in Dialogs

- Tab, Arrow, Enter and Escape Keys
- Character Mnemonic Keys

16-0

Keystrokes in Dialog Boxes

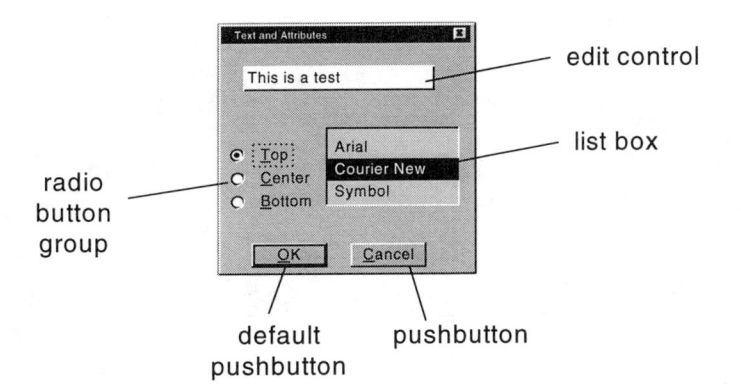

In this chapter, you will learn how dialog boxes process special keys. Now you might be wondering why this is important – after all, if the dialog box does it automatically, why worry about it? The answer is: the way keystrokes work is strongly influenced by how you design the dialog box.

For example, have you used a dialog box where as you pressed the tab key, the focus bounced all over the dialog? Or have you ever pressed the enter key expecting the dialog box to dismiss, but nothing happened? This chapter will teach you how to avoid these mistakes in the dialogs that you create.

We will use the dialog shown on this page to illustrate how keys work. This dialog has an edit control, a group of radio buttons, a list box, an OK pushbtton, and a Cancel pushbutton.
ı ̃Hint: it would be a good i...

- Dialogs provide special processing for certain keys: tab, arrow keys, enter, escape and mnemonic keys

16-1

The Dialog Focus

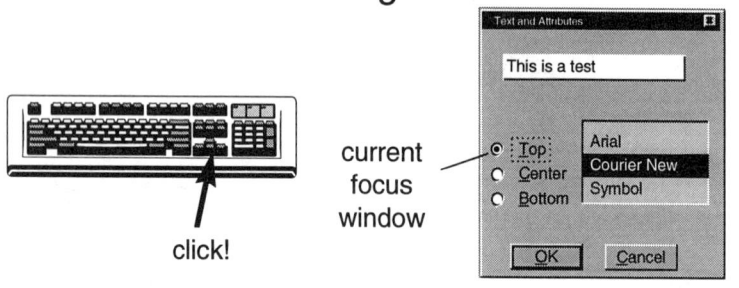

current focus window

click!

This page presents two major points:

First, the concept of focus. Windows uses the focus to determine which window receives keystroke messages. Only one window can have the focus at a time; in the picture shown here, it's the Top radio button. The focus window generally draws itself distinctively. For example, an edit control draws a flashing, text-entry caret, a radio button draws a half-tone focus rectangle around its text and so on.

Second, it's important to understand that dialog control windows are selective when it comes to keystrokes – they respond to some keystrokes, but ignore others. For example, if an edit control has the focus and the user presses the "a" key, the edit control responds to the message by displaying the "a" character. But that same edit control doesn't know what to do if the user presses the tab key – instead of inserting a character, the system chang...

- Only one control in the dialog ever has the focus at any given time - user can press special keys to switch the focus
- The focus window usually displays a caret, for example a flashing text-entry caret in edit boxes or a focus rectangle for buttons
- The system can only provide special key processing if the focus window doesn't handle the keystroke message

16-2

The Dialog Script

```
DLG_TEXTATTRS DIALOG DISCARDABLE  0, 0, 182, 145
STYLE DS_MODALFRAME | WS_POPUP | WS_CAPTION | WS_SYSMENU
CAPTION "Text and Attributes"
FONT 8, "MS Sans Serif"
{
    EDITTEXT        DLG_TEXTENTRY,16,14,129,14,ES_AUTOHSCROLL
    CONTROL         "&Top",DLG_TOP,"Button",BS_AUTORADIOBUTTON | WS_GROUP |
                    WS_TABSTOP,18,47,29,10
    CONTROL         "&Center",DLG_VCENTER,"Button",BS_AUTORADIOBUTTON,18,65,
                    36,10
    CONTROL         "&Bottom",DLG_BOTTOM,"Button",BS_AUTORADIOBUTTON,18,83,
                    37,10
    LISTBOX         DLG_FONTLIST,89,46,75,56,LBS_SORT | LBS_NOINTEGRALHEIGHT
                  | WS_VSCROLL | WS_TABSTOP | WS_GROUP
    DEFPUSHBUTTON   "&OK",IDOK,24,120,50,14,WS_GROUP | WS_TABSTOP
    PUSHBUTTON      "&Cancel",IDCANCEL,90,120,50,14,WS_TABSTOP
}
```
See The Dialog Script in Chapter 13 for a description of the script language

This page shows the dialog script for the sample dialog shown on the last page. The sequence of controls is quite important – it sets the order in which the focus changes within the dialog. So assuming that the focus starts on the first control, the edit control, the "Top" radio button would be next in line and so on.

When the dialog box is created, Windows internally organizes the dialog controls into a list and orders the list in the same order in which they are listed in the script. When it's time to change the focus, Windows consults the list to see which control receives the focus next.

But how do you specify the order when you create a dialog? By default, the dialog editor places controls in the script in the order in which they are created. Most dialog editors also let you change the order. For example, in the Microsoft Developer Studio, ...

- When you use a dialog editor to create a dialog box, the editor generates a script that lists the dialog controls
- The order in which controls appear controls the focus-change order

16-3

Keystrokes in Dialogs

The Tab Key

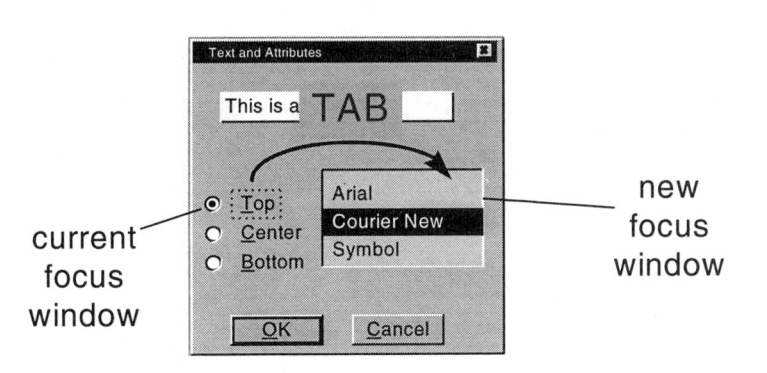

current focus window → (Top radio button)

new focus window → (Courier New in list: Arial / Courier New / Symbol)

- If the current focus window ignores the tab key, the dialog changes the focus to the next window that has the WS_TABSTOP style
- You can assign this style to a control in the dialog editor

16-4

The first special key we will examine is the Tab key. Most dialog controls do not handle this keystroke, even though that might not seem intuitive. On the dialog shown here, none of the controls process tab, so if the user presses it, you know that the focus will change.

The question is, which control will receive the focus? Here's what the system does: when the user presses Tab, the system first determines which control currently has the focus, and then finds it in the list specified by the dialog script. Windows then searches that list for the next control that has the WS_TABSTOP style, then switches the focus to that window. Note that the new focus window could be "above" the current focus window in the list, if the current focus window is at the end of the list, since Windows cycles back to the top of the list in that case.

So in this example, the focus will switch from the radio button to the list box, since t...

The Arrow Keys

current focus window → (This is a test edit control)

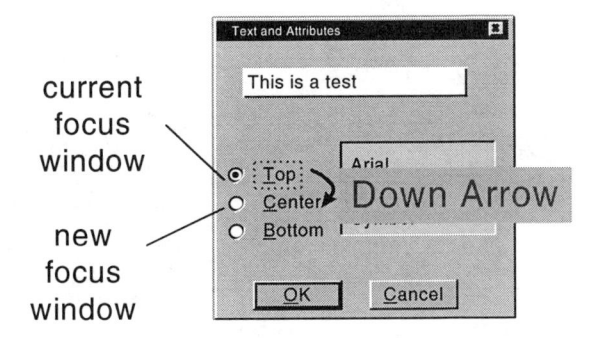

new focus window → (Center radio button — Down Arrow)

- If the current focus window ignores the arrow keys, the dialog changes the focus to the next member of the current group
- You create a group by assigning the WS_GROUP style to the first member of the group - the group continues until a subsequent window has the WS_GROUP style

16-5

The next set of keys to discuss is the directional, or arrow keys. These are a bit different from the tab key, because some dialog controls do handle them. For example, if an edit control has the focus when the user presses the left arrow key, the edit control moves its text-entry caret, and no focus change occurs.

However, if any kind of button has the focus and the user presses an arrow key, Windows will switch the focus, since buttons don't process arrow keys.

But which window gets the focus? When the system detects a non-handled arrow key, it first determines which control in the list currently has the focus. Then Windows changes the focus to the next member of the current group. You define a group by assigning the WS_GROUP style to the first member of the group – all subsequent windows are considered to b...

The Enter Key

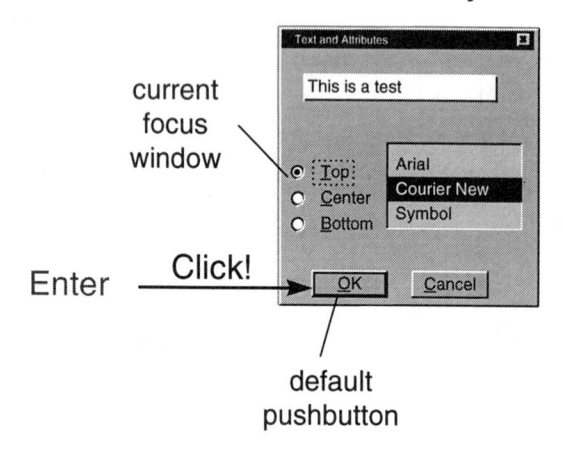

current focus window

Enter — *Click!*

default pushbutton

- If the current focus window ignores the Enter key, the dialog "clicks" the pushbutton the current default pushbutton (if any)
- You can specify which button is the default pushbutton in the dialog editor

16-6

The next key to talk about is the enter key. As with arrow keys, some dialog controls process the enter key. For example, a multiline edit control with the ES_WANTRETURN style inserts a new-line into its text when the user presses enter, and no special processing occurs. But in this dialog, none of the controls handle the enter key, so Windows will take action if the user presses it.

Windows processes the enter key a little differently than the other keys we've discussed – no focus change occurs. Instead, Windows queries the dialog box, asking for the default pushbutton. When it finds the default pushbutton, Windows simulates a mouse click on the button.

You assign the default pushbutton when you create the dialog – on this page, it's the OK button. The user can tell which is the default pushbutton, because that button draws itself with a darker border. So in this exa...

The Escape Key

current focus window

Escape Key

```
dialogfunction (...)
{
    case WM_COMMAND:

        case IDCANCEL:

}
```

pushbutton ID = 2

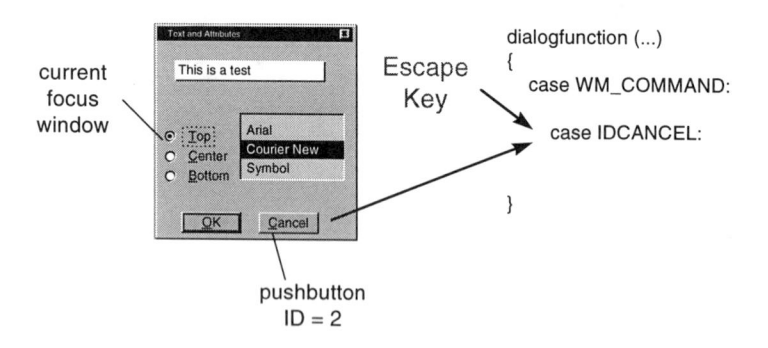

- If the current focus window ignores the Escape key, the dialog sends a WM_COMMAND message to the dialog function, specifying an ID of value 2 (IDCANCEL)
- Therefore, you should assign ID = 2 to any Cancel pushbutton (or equivalent) so that the same thing happens if the user presses the pushbutton or presses the Escape key

16-7

Now for the escape key. None of the dialog controls on this dialog handle the escape key, so if the user presses it, Windows will take action. When the system detects the escape key, it sends a WM_COMMAND message to the dialog function. Remember that the low-word of wParam in WM_COMMAND contains an ID – in this case, Windows hard-codes the ID to the numeric value two.

Since you can't change the way that the system processes the escape key, if you want the escape key to work the same as a "Cancel" button, you should assign your Cancel button the ID of two! That way, the dialog function will be invoked in the same fashion if the user clicks the Cancel button or presses the escape key. Windows makes this easier by defining the symbol IDCANCEL in the WINUSER.H header – and guess what its value is? That's right – two! Therefore you sh...

Character Mnemonic Keys

current focus window

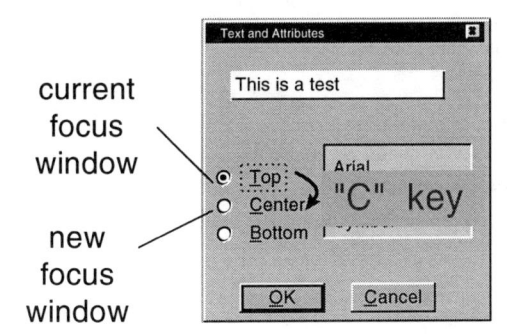

new focus window

"C" key

- If the current focus window ignores character keys - for example, checkboxes ignore them - the dialog "clicks" the button, if any, that recognizes the character as a keyboard mnemonic (underlined character)
- You can assign keyboard mnemonics by inserting an ampersand (&) in the button's text

Review Quiz

Before you move on to the next chapter, you should test your comprehension of this chapter by taking the review quiz. The quiz assumes that you have already done the lab exercise.

The quiz will be displayed in a separate window so that you can page through the chapter to help you find the answers. In other words, this is an open book quiz!

After you have answered all of the questions, press the button at the bottom of the quiz window to see how you did. If you didn't score as well as you think you should, you should review the chapter before continuing on.

Chapter Summary

- Windows treats certain keys specially in modal dialog boxes. The special keys are tab, enter, escape, directional (arrow) and character keys

- To determine how to respond to a key, Windows examines which window currently has the focus and then consults the order of the dialog controls as specified by the dialog script

- Developers should carefully design their dialogs so that these special keystrokes work in an intuitive fashion so as not to confuse users

Chapter 17: Modeless Dialogs

- ◆ Why Use a Modeless Dialog?
- ◆ Communicating with a Modeless Dialog
- ◆ Modeless Dialog Keystroke Processing

17-0

What is a Modeless Dialog?

Parent Window (WS_OVERLAPPED)

Modeless Dialog Box (WS_POPUP)

Modeless dialogs differ from the modal dialogs that you've learned about in the previous chapters in that they don't prevent their parent window from receiving user input. Modal dialogs do restrict the user – the user must dismiss a modal dialog before they can interact with the parent window. Modeless dialogs impose no such restrictions and thus are preferred by many users.

In the example shown here, the user can interact with either the main window or the modeless dialog.

There's not much difference between using a modeless dialog and just creating a secondary, overlapped window. The big difference is that modeless dialogs are easier to design since you can use a dialog-box editing tool to lay out the child windows.

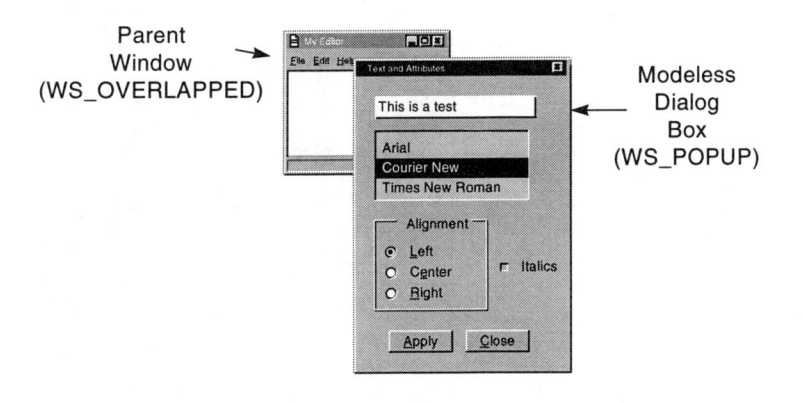

- Unlike modal dialogs, modeless dialogs do not disable their parent window - the user can interact with either the modeless dialog or the parent window
- The difference between a modeless dialog and a normal overlapped window is that you can design modeless dialogs in a dialog box editor

17-1

Why Use a Modeless Dialog?

Modeless   Modal

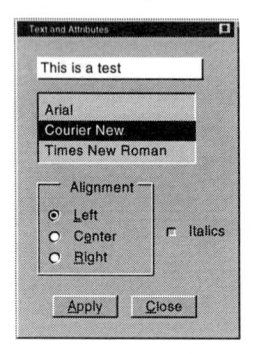

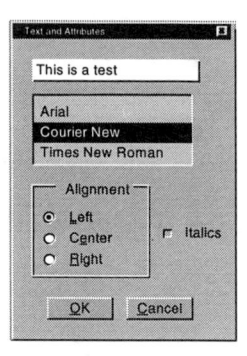

- Modal dialogs require the user to dismiss them before continuing - this is inconvenient if the user must reference the dialog often
- Modeless dialogs give the user more control over the application's flow, but may clutter the desktop

So how do you decide whether to use a modal or a modeless dialog? It depends on how often the user will wish to use the dialog box, and on how much structure you want to impose on the user's actions.

If you anticipate that the user will use the dialog box repeatedly, it's a good idea to create the dialog box as modeless. In the example shown on this page, if we use a modal box, to change a text attribute, the user must display the dialog box, select attributes and then press OK, which dismisses the dialog. If they want to change the attributes again, they must redisplay the dialog and repeat the entire process.

A modeless dialog box would make it easier on the user – they could leave the dialog box up and press the Apply button whenever they make a change to the text attributes – they don't have to keep showing and destroying the dialog box.

Creating a Modeless Dialog

```
HWND CreateDialogParam (
        HINSTANCE hInstance
      , LPCSTR lpTemplateName
      , HWND hWndParent
      , DLGPROC lpDialogFunc
      , LPARAM dwInitParam );
```

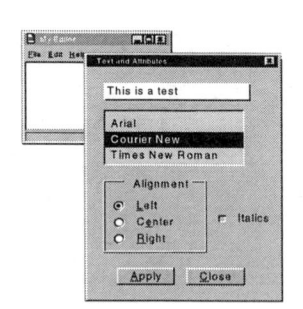

- CreateDialogParam returns the new dialog's window handle
- Unlike DialogBoxParam for modal dialogs, this call doesn't wait for the dialog to be dismissed before returning
- You can get rid of the modeless dialog by calling DestroyWindow

This call creates a modeless dialog and returns its handle. We pass the instance handle that indicates where the dialog resource resides, the name or ID of the dialog resource, the modeless dialog's parent, the address of the dialog function, and an application-defined argument.

These parameters are identical to DialogBoxParam, but one argument is interpreted differently – the parent window handle. A modal dialog disables its parent from receiving user input, but a modeless dialog doesn't. Windows does use this argument for modeless dialogs, however – Windows ensures that the modeless dialog never "goes behind" its parent in the Z-order. In other words, if the modeless dialog box is on top of its parent, and the user clicks on the parent, Windows will not surface the parent. That's nice because it shows the user that there's a relationship between the mo...

Communicating with a Modeless Dialog

```
#define WM_USER_APPLY WM_USER
#define WM_USER_CLOSE WM_USER + 1
```

As discussed on the last page, the CreateDialogBox call returns immediately, not waiting for the dialog box to be dismissed. But how then does the dialog inform the main window that something's happened? For example, how does the main window know when the dialog closes?

One easy way to provide the notification is to use messages – the dialog can send or post messages to the parent's window procedure whenever the user presses a button, for example. The question is: what message should we post? Although Windows doesn't explicitly define messages for modeless dialogs, Windows does allow you to define your own messages, as long as their IDs don't conflict with Windows messages. To avoid any conflict, just make sure the message's ID falls between the WM_USER constant defined in WINUSER.H and 0x7fff.

In this sample, we define two messages – one for when th...

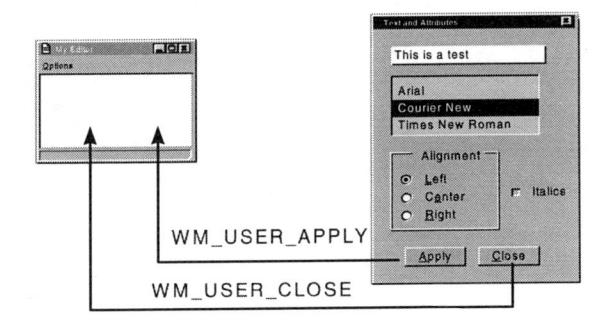

- Since modeless dialogs aren't synchronized with the parent window, you must use some other technique to communicate
- Application-defined messages work well for communication - you can define wParam and lParam to be whatever you want

17-4

Enabling and Disabling a Menu Item

```
#define WM_USER_APPLY WM_USER
#define WM_USER_CLOSE WM_USER + 1

WndProc (...)
{
  case WM_COMMAND:    // menu selection
         .
         .
    hwndModeless = CreateDialogParam (...);
    EnableMenuItem ( ... MF_GRAYED );
         .
         .
  case WM_USER_CLOSE:
    EnableMenuItem ( ... MF_ENABLED );
    return 0;
}

DialogProc ( HWND hwndDlg ... )
{
  case DLG_CLOSE:
    SendMessage ( GetParent (hwndDlg)
                , WM_USER_CLOSE, 0, 0 );

    DestroyWindow ( hwndDlg );
         .
         .
}
```

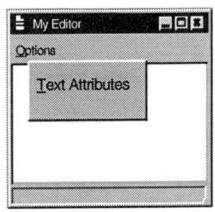

This page shows an example of a modeless dialog sending application-defined messages to a main window. Here, the user displays the modeless dialog by choosing from a menu.

When the user chooses from the menu, the main window displays the modeless dialog, and then grays-out the menu item to prevent the user from choosing the menu item again – if we didn't do this, the program would create another modeless dialog each time the user chose from the menu!

The question is: how does the main window procedure know when it's OK to re-enable the menu item? That's where the application-defined message comes in: the dialog can send WM_USER_CLOSE when the user clicks the Close button, and then destroy itself. When the main window procedure receives the message, it responds by re-enabling the menu item.

- In this example, the user displays the modeless dialog by choosing a menu item - the program disables the menu item while the dialog is visible to prevent multiple copies
- When the dialog exits, the program must re-enable the menu item - this program uses an application-defined message for notification

17-5

Keystroke Processing

```
HWND      hwndModeless = 0; // global variable
WinMain ( ... )
{
       .
       .
       .
    while ( GetMessage ( &msg, NULL, 0, 0 ) )
    {
        if ( IsWindow ( hwndModeless ) )
            if ( !IsDialogMessage ( hwndModeless, &msg ) )
                continue;

        DispatchMessage ( &msg );
    }
       .
       .
       .
}
```

- In Chapter 16, you learned about how keystrokes work in modal dialogs, for example the Tab key
- To provide the same support for modeless dialogs, you must call the IsDialogMessage Windows system call in your program's message loop

Here's some bad news – if your program does nothing special, then the tab, arrow and other keys we covered in Chapter 16 will not work in a modeless dialog. For example, if the user presses the tab key, expecting a focus change, nothing will happen!

To enable the special keys, you need to call IsDialogMessage from the message loop in WinMain, passing the modeless dialog's handle and the message structure dequeued by GetMessage.

IsDialogMessage does more than its name implies – it does check to see if a message corresponds to a special dialog-box key. But if it is a special key, IsDialogMessage also processes the keystroke, perhaps changing the focus in the dialog. That's why we coded the C-language continue statement – if IsDialogMessage does its work, we don't need to dispatch the message.

But we don't want to call IsDi...

Multiple Modeless Dialogs

```
DialogProc ( HWND hwndDlg ... )
{
case WM_ACTIVATE:
    switch ( LOWORD ( wParam ) )
    {
        case WA_ACTIVE:
        case WA_CLICKACTIVE:
            hwndModeless = hwndDlg;   // global variable
            break;

        case WA_INACTIVE:
            hwndModeless = 0;         // global variable
            break;
    }
    return 0;
       .
       .
       .
}
```

- The IsDialogMessage system call accepts the window handle of a modeless dialog - if you have multiple modeless dialogs, you cannot hard-code the handle
- The trick is to use a global variable to hold the window handle and set the global variable to the currently active modeless dialog's window handle

If you have multiple modeless dialog boxes in your program, you can simplify your message loop by including the code shown here in each modeless dialog function.

On the last page, we showed defining a global variable named hwndModeless. In each modeless dialog function, we process the WM_ACTIVATE message, which Windows sends when a window becomes active or inactive. If the dialog is becoming active, we store its handle in the global variable. If the dialog is losing activation, we set the global variable to zero.

This trick works because Windows allows only one active window at a time. With this code, each time any modeless dialog becomes active, it stores its handle in the global variable. If the user activates a non-dialog window, the dialog stores zero in the global variable as part of bei...

Modeless Dialog Sample

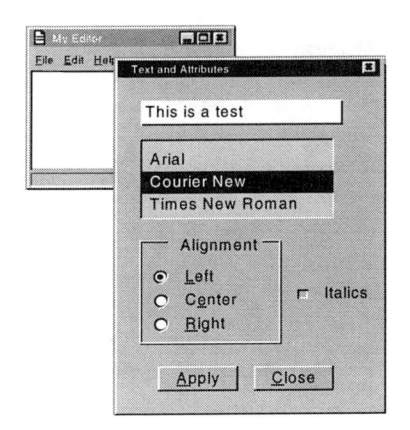

When you run this sample, try displaying the modeless dialog box by choosing from the menu. Then examine the menu item and note that it's disabled to prevent you from creating another modeless dialog. Then try interacting with either the main window or the modeless dialog – for example, try changing the main window's size while the dialog is visible. Since the dialog is modeless, you should be able to – and you couldn't if the dialog was modal.

- This program is similar to the complex dialog sample from Chapter 14, except that it uses a modeless dialog

Review Quiz

Before you move on to the next chapter, you should test your comprehension of this chapter by taking the review quiz. The quiz assumes that you have already done the lab exercise.

The quiz will be displayed in a separate window so that you can page through the chapter to help you find the answers. In other words, this is an open book quiz!

After you have answered all of the questions, press the button at the bottom of the quiz window to see how you did. If you didn't score as well as you think you should, you should review the chapter before continuing on.

Chapter Summary

- Unlike modal dialogs, modeless dialogs do not prevent their parent windows from receiving user input

- Since Windows doesn't automatically synchronize a modeless dialog with the window procedure that created the box, developers often use application-defined messages to communicate between the dialog function and the calling window function

- Since Windows doesn't automatically provide dialog-box keystroke processing for modeless dialogs, applications must modify their message loops or else the tab, arrow and other keys will not change the focus in a modeless dialog

Chapter 18: Property Sheets and Wizards

- ◆ What is a Property Sheet?
- ◆ Creating a Property Sheet
- ◆ Property Sheet Notifications and Messages
- ◆ What is a Wizard?
- ◆ Wizard Notifications and Messages

What is a Property Sheet?

Tabs — Property Sheet

Page Dialog

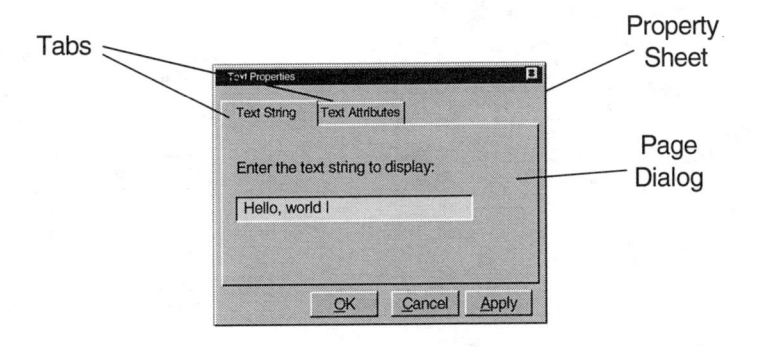

- A property sheet is a window that contains a collection of dialog boxes - the user can switch pages by clicking on the tabs
- Programs can use property sheets to let users configure application settings or properties of objects that the application creates
- Property sheets use the Windows common-control library

Property sheets let you collect many dialogs into a compact, easy-to-use package. Here, we have a property sheet that contains two dialogs that let a user configure a text string. The property sheet displays one dialog at a time and lets the user display a hidden dialog by clicking on the tab for that dialog. Each dialog in a property sheet is referred to as a property sheet page.

Before we had property sheets, we had to use separate dialogs, and typically each dialog had a corresponding menu item. That made the menus quite cluttered and hard to use. Using a property sheet, the program only needs a single menu item.

Structure of a Property Sheet

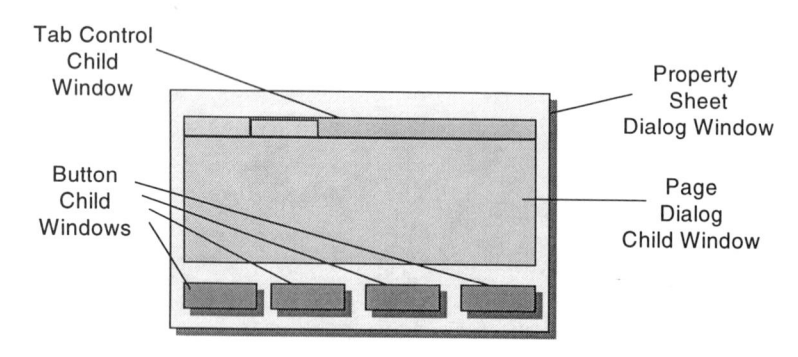

Diagram showing a property sheet with labels: Tab Control Child Window, Button Child Windows, Property Sheet Dialog Window, Page Dialog Child Window

- Each page in a property sheet is a separate modeless dialog - the developer must provide a dialog resource script and dialog function for each page
- Only one of the page dialogs is visible at a time -- the user selects which one by clicking on the tabs
- The property sheet creates the buttons and tab window and handles the user's selection of pages

Before you can create a property sheet, you must create a dialog for each page – you can design the page dialogs in your dialog editor. The page dialogs don't contain OK and Cancel buttons, since these are provided by the property sheet. You will also need to write a dialog function for each page dialog – we will discuss how to do that in a later part of this chapter, but it's quite similar to writing the dialog function for a regular dialog.

The window hierarchy in a property sheet is interesting. The parent window is the property sheet window itself, which is a WS_POPUP window. Each page of the property sheet is a child window, so the pages are siblings. Each page has the same size and position, but the user can see only the page that's on top of the Z-order. When the user selects a new page, the property sheet changes the Z-order so that the newly selected page rises to the top.
I˝The buttons are each sep...

18-2

Designing a Page Dialog

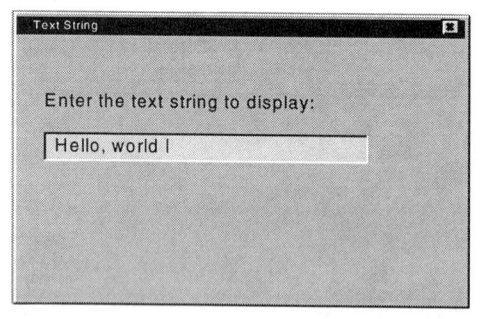

Screenshot of a dialog titled "Text String" with label "Enter the text string to display:" and text field containing "Hello, world !"

- The dialog for a page should not include OK and Cancel buttons since these are provided by the property sheet
- The property sheet hides the page dialog's titlebar but displays the title text in the tab for the page
- The dialog should have the WS_CHILD style since it will be a child of the property sheet window
- All pages in a property sheet should be about the same size

You have to design page dialogs a little differently than normal dialogs.

First, each page dialog must have the WS_CHILD style instead of WS_POPUP, or else the pages will not display properly.

Second, you should put a titlebar on the page dialog. The property sheet will hide the titlebar, but will use the title text in the tab for the page.

Third, the property sheet automatically sizes itself so that it can display the largest page, so if you don't make all of the page dialogs about the same size, the user will see a lot of blank space in the smaller pages.

18-3

Property Sheet Styles

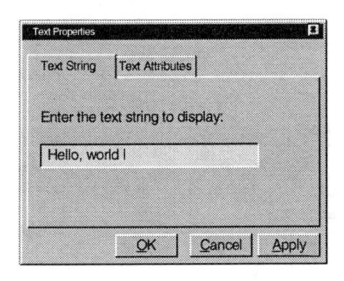

default style

PSH_WIZARD

There are two basic kinds of property sheets – normal property sheets and wizards. We will cover wizards later in the chapter. The default style is a normal property sheet. You also must decide if the property sheet will be modal or modeless. We will only cover modal property sheets in this chapter.

- By default, property sheets are modal - the user must dismiss them before continuing - but you can specify the PSH_MODELESS flag when you create the property sheet to create it as modeless. See Chapter 17 for more information on modeless dialogs
- A Wizard is a special kind of property sheet that has no tabs and walks the user through a sequence - we will cover them more at the end of this chapter

18-4

Notifications and Message Macros

Notification codes

PSN_APPLY
PSN_HELP
PSN_KILLACTIVE
PSN_QUERYCANCEL
PSN_RESET
PSN_SETACTIVE
PSN_WIZBACK
PSN_WIZFINISH
PSN_WIZNEXT

Message Macros

PropSheet_AddPage
PropSheet_Apply
PropSheet_CancelToClose
PropSheet_Changed
PropSheet_GetCurrentPageHwnd
PropSheet_GetTabControl
PropSheet_IsDialogMessage
PropSheet_PressButton
PropSheet_QuerySiblings
PropSheet_RebootSystem
PropSheet_RemovePage
PropSheet_RestartWindows
PropSheet_SetCurSel
PropSheet_SetCurSelByID
PropSheet_SetFinishText
PropSheet_SetTitle
PropSheet_SetWizButtons
PropSheet_UnChanged

- The notifications are sent as WM_NOTIFY messages. See Notification Messages in Chapter 15 for a review of WM_NOTIFY
- The message macros send property-sheet messages but are easier to use than sending the messages explicitly

This page lists the macros that you can use to manipulate a property sheet. We will cover some of the more useful macros in more detail in the next few pages.

Each of these macros is defined in PRSHT.H and each of them simply sends a message to the property sheet. The advantage of using the macros is that they are easier than sending the messages yourself. That's because the macros aren't limited to the generic wParam and lParam arguments that SendMessage uses -- the macros essentially take care of packaging the macro arguments into wParam and lParam and then sending the message.

18-5

Configuring a Page

```
static char sz[100];

strcpy ( sz, "Hello, world" );

PROPSHEETPAGE    psp[2];

psp[0].dwSize = sizeof (PROPSHEETPAGE);
psp[0].dwFlags = 0;
psp[0].hInstance = hInst;
psp[0].pszTemplate =
     MAKEINTRESOURCE (DLG_TEXT);
psp[0].pfnDlgProc = TextDialogProc;
psp[0].lParam = (LONG)sz;

psp[1].dwSize = sizeof (PROPSHEETPAGE);
psp[1].dwFlags = 0;
        .
        .
        .
```

resource ID = DLG_TEXT

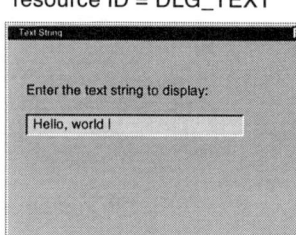

- For each page, you must fill in a PROPSHEETPAGE structure that describes the page
- Windows passes the lParam field to the dialog function in its WM_INITDIALOG message

Before you create the property sheet, you must configure the property sheet pages. To do so, you allocate an array of PROPSHEETPAGE structures – one array element for each page. Then you must initialize the structure fields for each page.

In the structure for each page, we fill in the size of the structure itself, a set of bit flags, the instance handle that contains the page dialog resource, the ID or name of the page dialog, the address of the page dialog function and an application-defined field.

The application-defined field is quite useful: Windows passes it to the dialog function's WM_INITDIALOG message. You can use this field to pass the address of the data that the page represents – in this case, the address of string. Since we passed an address, the dialog function can both read and modify the string – it will modify the string if the user changes the data in the edit control and then presses the...

Creating a Property Sheet

```
PROPSHEETHEADER psh;

psh.dwSize = sizeof (PROPSHEETHEADER);
psh.dwFlags = PSH_PROPSHEETPAGE;
psh.hwndParent = hwnd;
psh.nPages = 2;
psh.pszCaption = "Text Properties";
psh.ppsp = psp;

// display the property sheet
int nErr = PropertySheet ( &psh );
```

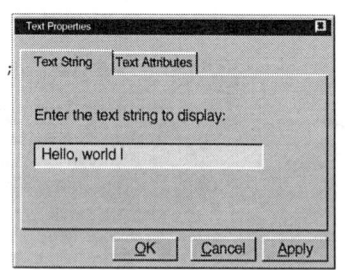

- Unlike "normal" dialogs, property sheets must be constructed at runtime instead of being defined by a resource script (the page dialogs can be resource scripts)
- You must fill in the PROPSHEETHEADER structure that describes the property sheet and then call the PropertySheet system call
- By default, property sheets are modal - the PropertySheet call doesn't return until the user dismisses the sheet

Once you have filled in the array of page-description structures, you have to initialize one more structure. This is the PROPSHEETHEADER structure that describes the property sheet window itself.

Here, we specify the size of the structure itself, a flags parameter that configures the property sheet, the parent window handle – since by default the property sheet is modal, Windows will disable the parent, the page count, the titlebar text and the address of the array that describes the pages.

We then pass the address of this structure to the PropertySheet system call to create and display the property sheet dialog. Since this property sheet is modal, this call will not return until the user dismisses the property sheet.

The PSH_PROPSHEETPAG...

Property Sheet Buttons

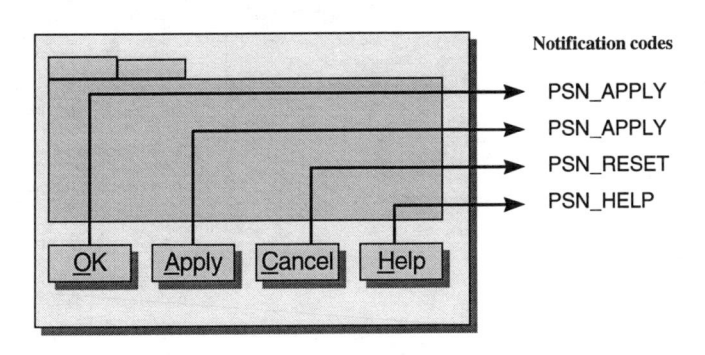

Notification codes

- PSN_APPLY (OK)
- PSN_APPLY (Apply)
- PSN_RESET (Cancel)
- PSN_HELP (Help)

Notice that the OK and Apply buttons generate the same notification – the page dialog function can't really differentiate them. The only real difference is that OK automatically dismisses the property sheet. We will see some code to handle these buttons in a moment.

If the user presses the Cancel button, each page dialog receives the PSN_RESET notification and the property sheet is automatically dismissed. We will see code for Cancel on the next page.

We don't cover help in this workshop, but help for property sheet pages is pretty easy. When a page dialog receives the PSN_HELP notification, it should call WinHelp and specify the ID of the help text for the page dialog window.

- When the user clicks a property sheet button, the sheet sends WM_NOTIFY messages to the page dialog functions
- Both OK and Cancel buttons automatically dismiss the property sheet, so the page dialog function shouldn't call EndDialog
- The difference between the "OK" and "Apply" buttons is that "OK" dismisses the property sheet

---

Handling the Cancel Button

```
PageDialogProc (...)
{
static char *pszName;    // points to caller's string
static char szSave[100]; // backup copy

case WM_INITDIALOG:
{
  PROPSHEETPAGE *psp = (PROPSHEETPAGE *)lParam;
  pszName = (char *)psp->lParam;

  strcpy ( szSave, pszName );
}
case WM_NOTIFY:
{
  .
  .
  case PSN_RESET:
    strcpy ( pszName, szSave );
  .
  .
}
```

When the user presses the Cancel button, each page dialog receives the PSN_RESET notification. This notification means that the user wants to revert back to the state that existed before they displayed the property sheet.

Handling the Cancel button is easy if you specify the PSH_NOAPPLYNOW flag when you create the property sheet. Then, the property sheet has no Apply button, and you can write the page dialog function like a normal dialog function: in WM_INITDIALOG, initialize the controls, and when the user presses OK, read the data from the controls.

If you have an apply button, however, life is more difficult. When the user presses Apply, they expect the data in the main window to be updated with the values entered into the property sheet – but the property sheet isn't dismisse...

- Upon initialization, each page dialog function should make a backup copy of the data to which it refers - then if the user presses Cancel, the dialog function can restore the data

Handling OK and Apply Buttons

```
PageDialogProc ( HWND hwndDlg, ...)
{
static char *pszName;
static char szSave[100];

case WM_NOTIFY:
{
    .
    .
    case PSN_APPLY:
      GetDlgItemText ( hwndDlg, DLG_TEXTSTR, pszName );
      HWND hwndSheet = GetParent ( hwndDlg );
      HWND hwndMain  = GetParent ( hwndSheet );
      SendMessage ( hwndMain, WM_USER_APPLY
                    , 0, 0 );
    .
    .
}
```

- When the user presses OK or Apply, the page dialog function should read the controls on the page
- If the user presses Apply, the property sheet isn't dismissed, but the user expects the application to update its display - to accomplish this, the page dialog function can send an application-defined message

If the user presses the OK or Apply buttons, the property sheet passes the PSN_APPLY notification to each page.

If you create the property sheet using the PSH_NOAPPLYNOW flag, the code is easy. When the user presses OK, all you need to do is read the page dialog controls and update the caller's data, much like you would in a normal dialog.

But if you have an Apply button, the user expects the main window's data to be updated when they press the button. However, when the user presses Apply, the property sheet is not dismissed. How can the page inform the main window that it's data has changed so the main window can update its display?

The solution is to use an application-defined message – in this example, we named the message WM_USER_APPLY. We first read the text from the edit control and write it into the caller's string (we initialized ...

18-10

Enabling the Apply Button

```
case WM_COMMAND:
  switch ( LOWORD ( wParam ) )
  {
    case DLG_TEXTSTR:
      switch ( HIWORD ( wParam ) )
      {
        case EN_CHANGE:
          PropSheet_Changed ( GetParent ( hwndDlg )
                              , hwndDlg );
          return TRUE;
      }
      break;
  }
  return FALSE;
```

- The property sheet initially disables the Apply button - when the user changes data in a dialog control, the page dialog function can call PropSheet_Change to enable it
- The property sheet automatically re-disables the Apply button whenever the user presses it

When the property sheet first comes up, Windows disables the Apply button, indicating that there's not yet any changes to apply. It's the page dialog's job to tell Windows when it should enable the Apply button.

The code shown here is from the page dialog function for a page with an edit control. When the user modifies the text in the edit control, the edit control sends a WM_COMMAND message to the dialog function. Here, we process WM_COMMAND by first looking for the edit control's ID, then by looking for the EN_CHANGE notification code that indicates that the user modified the text. We then call the PropSheet_Changed macro, which tells the property sheet to enable the Apply button.

If the user subsequently presses the Apply button, Windows will again disable it. If your page dialogs have...

18-11

Notification Result

```
PageDialogProc ( HWND hwndDlg, ... )
{
    .
case WM_NOTIFY:
{
    .
    .
    switch ( pnmdhr->code )
    {
      case PSN_APPLY:
        .
        .
        SetWindowLong ( hwndDlg, DWL_MSGRESULT, PSNRET_NOERROR );
        return TRUE;
    }
}
return FALSE;
```

Window Data Structure

SetWindowLong → msg result DWL_MSGRESULT

- Some property sheet notification messages require that the page dialog function set the DWL_MSGRESULT field in the page dialog's window data
- Remember that in any dialog function, you should return TRUE if you processed the message, FALSE otherwise - the DWL_MSGRESULT technique lets you return additional information back to the property sheet

18-12

For some notifications, the property sheet expects the page dialog to return a value that the property sheet examines. The problem is: We can't just use the value on the return statement, since Windows uses that value for something else. So, we set a special field in the window data structure instead. After the return, the property sheet will retrieve the value from the window data structure.

When the user presses the OK button on a property sheet, each page dialog receives the PSN_APPLY notification. Here, when we receive that notification, we store the constant PSNRET_NOERROR in the window data structure to indicate that it's OK for Windows to dismiss the property sheet. If for some reason, we didn't want Windows to dismiss the property sheet, we could instead store PSNRET_INVALIDNOCHANGE.

For example, suppose the p...

Property Sheet Sample

- This program displays a text string in its client area. The user can change the text string and its attributes by entering data into a property sheet

18-13

This sample program illustrates using a property sheet to gather two related dialogs into a package. The dialogs let the user configure the text that the program displays, and the text attributes, such as italic and underline. You can display the property sheet by choosing from the program's menu.

The property sheet includes an apply button – you can change the text or attributes and then press Apply – the changes should be displayed in the main window, but the property sheet will not be dismissed. The program does this by sending an application-defined message whenever the user presses Apply.

The Cancel button also is functional – if you change an attribute and apply it without dismissing the sheet, you can roll back the change by pressing the Cancel button. The property sheet will dismi...

What is a Wizard?

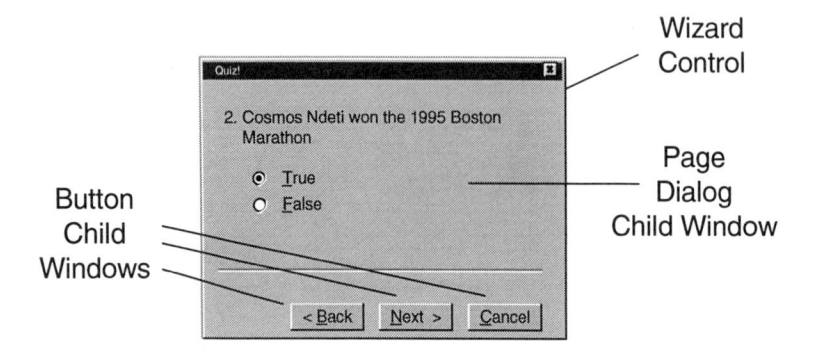

(Diagram labels: Wizard Control, Page Dialog Child Window, Button Child Windows)

- A wizard is a type of property sheet - it contains a collection of page dialogs. It differs from a normal property sheet in that it has no tabs and the buttons are labeled Back and Next instead of OK and Cancel
- You can use wizards to force the user into a sequence

Wizards are a special style of property sheet. Like a normal property sheet, a wizard contains a set of page dialogs, each of which is a child of the wizard. Users can click on the buttons to navigate the wizard – that causes the wizard to surface a different dialog child window.

The fundamental difference between a wizard and a property sheet is that a property sheet gives the user random access to the pages, while the wizard imposes sequential access. Thus, a wizard is appropriate if you want walk the user through an activity, step by step.

For example, the wizard on this page walks the user through a quiz, where the questions are numbered. The student can go forward or backward through the quiz, but cannot jump to any particular question.

Another example is the Add Printer wizard that Windows uses to let the user configure a new printer. The wizard's op...

18-14

Creating a Wizard

```
PROPSHEETHEADER psh;

psh.dwSize = sizeof (PROPSHEETHEADER);
psh.dwFlags = PSH_PROPSHEETPAGE |
              PSH_WIZARD;
psh hwndParent = hwnd;
psh.nPages = 2;
psh.pszCaption = "Quiz!";
psh.ppsp = psp;

// display the wizard
int nErr = PropertySheet ( &psh );
```

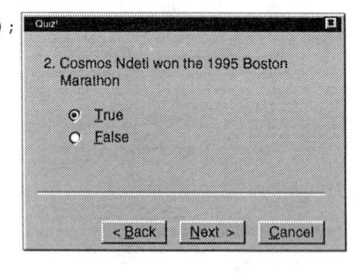

The only substantial difference between creating a wizard and a normal property sheet is that you specify the PSH_WIZARD flag. You still need to create an array of page-description structures and so forth. By default, as the user presses the Next button, the wizard will step through the pages in the order in which are contained in the page-description array.

- You create a wizard in the same way you create a property sheet except that you specify PSH_WIZARD in the flags of the PROPSHEETHEADER structure

18-15

Property Sheets and Wizards

The Next and Back Buttons

First page — Middle Page — Last Page

When the user displays the first page in a wizard, the Back button should be disabled. When a page in the middle is displayed, both Back and Next should be enabled. When the last page is displayed, the Next button should be replaced by a Finish button. When the user clicks on the Finish button, Windows will dismiss the wizard.

The bad new is that enabling and disabling the buttons doesn't happen automatically – the page dialog functions must have code in them to make it happen.

- When the user displays the first page in the wizard, the Back button should be disabled
- When the user displays the last page in the wizard, the Next button should be replaced with a "Finish" button
- You must write code to support this

18-16

Handling the Next and Back Buttons

```
case WM_NOTIFY:

  case PSN_SETACTIVE:
    {
    HWND    hwndWiz = GetParent ( hwndDlg );

    if ( first_question () )
      PropSheet_SetWizButtons ( hwndWiz
                         , PSWIZB_NEXT );

    else if ( last_question () )
      PropSheet_SetWizButtons ( hwndWiz
                         , PSWIZB_BACK | PSWIZB_FINISH );

    else
      PropSheet_SetWizButtons ( hwndWiz
                         , PSWIZB_NEXT | PSWIZB_BACK );
       .
       .
       .
```

- This code determines which page has been activated and then calls PropSheet_SetWizButtons to correctly set the wizard button state

To set the button state properly, each page function needs to process the PSN_SETACTIVE notification, which the wizard sends when the user selects the page.

In the sample code shown here, the newly activated page first determines if it's the first page by calling a local function. If it is, we call PropSheet_SetWizButtons with the PSWIZB_NEXT flag, which causes the wizard to disable the Back button and enable the Next button.

If we're not the first page, we then call another local function to determine if we are the last page. If so, we call PropSheet_SetWizButtons with the PSWIZB_BACK and PSWIZB_FINISH flags, which causes the wizard to enable the Back button and display a Finish button.

If we're not the first or last page, we must be a middle page, so we call PropSheet_...

18-17

Branching Pages

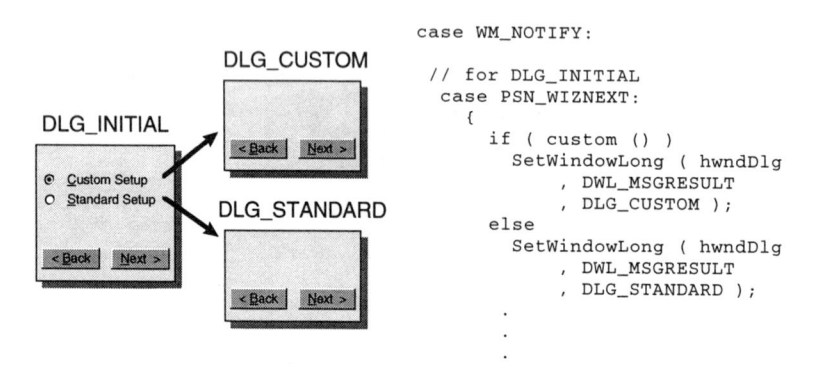

```
case WM_NOTIFY:

// for DLG_INITIAL
case PSN_WIZNEXT:
    {
        if ( custom () )
            SetWindowLong ( hwndDlg
                , DWL_MSGRESULT
                , DLG_CUSTOM );
        else
            SetWindowLong ( hwndDlg
                , DWL_MSGRESULT
                , DLG_STANDARD );
        .
        .
        .
```

- By default, the Next and Back buttons navigate the wizard pages in the order in which they appear in the PROPSHEETPAGE array
- However, you can change the sequence by setting a dialog resource ID as the message result when the user presses Next or Back - the property sheet will switch to the specified page

By default, the sequence of pages is determined by their position in the array that we use to initialize the wizard. However, sometimes you might want to create a wizard where the sequence depends on the user's actions. For example, a setup wizard may offer the user two ways to set up an application: a standard setup and a custom setup. This wizard's initial page could have a pair of radio buttons that let the user choose. And then based on the choice, the wizard can branch to a different page.

If you want to do this sort of thing, you need to process the PSN_WIZNEXT and PSN_WIZBACK notifications in the page dialog function. To override the default ordering, the page dialog must set the message result to a dialog ID – the ID of the page to which to branch.

This code is taken from the initial page dialog. We process the PSN_WIZNEXT notification generated when the user presses the Next bu...

18-18

Wizard Sample Program

- This program displays a wizard that lets the user take a quiz -- each page in the wizard is a separate quiz question

This sample program displays a trivia quiz which has four questions. When you complete the quiz, the program displays your score in a message box.

Please note that all of the pages look the same, except that the question text is different. Therefore, I decided to use the same dialog resource and dialog function for all of the pages – the dialog function sets the question text in the WM_INITDIALOG message. This works because even though I re-use the dialog resource, the wizard still creates a separate window for each page – the dialog function will be called four times in the WM_INITDIALOG case.

18-19

Lab Exercise 14: Property Sheets

In this lab, you will write a program that displays a property sheet that lets the user enter information about a student, including the student's name and test score.

Press the "Run Lab Solution" button to see what your completed program should look like -- click the right mouse button on the client area to see the floating popup menu.

To view the lab exercise instructions, press the "Lab Write Up" button. This will display the lab document and let you print it if you wish. When you are finished with the lab, continue to the next page to take a review quiz.

Review Quiz

Before you move on to the next chapter, you should test your comprehension of this chapter by taking the review quiz. The quiz assumes that you have already done the lab exercise.

The quiz will be displayed in a separate window so that you can page through the chapter to help you find the answers. In other words, this is an open book quiz!

After you have answered all of the questions, press the button at the bottom of the quiz window to see how you did. If you didn't score as well as you think you should, you should review the chapter before continuing on.

Chapter Summary

- A property sheet is a collection of dialogs called pages. The property sheet displays tabs to let the user select pages

- A wizard is a special style of property sheet that guides the user through a sequential set of pages

- Each page in a property sheet or wizard is a dialog for which the developer must provide a resource script and a dialog function

- When the user clicks a button on a property sheet or wizard, the property sheet sends notification messages to the pages. The page dialog can then respond to the click

Chapter 19: Common Dialogs

- The Find Text Dialog
- The Open File Dialog
- The Save File Dialog
- The Page Setup Dialog
- The Print Dialog
- The Replace Text Dialog

What is a Common Dialog?

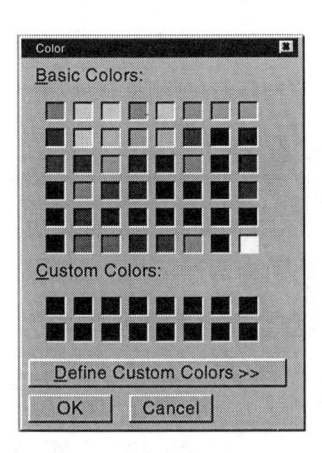

Common Dialog Display Functions

ChooseColor
ChooseFont
FindText
GetOpenFileName
GetSaveFileName
PageSetupDlg
PrintDlg
ReplaceText

Common dialogs save you, the developer, time and effort. They are a set of dialog resources and dialog functions, provided by Microsoft and shipped with Windows. They include: a choose-color dialog, which is shown on this page, a choose-font dialog, a search-for-text dialog, a file-open dialog, a save-file dialog, a page-setup dialog, a print dialog and a replace-text dialog. If these dialogs didn't exist, there's a good chance you would end up having to write some or all of them yourself.

But more importantly, at least to users, is the fact that the dialogs are available to all programs. That makes it easier for users to learn new programs.

Another plus is that for the most part, the programming for all of the dialogs is the same. So once you learn how to program one of them, you'...

- The common dialogs are a set of dialog boxes defined by Windows that provide a standard user interface
- To use a common dialog, your program must link to COMDLG32.LIB

Displaying a Common Dialogs

① Allocate and initialize a dialog-specific structure

② Call the dialog display function

③ Check for which button user pressed or for error

- Each common dialog function has an associated structure that you must allocate and initialize - you then pass the address of the structure
- Most common dialogs are modal (FindText and ReplaceText are modeless)

The programming interface for all of the common dialogs is similar – the three steps shown here. You start by filling in a structure, and then you pass the structure's address to a dialog-display system call. This will create and show the dialog, and then return you some indication of how the user dismissed the dialog box, or if an error occured.

The big difference between each common dialog is the structure – that's where your learning curve will be the steepest. Whenever you want to display a common dialog that you've never used before, your first step should be to study the structure used by that dialog. Don't be intimidated by the structures – some of them have quite a few fields. Luckily, most of the fields have reasonable defaults so in most cases, you can initialize the entire structure to zero and then fill in only the fields that you think are important.

With the exception of the FindText and ReplaceText di...

Checking for Response and Errors

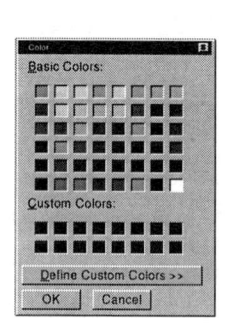

```
BOOL fRet = ChooseColor ( ... );

if ( fRet == 0 )
{
    DWORD dwErr = CommDlgExtendedError ();
    if ( dwErr == 0 )
    {
        // user pressed cancel
    }
    else
    {
        // commmon dialog error
    }
}
else
{
  // user OK'ed the dialog
}
```

- The common dialog functions return zero if the user cancels the box or if an error occurs (e.g. bad parameter)
- You can look up the error codes in CDERR.H

When the user dismisses a modal common dialog, your program must take action only if the user pressed the OK button. This code shows how you can determine which button the user pressed to dismiss the dialog.

We start by examining the return from the common dialog call, in this case ChooseColor. The documentation states that if the return value is zero, then the user pressed the OK button. We could then determine which color the user chose and take appropriate action (we'll cover the color dialog in more detail in a moment).

If the return value is non-zero, that means that the user must have pressed Cancel, right? Well, there's actually another possibility – we might have committed a programming error. The question is: how do you differentiate between programming errors and the Cancel button? After all, you ...

The Choose Color Dialog

Example:

```
DWORD       adwColors[16];
CHOOSECOLOR cc;

memset ( &cc, 0, sizeof ( cc ) );
cc.lStructSize = sizeof ( cc );
cc.hwndOwner = hwnd;
cc.lpCustColors = adwColors;
cc.rgbResult = RGB (0, 0, 0 );
cc.Flags = CC_RGBINIT;

BOOL fRet = ChooseColor ( &cc );

// check response

HBRUSH hbrBack =
    CreateSolidBrush ( cc.rgbResult );
```

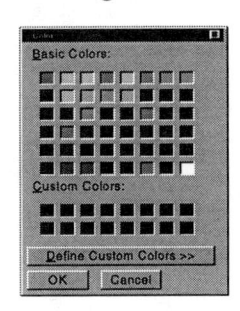

The ChooseColor dialog is useful to let the user choose window's background color, or the color of graphics drawn in the client area, for example, the bars in a bar chart. We don't normally use this dialog to let the user choose text color, since the font dialog does that for us.

The dialog displays a set of 48 color swatches, on which the user can click to select. The colors in the swatches are a subset of the 256 Windows standard colors. If your display hardware cannot physically show some of the standard colors, Windows simulates them by mixing other colors using a process called dithering.

The dialog contains a button labeled "Define Custom Colors". When the user pushes that button, the dialog expands to let the user choose the so-called custom colors, which are shown at the bottom of the dialog. And just as with the standard colors, the Windows uses dithering to simulate colors that the displ...

- This dialog lets the user select a color and also lets them define "custom" colors
- You could display this dialog to let the user choose your window's background color, for example

19-4

The Choose Font Dialog

Example:

```
LOGFONT     lf;
CHOOSEFONT  cf;

memset ( &lf, 0, sizeof ( lf ) );
memset ( &cf, 0, sizeof ( cf ) );

cf.lStructSize = sizeof ( cf );
cf.hwndOwner = hwnd;
cf.lpLogFont = &lf;
cf.Flags = CF_TTONLY | CF_SCREENFONTS |
           CF_EFFECTS;

BOOL fRet = ChooseFont ( &cf );

// check response

HFONT hf = CreateFontIndirect ( &lf );
SetTextColor ( hdc, cf.rgbColors );
```

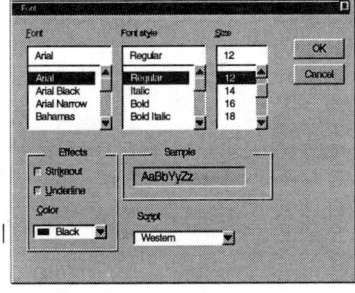

The Choose-Font dialog lets the user select a font, including its style, size, special effects and color.

It displays a combo box listing the available font names, a combo box that lists the available styles for the highlighted font name, for example Bold, a font-size combo box, from which the user can select a point size, a set of controls called the font effects – these let the user choose underline or strikeout as well as the text color, and the Script combo box, which lets the user choose a language-specific character set for the font.

In the code on this page, we first allocate and initialize two structures – a LOGFONT structure that the dialog will fill in, and the CHOOSEFONT structure, which we pass to the dialog-display system call. As before, we zero-out the structures so that we don't have to manually initialize all...

- This dialog lets the user select a font and optionally lets the user select a text color
- You could display this dialog to let the user configure the font that your program uses to display its text

19-5

The Find Text Dialog

Example:

```
static    FINDREPLACE  fr;
static    char         szFind[80];

szFind[0] = '\0';
memset ( &fr, 0, sizeof (fr) );

fr.lStructSize = sizeof (fr);
fr.hwndOwner = hwnd;
fr.lpstrFindWhat = szFind;
fr.wFindWhatLen = sizeof (szFind);

HWND hwndModeless = FindText ( &fr );

// check response
```

- This dialog displays a dialog into which the user can enter a search string - when the user presses the "Find" button, your program receives the FNDMSGSTRING message
- Upon receipt of this message, your program can search for the string
- This dialog is a modeless dialog, so you must call IsDialogMessage in your program's message loop

19-6

The Find Text dialog lets the user enter a search string and some searching options, such as whether to search forward or backward and whether or not to search without regard to case. It's important to note that this dialog doesn't do any searching – that's your job! All the dialog does is return to you the string for which user wants to search.

Unlike the other common dialogs, this dialog is modeless – it doesn't disable its parent window. When the user presses the Find Next button, the dialog sends us the FINDMSGSTRING message. We'll discuss how to handle this message on the next page.

In the code on this page, we first allocate a FINDREPLACE structure and a character array into which the dialog will write the search string. We then zero out the structure as before and initialize the character array to a zero-length string.

We then fill in the structure s...

The FINDMSGSTRING Message

```
LRESULT CALLBACK WndProc ( HWND hwnd, UINT iMsg
                         , WPARAM wParam, LPARAM
lParam )
{
static    UINT      iFindMsg = 0;

  if ( iMsg == iFindMsg )
  {
    FINDREPLACE *pfr = (FINDREPLACE *)lParam;

    if ( pfr->Flags & FR_FINDNEXT )
    {
      // user's string is in pfr->lpstrFindWhat
    }
    return 0;
  }
  else switch ( iMsg )
  {
    case WM_CREATE:
      iFindMsg =
         RegisterWindowMessage ( FINDMSGSTRING );
      return 0;
      .
      .
      .
  }
}
```

- The FindText and ReplaceText dialogs are modeless -- they send this message when the user interacts with them
- This message's ID is determined at runtime -- you cannot use the normal "switch" statement to process it

19-7

This page shows the gyrations you must perform to respond to the user clicking a pushbutton on the Find Text or Replace Text common dialogs. When something happens to the dialog, it sends a message to its parent window – that's similar to what we've covered before. What's different is that these messages do not have a predefined message identifier. Instead, Windows determines the message ID at run time. This is very flexible and prevents any conflicts with any application-defined messages, but it is cumbersome.

Instead of having an predefined ID, this message has a string name, FINDMSGSTRING, which is defined in COMMDLG.H. When the common dialog library loads, it invokes the RegisterWindowMessage system call, passing the string name. That establishes the message ID. We can obtain the ID by calling RegisterWi...

The Open File Dialog

Example:
```
OPENFILENAME    ofn;
char szFname[ _MAX_PATH ];

szFname[0] = '\0';

memset ( &ofn, 0
        , sizeof ( OPENFILENAME) );
ofn.lStructSize =
          sizeof ( OPENFILENAME );
ofn.hwndOwner = hwnd;
ofn.lpstrFile = szFname;
ofn.nMaxFile = _MAX_PATH;
ofn.lpstrTitle = "Open Text File";
ofn.Flags = OFN_FILEMUSTEXIST | OFN_HIDEREADONLY;
ofn.lpstrFilter = "Text Files(*.TXT)\0*.TXT\0";
ofn.lpstrDefExt = "TXT";

BOOL fRet = GetOpenFileName ( &ofn );

// check response

FILE *f = fopen ( szFname, "r" );
```

- This dialog lets the user select a file that your program can then open - the function retrieves the fully qualified filename

19-8

The Open File dialog retrieves a file name string from the user that your program can use to open a file. This dialog is very similar to the Save File dialog that we'll cover in a moment – the two dialogs look much the same and use the same structure and flags.

The Open File dialog displays a "Look In" combo box that shows drives and directories. Next to that combo box are a series of buttons that let the user change to the parent directory, create a new directory and change the file list from list view to details view. Below that, in the large rectangle, the dialog displays a list of files. Next is a "File Name" edit control where the user can manually enter a file name. Next is a "Files of Type" combo box that contains one or strings, called filter strings, each of which specifies a file extension. The dialog uses the current filter extension to exclude files from the list. In the dialog shown on this page, only files with .TXT as an extension are displayed.
ιTo display an Open File ...

The Save File Dialog

Example:
```
OPENFILENAME    ofn;
char szFname[ _MAX_PATH ];

szFname[0] = '\0';

memset ( &ofn, 0
        , sizeof ( OPENFILENAME) );
ofn.lStructSize =
          sizeof ( OPENFILENAME );
ofn.hwndOwner = hwnd;
ofn.lpstrFile = szFname;
ofn.nMaxFile = _MAX_PATH;
ofn.lpstrTitle = "Save Text File";
ofn.Flags = OFN_OVERWRITEPROMPT | OFN_HIDEREADONLY;
ofn.lpstrFilter = "Text Files(*.TXT)\0*.TXT\0";
ofn.lpstrDefExt = "TXT";

BOOL fRet = GetSaveFileName ( &ofn );

// check response

FILE *f = fopen ( szFname, "w" );
```

- This dialog lets the user enter a file name under which your program can save its data - the function returns the fully qualified filename

19-9

The Save As dialog is almost the same as the Open File dialog covered on the last page. The main difference is that programs display this dialog in response to the user asking to save a file rather than open a file. Another difference is the flags field in the structure – as shown in the example, it's common to specify the OFN_OVERWRITEPROMPT flag so the dialog asks the user if they want to overwrite an existing file.

For more programming details, see page 19-8, where we cover the Open File dialog.

The Page Setup Dialog

Example:

```
PAGESETUPDLG    psd;

memset ( &psd, 0, sizeof (psd) );

psd.lStructSize = sizeof (psd);
psd.Flags = PSD_INTHOUSANDTHSOFINCHES;
psd.hwndOwner = hwnd;

BOOL fRet = PageSetupDlg ( &psd );

// check response

// psd.ptPaperSize.x has paper width
// psd.ptPaperSize.y has paper height
// psd.rtMargin.left has left margin width
    .
    .
    .
```

- This dialog lets the user configure printing characteristics such as margins and page orientation

Many programs display this dialog in response to a Page Setup menu item to let the user set the page margins, size and orientation. It's again important to note that this dialog really doesn't affect the printed output directly – the dialog simply retrieves information from the user. It's up to your program to do something with the data that the user enters.

Taking a look at the dialog, you'll notice that the dialog displays a page preview that shows the page orientation and margins. Below the preview, the next set of controls let the user choose a paper size and source – the dialog queries the default printer for this information. The radio buttons on the bottom left of the dialog let the user choose the page orientation – portrait for normal printing and landscape for printing sideways on the page. The next set of edit boxes let the user select the margins – the margins default to one inch, but you can instead have the dialog query the minimum m...

The Print Dialog

Example:

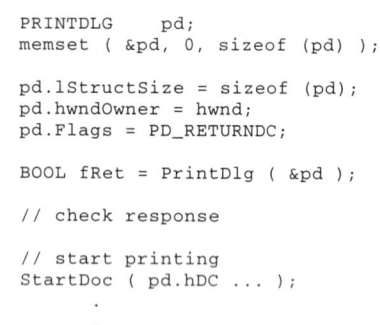

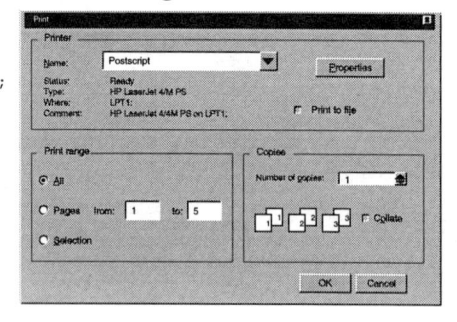

```
PRINTDLG    pd;
memset ( &pd, 0, sizeof (pd) );

pd.lStructSize = sizeof (pd);
pd.hwndOwner = hwnd;
pd.Flags = PD_RETURNDC;

BOOL fRet = PrintDlg ( &pd );

// check response

// start printing
StartDoc ( pd.hDC ... );
    .
    .
    .
```

- This dialog lets the user choose a printer and other printing options, such as the number of pages
- After displaying this dialog, your program can then print to the selected printer

This dialog lets the user choose a printer and printing options. The dialog has three groups of controls. The first group, labeled "Printer" lets the user select a printer from the "Name" combo box and set its properties, such as resolution, by pressing the "Properties" button. The second group, the "Print Range" group, lets the user select how much of your program's data should be printed. The third group, labeled "Copies", lets the user select how many copies should be printed, and if multiple-page print jobs should be collated.

Before we look at the code, let's discuss how printing works in a Windows program. First, a brief review of how Windows treats graphical output devices. Before you can output to any device, you first need to retrieve a device context handle for the device. In this workshop, mostly we've used the GetDC function to r...

The Replace Text Dialog

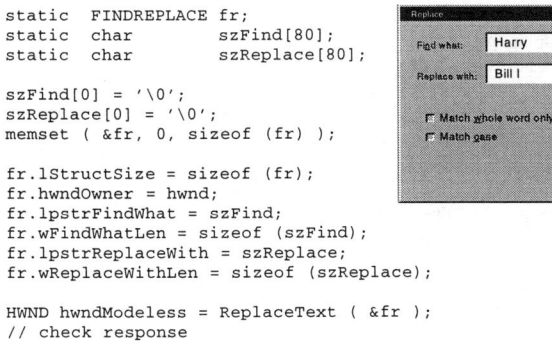

Example:
```
static  FINDREPLACE   fr;
static  char          szFind[80];
static  char          szReplace[80];

szFind[0] = '\0';
szReplace[0] = '\0';
memset ( &fr, 0, sizeof (fr) );

fr.lStructSize = sizeof (fr);
fr.hwndOwner = hwnd;
fr.lpstrFindWhat = szFind;
fr.wFindWhatLen = sizeof (szFind);
fr.lpstrReplaceWith = szReplace;
fr.wReplaceWithLen = sizeof (szReplace);

HWND hwndModeless = ReplaceText ( &fr );
// check response
```

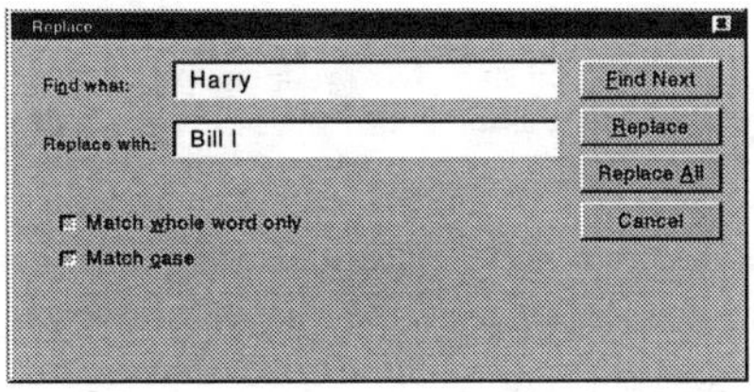

The Replace Text dialog is very similar to the Find Text dialog discussed earlier in this chapter. The main difference is that this dialog returns two strings instead of one: it returns both a find string and a replace string. But other than that, the programming is the same as the Find Text dialog. See Page 19-6 for more information.

- This dialog displays a dialog into which the user can enter both a search string and a replacement string- when the user presses the "Replace" button, your program receives the FNDMSGSTRING message
- Upon receipt of this message, your program can search for the string and replace it
- This dialog is a modeless dialog, so you must call IsDialogMessage in your program's message loop

19-12

Common Dialog Sample Program

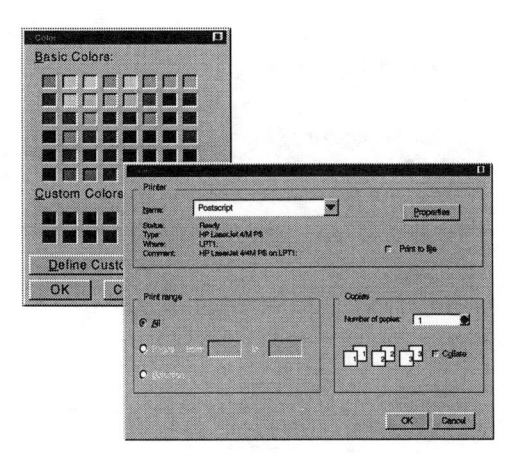

This sample program demonstrates five of the common dialogs: the File Open and File Save dialogs, the Choose Font and Choose Color dialogs and the Print dialog.

When you run the program, you can enter information about a student's test score by choosing Student Information from the Edit menu. When you OK this dialog, the program displays the student information in the client area. You can change the display font and background color via common dialogs by choosing the appropriate menu items on the Edit menu. You can then save the student information in a file or retrieve a previously saved student by choosing entries from the File menu. Finally, you can print the student information by choosing Print from the File menu.

- This program displays a student's test score and uses several kinds of common dialogs to let the user configure colors and read or write to a file

19-13

Review Quiz

Before you move on to the next chapter, you should test your comprehension of this chapter by taking the review quiz. The quiz assumes that you have already done the lab exercise.

The quiz will be displayed in a separate window so that you can page through the chapter to help you find the answers. In other words, this is an open book quiz!

After you have answered all of the questions, press the button at the bottom of the quiz window to see how you did. If you didn't score as well as you think you should, you should review the chapter before continuing on.

Chapter Summary

- Common dialogs save the developer time and effort by providing dialogs that are needed by many programs
- Each common dialog uses a structure that you must fill in before calling the dialog-display function. Each of the structures contains common fields, for example the structure-size and flags field. Therefore, once you know how to program one common dialog, it's not hard to learn another

Lab Exercises

Windows 32-bit API Programming Workshop

Windows 32-bit API Programming
THE USER INTERFACE

Dr. Dobb's
JOURNAL

Table of Contents

LAB 1: FIRST WINDOWS PROGRAM 5

LAB 2: A SIMPLE WINDOWS PROGRAM 9

LAB 3: MESSAGES 17

LAB 4: ICONS 23

LAB 5: THE GRAPHICAL DEVICE INTERFACE (GDI) 25

LAB 6: WINDOW STYLES AND INFORMATION 29

LAB 8: THE KEYBOARD 35

LAB 9: MENUS 41

LAB 10: TOOL BARS 51

LAB 11: A SIMPLE MODAL DIALOG BOX 57

LAB 12: DIALOG CONTROLS 63

LAB 13: LIST VIEW CONTROLS 69

LAB 14: PROPERTY SHEETS 75

Lab 1: First Windows Program

Note: If you are viewing this with Windows Write, you will get best results if you choose Tabs from the Document menu and set the first three tab stops to .5", 1.0" and 1.5".

Objectives:

- To write the minimum Windows program.
- To become familiar with the Visual C++ development environment

Steps:

1. Start the Microsoft Developer Studio by choosing it from the Microsoft Visual C++ group. If this is the first time you have run the Developer Studio, it may display a "tip of the day". If you don't want to see these tips in the future, click on the appropriate check box on the dialog. In either case, close the dialog.

2. Create a new project for the lab by choosing *New* from the *File* menu and selecting *Project Workspace*. Then fill in or select the following:

Type:	Application (not MFC Application or Console Application)
Name:	lab1
Platform:	Win32
Location:	Enter the directory on your hard disk where the online workshop labs are installed, followed by "lab1". For example:

   c:\descript\labs\lab1

   Note: the *lab1* sub-directory should already exist. Make sure that the "lab1" text appears only once in the Location directory.

   If you cannot remember where you installed the online workshop labs, click on the *Lab Setup* button in the Chapter 1 online workshop Lab Exercise page.

   Then click on the Create button to cause the Developer Studio to build the initial project files.

   If the InfoViewer window appears, you can close it or ignore it. You will manipulate it in a moment.

3. Next you need to create a text file that will contain the source code for your program. Choose *New* from the *File* menu and select *Text File*. Then choose *Save As* from the *File* menu and save the file as LAB1.CPP.

4. Even though you have created the file from within the Developer Studio, it doesn't automatically add the file to the current project. To do that, choose *Files Into Project* from the *Insert* menu and select LAB1.CPP. This adds the new source file into the project.

Lab 1: First Windows Program   6

5. Now you are ready to write the minimum Windows program. This program will be very simple -- it will display only a message box.

    Click the mouse on the large empty window pane on the right side of the Developer Studio window. Then enter the following text:

    ```
    #define STRICT
    #include <windows.h>
    ```

    These lines include all of the symbols required for Windows programming, including function prototypes for the Windows system calls, constant definitions and so forth. The STRICT directive causes the C++ compiler to perform more stringent error checking so the compiler catches more programming errors at when you compile.

6. Next, write the *WinMain* function that's required by all Windows programs -- it replaces the main function found in "normal" C or C++ programs. You will learn more about WinMain in later chapters, so for now, just type it in:

    ```
    int WINAPI WinMain ( HINSTANCE hInstance, HINSTANCE hPrevInstance
                       , LPSTR lpCmdLine, int nCmdShow )
    {
        return 0;
    }
    ```

    The *WINAPI*, *HINSTANCE* and *LPSTR* symbols are all defined by WINDOWS.H.

7. At this point, the WinMain function is empty, except for the return statement. Now you will modify WinMain so that it displays a message box that looks like:

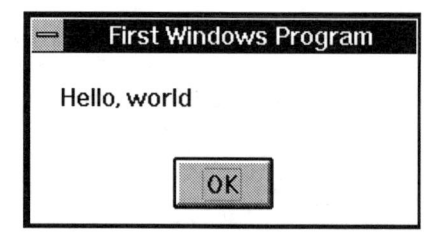

    Figure 1: Message Box WIndow

    To display the message box, code the *MessageBox* system call: put it immediately in front of the *return* statement. To look up help on a system call, type it into the source file, move the text-entry cursor over it, and then press the F1 key. Choose the help-file entry from the Win32 SDK.

    The Developers Studio should display the online help for MessageBox. You can toggle between your source file and the online help by pressing Ctrl-F6 or by choosing from the *Window* menu.

    However, by default, you might not be able to see both your source file and the online help! But with a little work, it's not too hard to do. Press the right mouse button immediately to the right of the "Overview Group" text to display a popup menu. From the menu, choose docking view, which moves the online help into a separate *InfoViewer Contents* window. You can move the window around by dragging its miniature titlebar. Drag the window to the bottom center of the Developer

Lab 1: First Windows Program 7

Studio window and watch the border – when the border changes to a thin wide rectangle, that means you can dock the window at that location. To dock the window, release the mouse button. The InfoViewer window should now be a window pane at the bottom of the Developer Studio window. If it isn't where you want it to be, you can move it by pressing the left mouse button immediately to the right of the InfoViewer toolbar and then dragging it to another location.

Unfortunately, after docking, the online help window is probably too small to show much text. To expand it, move the mouse cursor to the thick line above the online help window pane – watch the mouse cursor change to a pair of sizing arrows. Drag the thick line upward until you can see a good portion of both the online help and source-code windows.

8. Here are some hints for coding the MessageBox call:

   a. Use *NULL* for the owner window.
   b. You can ignore the return value from the call.
   c. Your message box needs only an *OK* button.

9. Then choose *Save All* from the *File* menu to make sure everything's saved to the disk.

10. To compile and link your program, choose *Build lab1.exe* from the *Build* menu. The Developer Studio opens an *Output window* to display the results of compiling and linking, including any error messages. If you have any error messages, press the left mouse button on the error message text to highlight it, then press the right mouse button on the message to display a popup menu. From the popup menu, choose *Goto Error/Tag* – the Developer Studio positions the text-entry cursor on the offending line so you can fix it.

11. To run your new program, choose *Execute lab1.exe* from the *Build* menu. Do you see your message box? Press OK to terminate it. Then return back to the Descriptor Systems Online Course Viewer to continue your workshop.

    Change to the *Review Quiz* page in Chapter One and answer the review questions to test your understanding of the material you've covered so far.

Lab 2: A Simple Windows Program

Note: If you are viewing this with Windows Write, you will get best results if you choose Tabs from the Document menu and set the first three tab stops to .5", 1.0" and 1.5".

Objectives:

- To write a minimal but complete *WinMain* function and a window procedure
- To learn how to retrieve error codes after calling Windows system calls
- To perform simple output to a client area
- To learn how to use the Microsoft Developer Studio for debugging

Part 1: A Complete Windows Program

In this part, you will write both the *WinMain* function and a window procedure for a simple Windows application. While the program will not be very visually exciting, it will provide a base for future labs.

Steps:

1. Start the Microsoft Developer Studio by choosing it from the Microsoft Visual C++ group. Close any current project by choosing *Close Workspace* from the *File* menu.

2. Create a new project for the lab by choosing *New* from the *File* menu and selecting *Project Workspace*. Then fill in or select the following:

Type:	Application
Name:	lab2
Platform:	Win32
Location:	Enter the directory on your hard disk where the online workshop lab exercises are installed, for example:

    c:\descript\labs\lab2

    Note: the *lab2* sub-directory should already exist. Make sure that the "lab2" text appears only once in the Location directory.

    If you cannot remember where you installed the online workshop lab exercises, click on the *Lab Setup* button in the Chapter 2 online workshop Lab Exercise page.

    Then click on the Create button to cause the Developer Studio to build the initial project files.

3. To save you some typing, we have provided you with a partially-completed source file that you will fill in. Choose *Open* from the *File* menu and select LAB2.CPP. The Developer Studio will display the file. Please examine it so that you understand what has been provided for you.

Lab 2: Complete Windows Program   10

4. Even though you have opened the file from within the Developer Studio, it doesn't automatically add the file to the current project. To do that, choose *Files Into Project* from the *Insert* menu and select LAB2.CPP. This adds the source file into the project.

5. Your first job is to complete the *WinMain* function so that it:

    a. Registers a window class.
    b. Creates an overlapped window of that class.
    c. Executes a message processing loop.

    The next few steps will describe each task in more detail.

6. *WinMain* should register the class only for the first instance of the program (see Chapter 3 for a discussion of instances.) To register the class, call the Windows *RegisterClass* call.

    Remember that you can see online help on Windows calls by typing them in and then pressing the F1 key and choosing from the Win32SDK help selection. One other helpful hint: you can copy text from the Descriptor Systems online course viewer by clicking the right mouse button on the text and selecting *Copy to Clipboard* from the popup menu. You can then insert the text into your source file in the Developer Studio by choosing *Paste* from the *Edit* menu.

    Here are the specifications for the RegisterClass call (use the provided *wndclass* variable):

    a. Use no special class styles.

    b. Use the provided window procedure.

    c. You need no class or window extra bytes.

    d. Use the instance handle passed to *WinMain* (*hInstance*, not *hPrevInstance*.)

    e. Load the generic application icon (use *LoadIcon.*)

    f. Load the titled-arrow mouse cursor (use *LoadCursor.*)

    g. Retrieve a WHITE_BRUSH for the client-area background (use *GetStockObject.*)

    h. Your window will have no menu.

    i. Use "Lab2" as the class name string.

    If RegisterClass fails, your program should call MessageBox and display a title of "Error" and a message of "Unable to register class". The program should exit by returning the value one "1" from WinMain if unable to register the class.

7. Next, create a window for your program by calling *CreateWindow*. Store the returned window handle in the provided *hwnd* variable.

    Here are the specifications for the CreateWindow call:

    a. Use the class name string from the RegisterClass call.

    b. Use any title (window name) string that you want.

    c. Use WS_OVERLAPPEDWINDOW for the window style.

    d. Use the default size and position for you window.

    e. Your window will have no parent, menu or creation parameters.

Lab 2: Complete Windows Program   11

If CreateWindow fails, your program should call MessageBox and display a title of "Error" and a message of "Unable to create window". The program should exit by returning the value one "1" from WinMain if unable to create the window.

8. Make the new window visible by calling *ShowWindow*. Use the *nCmdShow* argument passed to WinMain.

9. Code a standard Windows message loop by calling *GetMessage* and *DispatchMessage* in a loop until GetMessage returns *FALSE*. You can pass zero for the last three arguments of GetMessage. Use the provided *msg* variable. See Chapter 3 for help on coding the message loop.

10. Your next job is to complete the window procedure. Start by adding a *switch* statement based on the *iMsg* argument. In the *default* case, call the default window procedure. The default window procedure will give your window the standard behavior of all windows, for example, the user will be able to move, size and close your window. See Chapter 2.

11. Add a *WM_DESTROY* case to the window procedure so that your program exits when the window is destroyed by calling *PostQuitMessage*. See Chapter 3 for details.

12. Add a WM_PAINT case to the window procedure:

```
case WM_PAINT:
{
        PAINTSTRUCT        ps;

        HDC    hdc = BeginPaint ( hwnd, &ps );

        EndPaint ( hwnd, &ps );
}
return 0;
```

This code doesn't draw anything, so your client area will be blank. However, this code does act as scaffolding to which you will add in later parts of this lab.

13. Choose *Save All* from the *File* menu, then develop your program by choosing *Build lab2.exe* from the *Build* menu. If there are any errors, fix them before continuing. See the first lab for a review on editing errors in the Developer Studio.

14. To run your program, choose *Execute lab2.exe* from the *Build* menu. Can you move, size, minimize and maximize your window? Is the titlebar text correct? What happens if you click the mouse on the client area? What happens if you press a key when the window is the active window?

Refer to the LAB2 FAQ in Chapter 3 if you have any problems.

Close your window. Then continue with Part 2 of this lab.

Part 2: Retrieving Error Codes from Windows System Calls

In this part of lab, you will learn how to retrieve system error codes. This technique makes it much easier to debug Windows programs, since Windows itself will tell you why a system call failed. Note that this technique doesn't work in 16-bit Windows – only 32-bit versions of Windows such as Windows NT and Windows 95 or greater have this capability.

Lab 2: Complete Windows Program   12

The error codes by themselves aren't all that helpful, but you look up the error codes in a file provided by Visual C++. The file is called WINERROR.H and you can find it in the \MSDEV\INCLUDE directory where Visual C++ is installed on your system. You should open this file into the Developer Studio now, since you will need it in a few moments. Once you have it opened, you can toggle between the LAB2.CPP file and the WINERROR.H file by pressing Ctrl-F6 or by choosing from the *Window* menu.

Steps:

1. If not already running, start the Microsoft Developer Studio by choosing it from the Microsoft Visual C++ group. If not already open, open the *lab2* project by choosing *Open Workspace* from the *File* menu.

2. Write a function at the bottom of the LAB2.CPP source file:

   ```
   void err_msg ( HWND hwnd, char *p )
   {
           char   szMsg[1000];            // error message string
           DWORD  dwEcode;                // error code

   }
   ```

   At this point, the function is empty but you will complete it in a moment.

3. Write a function prototype for the new function near the top of LAB2.CPP. You can prototype a function by copying its definition and appending a semicolon (see the existing prototype for the window procedure.) To copy text in the editor, highlight the text with the mouse or keyboard, then choose *Copy* from the *Edit* menu (or press Ctrl-C.) Move the cursor to the desired location and choose *Paste* from the *Edit* menu (or press Ctrl-V.)

4. Complete the error-message function so that it:

   a. Calls *GetLastError* to retrieve an error code into the *nEcode* variable.
   b. Call *wsprintf* to format the string argument and the error code into the *szMsg* string (*wsprintf* is a indows system call that's equivalent to the C-library *sprintf* call):

   ```
   wsprintf ( szMsg, "%s, error code = %d", p, nEcode );
   ```

   c. Display a message box with "Error" for the title and error-message string as the text. Use the *hwnd* argument as the message box owner.

   Remember that you can obtain help on a Windows system call like *GetLastError* by positioning the text-entry cursor on it and pressing the F1 key – then choose the Win32SDK selection.

5. In *WinMain*, call the error-message function after the *RegisterClass* and *CreateWindow* calls to verify that they worked correctly. For example, the RegisterClass call returns FALSE if it fails, so you could code:

   ```
   ATOM  ret = RegisterClass ( . . . );
   if ( ret == 0 )
   {
           err_msg ( NULL, "Unable to create class" );
           return 1;
   }
   ```

Lab 2: Complete Windows Program 13

The testing after CreateWindow will be similar except that CreateWindow returns zero for the window handle if it fails.

6. To test your new error function, modify the CreateWindow call so that it passes an invalid (unregistered) class name string, such as "xyz123".

7. Then develop and run your program. Do you see the error message box, complete with error code? You can look up the error code in the \MSDEV\INCLUDE\WINERROR.H file in the Visual C++ directory – use the *Find* command from the *Edit* menu to locate the error code. Does the description there make sense?

8. Be sure to fix the intentional error before continuing. Then go on to Part 3.

Part 3: Displaying Text in the Client Area

In this part of lab, you will decorate your client window by displaying the classic "Hello, world" string at the top of the client area. At this time, you should review Chapter 2, especially the page(s) on coordinates.

Steps:

1. If not already running, start the Microsoft Developer Studio by choosing it from the Microsoft Visual C++ group. If not already open, open the *lab2* project by choosing *Open Workspace* from the *File* menu.

2. Modify the WM_PAINT case in the window procedure so that it displays the string "Hello, world" at the top of the client area. To display the string, use the *TextOut* Windows system call. Be sure to code TextOut between the *BeginPaint* and *EndPaint* calls. Review Chapter 2 if you need help with the coordinates.

   Be sure to call your error-message function after calling TextOut to validate that it worked correctly. Pass the window procedure's *hwnd* argument as the first parameter to the error-processing function.

   Remember that you can obtain help on a Windows system call like *TextOut* by positioning the text-entry cursor on it and pressing the F1 key – then choose the Win32SDK selection.

3. Develop and run your program. Do you see the text? When you are satisfied with the program, close the window and continue in Part 4.

Part 4: Debugging with the Microsoft Developer Studio

In this part of lab, you will gain experience using the Developer Studio's integrated debugger. While it might seem strange to use the debugger on a working program, this part's goal is to make you familiar with the debugger so you can use it later labs when your program doesn't work.

Lab 2: Complete Windows Program

This part of lab is actually a tutorial for the debugger, so it's important to follow the steps as closely as you can. After you have run through the steps, you can play with the debugger yourself in a more free-form fashion.

Steps:

1. If not already running, start the Microsoft Developer Studio by choosing it from the Microsoft Visual C++ group. If not already open, open the *lab2* project by choosing *Open Workspace* from the *File* menu.

2. Display the *Build* menu and choose *Step Into* from the *Debug* cascaded menu. This changes the Developer Studio into debugging mode. The Developer Studio displays an arrow on the first executable line in *WinMain*. The arrow marks the current execution line.

3. Choose *Step Over* from the Debug menu (or press F10)– the arrow moves to the next executable line. The difference between Step Over and Step Into is that Step Into will enter an application-defined function and Step Over executes the entire function. In other words, if you know the function works correctly and don't want to single step through it, choose Step Over. If you want to debug the function, choose Step Into instead. Notice that they both work the same if the current executable line isn't a call to an application-defined function.

4. Move the text-entry cursor (the flashing vertical bar) to the *RegisterClass* line in WinMain, then choose *Run to Cursor* from the *Debug* menu (or press F7.) This command executes all of the lines from the current execution line to the text-entry cursor – it's handy for skipping lines that you know work properly so you don't have to keep single-stepping.

5. Next, step over the *RegisterClass* call, then examine the return from the call to see if it worked correctly. You can examine variables in the Developer Studio in several different ways.

    One way is to look in the *Variables* window pane in the lower-left corner of the Developer Studio – the pane with the *Auto*, *Local* and *this* tabs. If you select the *Auto* tab, the pane displays variables used in the current and previous statements; the *Local* tab displays local variables and arguments to the current function; and the *this* tab displays the local data of the current C++ object (if any.)

    Another way to examine a single variable is to move the mouse cursor over the variable and hold it there for a second or two – the Developer Studio displays a "fly-over" window with the variable's contents.

    Finally, if you want to see the contents of a variable even if you are debugging a different function, you can add it to the *Watch* window. Move the mouse cursor and click the right mouse button on the variable name and choose *Quick Watch* from the popup menu– the Developer Studio displays a dialog box (press the *Add Watch* button.) This adds an entry to the *Watch* window that the Developer Studio displays persistently.

6. While *Run to Cursor* is useful, sometimes you want to consistently stop at a line, especially if your program contains a loop. The Developer Studio lets you set persistent breakpoints for this purpose.

    Move the text-entry cursor down to the *BeginPaint* line in the window procedure. Then click the right mouse button on that line and choose *Insert / Remove Breakpoint* from the popup menu (or press the F9 key.) The Developer Studio displays a circle at the beginning of the line to show that there's a break point on that line.

Lab 2: Complete Windows Program   15

You can edit or examine the break point by choosing *Breakpoints* from the *Edit* menu. This dialog box also lets you set more sophisticated break points, such as when a variable changes, but we will leave those for later. Do you see your break point listed? Press OK to dismiss the dialog.

7. Try setting another break point on the *PostQuitMessage* call in the *WM_DESTROY* case.

8. To execute until a break point is encountered, choose *Go* from the *Debug* menu (or press the F5 key.) The Developer Studio should break on the *BeginPaint* line. At this point, you can single step or examine variables.

    Then remove the BeginPaint break point using the same technique you used to set it (or display the *Breakpoints* dialog box, highlight the break point and press the *Remove* button.)

9. Choose *Go* again and then close your program's window. The Developer Studio should break on the PostQuitMessage call.

10. Choose Go again – the program will execute to completion and the Developer Studio should display a message to that effect. The Developer Studio will also exit debug mode – you can re-enter debug mode at any time by single stepping.

    Note: there are two other useful commands that you can use while debugging:

    a. Stop Debugging from the Debug menu takes you out of debug mode at any time.

    b. Restart from the Debug mode starts the program back at the beginning in debug mode.

12. You are now finished with Lab 2. You should continue by taking the Review Quiz in Chapter 3.

Lab 3: Messages

Note: If you are viewing this with Windows Write, you will get best results if you choose Tabs from the Document menu and set the first three tab stops to .5", 1.0" and 1.5".

Objectives:

- To learn how to respond to messages from Windows
- To understand how to use *static* variables in a window procedure
- To send messages to other windows

Part 1: Receiving Messages

In this part of lab, you will write a window procedure that will keep a count of how many times the user switches focus to the window. The window will display the count at the bottom of the client area.

Steps:

1. Start the Microsoft Developer Studio by choosing it from the Microsoft Visual C++ group. Close any current project by choosing *Close Workspace* from the *File* menu.

2. Create a new project for the lab by choosing *New* from the *File* menu and selecting *Project Workspace*. Then fill in or select the following:

Type:	Application
Name:	lab3
Platform:	Win32
Location:	Enter the directory on your hard disk where the online workshop lab exercises are installed, for example:

    c:\descript\labs\lab3

    Note: the *lab3* sub-directory should already exist. Make sure that the "lab3" text appears only once in the Location directory.

    Then click on the Create button to cause the Developer Studio to build the initial project files.

3. To save you some typing, we have provided you with a partially-completed source file that you will fill in. Choose *Open* from the *File* menu and select LAB3.CPP. The Developer Studio will display the file. Please examine it so that you understand what has been provided for you. Note that *WinMain* is totally complete and that we have provided you with an *err_msg* function (similar to an earlier lab) that you can call to display error messages to the screen.

4. Even though you have opened the file from within the Developer Studio, it doesn't automatically add the file to the current project. To do that, choose *Files Into Project* from the *Insert* menu and select LAB3.CPP. This adds the source file into the project.

Lab 3: Messages   18

5. Your first job is to add some *static* variables to the window procedure. Insert these lines at the top of the window procedure, immediately above the switch statement:

    ```
    static   int nCount = 0;      // number of times we've gained focus
    static   int cyClient;        // client area height
    static   int cyChar;          // height of characters
    ```

    When you define a variable as *static*, the compiler allocates the variable in permanent storage so it retains its value. If you don't use the *static* keyword, the variable is allocated and de-allocated each time the function it resides in is called and returned from. Thus, you can use static variables to "remember" information from one message to another, since each message is a separate call to the window procedure.

6. Next add a new case to the window procedure. To make it easier to find things, we recommend that you sort message cases in the window procedure in alphabetical order. So in this case, add the WM_CREATE case immediately before the existing WM_DESTROY case.

    ```
    case WM_CREATE:
        {
            HDC           hdc;   // device context handle
            BOOL          f;     // return from system call
            TEXTMETRIC    tm;    // font characteristics

        }
        return 0;
    ```

    Windows sends the WM_CREATE message to a window procedure when a window is being created. This message gives the window procedure a chance to initialize itself. Since it is called only once for each window, it's a great place to perform processing that only needs to be done once. In your lab, you will use this opportunity to determine the height of characters in the default font; since your window won't change its font, the character height will never change.

7. Then complete the WM_CREATE case to:

    a. Retrieve a device context handle by calling *GetDC*, Store its handle in the *hdc* variable. Remember that you can obtain online help for Windows system calls – look back at Lab 2 if you can't remember how.

    b. Call *GetTextMetrics* to initialize the *tm* structure with information about the current (default) font. Be sure to pass the address of the *tm* structure.

    c. Store the font's character height in the *cyChar* static variable. The height is stored in the *tmHeight* field in the *tm* structure.

    d. Return the device context handle back to Windows by calling *ReleaseDC*.

    After each system call, be sure to check for errors and call the provided *err_msg* function to display an error message if one occurs.

8. Add another case to the window procedure:

    ```
    case WM_SETFOCUS:
        {

        }
    ```

Lab 3: Messages

```
        return 0;
```

Windows sends WM_SETFOCUS to a window whenever the window gains the input focus (the window receives WM_KILLFOCUS when it loses the focus.) The focus window is the one window in the system that receives keystroke messages – most windows use these messages to show or hide a text-entry caret (cursor.) However, your window will use WM_SETFOCUS to keep track of how many times the user "switches" to the window.

9. Complete the WM_SETFOCUS case to:

   a. Increment the *static* count variable.

   b. Call *InvalidateRect (hwnd, NULL, TRUE)* to force a *WM_PAINT* message so your window can update its display whenever it gains the focus. We will discuss what this call does in later chapters.

10. Add another case to the window procedure:

```
case WM_SIZE:
    {

    }
    return 0;
```

As you learned in Chapter 4, Windows sends this message to notify the window procedure whenever the window changes size. Since your window will display text at the bottom of the client area, it needs to keep track of the client area's height: in WM_SIZE, your program will store the current height in a *static* variable.

11. Complete the WM_SIZE case to:

   a. Store the client area's height in the cyClient static variable. See Chapter 4 for help, or use the online help to look up WM_SIZE.

   b. Call InvalidateRect (hwnd, NULL, TRUE) to force a WM_PAINT message so your window can update its display whenever it changes size.

12. In the WM_PAINT case, add code that:

   a. Allocates a character array:

   ```
   char sz[255];
   ```

   b. Calls *wsprintf* to format a string containing the count into the character array. The string should look like:

   focus count = n

   where n is the static *nCount* variable. The wsprintf function is a Windows system call that works much the same as the C-library *sprintf* and *printf* calls. Use the online help to find more information if you need it, or see the *err_msg* function at the bottom of LAB3.CPP for an example.

Lab 3: Messages

c. Calls *TextOut* to display the string at the lower-left corner of the client area. Hint: use the *cyClient* and *cyChar* static variables! Hint #2: the coordinates that you pass to TextOut specify the position of the string's upper left!

13. Choose *Save All* from the *File* menu, then build your program in the same way you did in Lab 2. If there are any errors, fix them before continuing.

14. Then run your program. Do you see the focus count at the bottom of the client area? Try clicking on another window and then clicking on yours (you may have to move or size your window to do this.) Does the count change?

    Refer to the LAB 3 FAQ in Chapter 4 if you have any problems or questions.

    Close your window. Then continue with Part 2 of this lab.

Part 2: Sending Messages

In this part of lab, you will create a listbox child window to which you will add a string whenever your window gains the focus. The string will contain the current time; this will give you a record of the times when your window gained the focus.

Your program will size and position the listbox child window so that it occupies the upper-left quarter of the client area. In other words, whenever the user sizes the main window, its window procedure will resize the child window based on the main window's new size.

The objective of this part is to learn how to send messages to another window; the listbox in this case. Even though we haven't yet covered listboxes in any detail, this lab write-up should contains enough information about listboxes so that you can complete the lab.

Steps:

1. If not already running, start your development environment and open the *lab3* project. Then open LAB3.CPP.

2. At the top of the file, immediately after the "internal function prototypes", add the following constant definition:

   ```
   const int        IDW_LIST = 10;
   ```

   You will use this symbolic name for the window ID of the listbox child window.

3. In the window procedure, define another *static* variable:

   ```
   static      HWND    hwndList;    // listbox window handle
   ```

   This variable will contain the listbox's window handle.

4. In the WM_CREATE case, add code that:

   a. Retrieves the current instance handle and stores it in a variable of type *HINSTANCE* (you will need to define the variable.) To retrieve the instance handle, call *GetWindowLong*, passing the current window's handle (*hwnd*) and the *GWL_HINSTANCE* command. You

Lab 3: Messages

will need to cast the return value of GetWindowLong to *HINSTANCE* to make the compiler happy.

b. Calls *CreateWindow* or *CreateWindowEx* to create the listbox child window, storing its handle in the static variable. Here are the specifications for the new window:

class: "LISTBOX"
styles: *WS_VISIBLE, WS_CHILD, WS_BORDER* and *WS_VSCROLL*
size and position: 0
parent: the main window
child window ID: *(HMENU)IDW_LIST*

The listbox window requires no creation parameters. Be sure to check that the window creation was successful.

The reason you set the size and position to zero is that you will change the child window's size and position in the main window's *WM_SIZE* message case.

5. In the WM_SIZE case, add code that calls *SetWindowPos* to set the listbox child window's position and size so that the child window occupies the upper-left quarter of the main window's client area. Position the child window at the top of the Z-order (you need no special sizing flags.)

6. In the WM_SETFOCUS case, add code that:

   a. Allocates a character array:

   ```
   char sz[9];
   ```

   This array will hold the a string representing the current time.

   b. Calls the *_strtime* C-library function to retrieve the current time string and store it in the character array. You will also need to *#include <time.h>* at the top of the file to include the definition for the _strtime function.

   c. Calls *SendMessage* to insert the time string into the listbox child window. Send the *LB_ADDSTRING* message. Please look up this message in the online help to obtain a description of the message parameters. You will need to cast the string's address to *LPARAM* to make the compiler happy.

7. Then develop and test your program as before. Try changing the focus to and from your window. Does the listbox contain a string for each time you change focus to your window?

8. You are now finished with Lab 3. You should continue by taking the review quiz in Chapter 4 in the online workshop.

Lab 4: Icons

Note: If you are viewing this with Windows Write, you will get best results if you choose Tabs from the Document menu and set the first three tab stops to .5", 1.0" and 1.5".

Objectives:

- To learn how to use the Microsoft Developer Studio to create an icon.
- To load and icon and associate it with a window class.

In this lab, you will exercise your artistic talents to create an icon for a Windows program. The goal here is to learn the steps to associate the icon, not to create the prettiest icon – you don't need to spend much time on your icon's appearance (unless you want to!)

Steps:

1. Start the Microsoft Developer Studio by choosing it from the Microsoft Visual C++ group. Close any current project by choosing *Close Workspace* from the *File* menu.

2. Create a new project for the lab by choosing *New* from the *File* menu and selecting *Project Workspace*. Then fill in or select the following:

Type:	Application
Name:	lab4
Platform:	Win32
Location:	Enter the directory on your hard disk where the online workshop lab exercises are installed, for example:

    c:\descript\labs\lab4

    Note: the *lab4* sub-directory should already exist. Make sure that the "lab4" text appears only once in the Location directory.

    Then click on the Create button to cause the Developer Studio to build the initial project files.

3. To save you some typing, we have provided you with a partially-completed source file that you will fill in. Choose *Open* from the *File* menu and select LAB4.CPP. The Developer Studio will display the file. Please examine it so that you understand what has been provided for you. The provided code includes a complete *WinMain* and window procedure. You will modify WinMain in a moment to load an icon.

4. Even though you have opened the file from within the Developer Studio, it doesn't automatically add the file to the current project. To do that, choose *Files Into Project* from the *Insert* menu and select LAB4.CPP. This adds the source file into the project.

5. Your first duty is to create and draw the icon. The Developer Studio contains an integrated icon editor; to start it, choose *Resource* from the *Insert* menu, then choose *Icon*. The Developer Studio

Lab 4: Icons   24

should display a blank icon at this point – each of the icon's pixels should be a greenish color that indicates that the pixel will be transparent. You can now use the tool palette (the window with the shapes) and the color palette to draw a picture on the icon's pixels. Unless you are a perfectionist, you don't need to spend a lot of time here making the icon perfect.

6. When you are finished drawing, double-click on the icon's window pane anywhere outside of the icon's pixels. The Developer Studio should display an *Icon Properties* window. Enter *IDI_MYICON* for the icon's ID and LAB4.ICO as the icon's file name. Then press the Enter key to assign the properties and close the properties window.

7. Then choose *Save* from the *File* menu and enter the name LAB4.RC. The Developer Studio will create three files for you:

    LAB4.ICO   Contains the binary data for the icon.

    LAB4.RC   Contains the resource script that includes the icon binary-data file.

    RESOURCE.H   Contains the #define for the icon's symbolic name (IDI_MYICON)

8. Even though you created the resources in the Developer Studio, you still need to include them in the Lab 4 project. To do that, choose *Files into Project* from the *Insert* menu and type LAB4.RC. Notice that the Developer Studio displays the project files in the *Project Workspace* pane – now there should be entries for both LAB4.CPP and LAB4.RC.

9. Next, you need to edit LAB4.CPP to associate the icon with the window class. Choose LAB4.CPP from the *Window* menu, or double-click its entry in the Project Workspace pane. The Developer Studio should display the LAB4.CPP file. Start by entering:

    ```
    #include "resource.h"
    ```

    at the top of the file after any other includes. This brings the icon's symbolic identifier into the source file.

10. Then modify the *RegisterClass* code so that it loads the new icon into the *WNDCLASS* structure. See Chapter 5 for details. You should check the return from *LoadIcon* for success and call the provided *err_msg* function to display an error message if LoadIcon fails.

11. Choose *Save All* from the *File* menu, then build your program in the same way you did in Lab 3. If there are any errors, fix them before continuing.

12. Then run your program. If you are running Windows 95 or Windows NT 4.0 or later, you should see your icon in the window's upper-left corner and on the task bar. If you are using Windows NT 3.51, you will need to minimize the window to see the icon on the desktop. If you don't see the icon, refer to the LAB 4 FAQ in Chapter 5 for hints.

    Close your window.

13. You are now finished with Lab 4. You should continue by taking the review quiz in Chapter 5 in the online workshop.

Lab 5: The Graphical Device Interface (GDI)

Note: If you are viewing this with Windows Write, you will get best results if you choose Tabs from the Document menu and set the first three tab stops to .5", 1.0" and 1.5".

Objectives:

- To gain experience creating and selecting brushes, pens and fonts
- To learn about the characteristics of text and fonts in Windows

Here's the situation: your entrepreneur cousin William has just opened a new business on nearby Sludge Lake and he needs a logo for his enterprise. To that end, he contacted another cousin, Becky the graphic artist to design the logo and now he wants you, an acknowledged computer expert, to render the logo under Microsoft Windows. Here's Becky's specification for the logo:

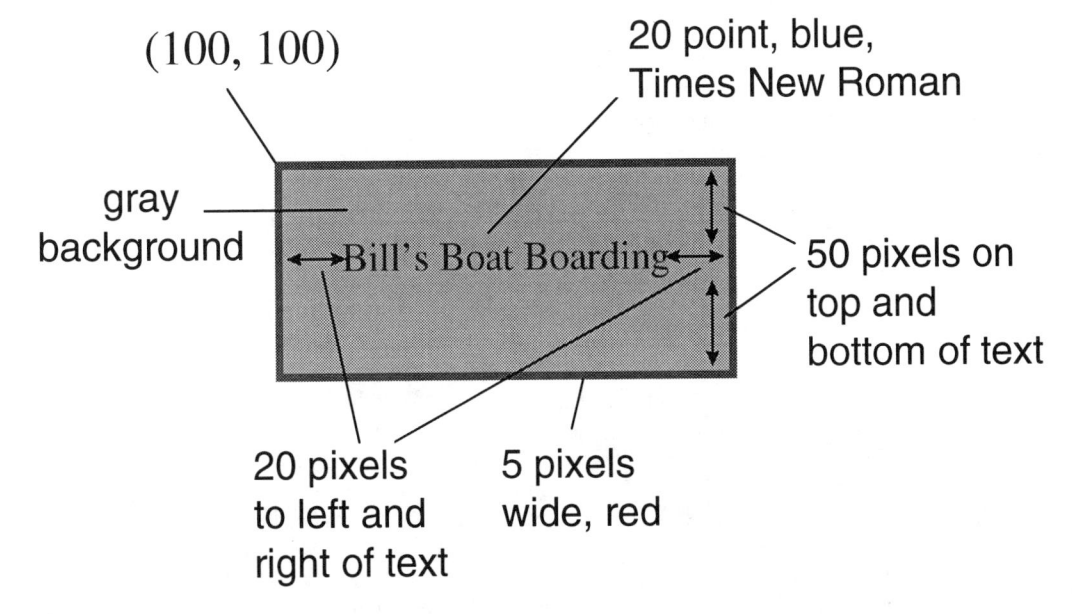

Figure 2: Bill's logo

The logo contains the string "Bill's Boat Boarding" in a blue, 20-point Times New Roman font, centered in a gray rectangle with a 5-pixel-wide red border. There should be 20 pixels on each side of the text. There should be 50 pixels from the top of the rectangle to the top of the text, and 50 more pixels from the bottom of the text to the rectangle's bottom. The rectangle's upper-left corner should be at coordinate (100, 100) in the client area.

Your job is to use Windows GDI calls to display the logo in a window. Of course, your picture should not include the captions and lines, such as the "20 pixels" text.

Steps:

Lab 5: GDI

1. Start the Microsoft Developer Studio by choosing it from the Microsoft Visual C++ group. Close any current project by choosing *Close Workspace* from the *File* menu.

2. Create a new project for the lab by choosing *New* from the *File* menu and selecting *Project Workspace*. Then fill in or select the following:

   Type: Application
   Name: lab5
   Platform: Win32
   Location: Enter the directory on your hard disk where the online workshop lab exercises are installed, for example:

   c:\descript\labs\lab5

   Note: the *lab5* sub-directory should already exist. Make sure that "lab5" appears only once in the Location directory.

   Then click on the Create button to cause the Developer Studio to build the initial project files.

3. To save you some typing, we have provided you with a partially completed source file that you will complete. Choose *Open* from the *File* menu and select LAB5.CPP. The Developer Studio will display the file. Please examine it so that you understand what has been provided for you. The provided code includes a complete *WinMain,* a partially completed window procedure, and a partially completed function named *mycreatefont*. You will complete these in a moment.

4. Even though you have opened the file from within the Developer Studio, it doesn't automatically add the file to the current project. To do that, choose *Files Into Project* from the *Insert* menu and select LAB5.CPP. This adds the source file into the project.

5. First, insert some *static* variables into the window procedure:

   ```
   static      HFONT       hfont;      // font handle for logo
   static      HBRUSH      hbrGray;    // gray brush
   static      HPEN        hpenRed;    // red pen
   ```

6. Your next job is to complete the *mycreatefont* function (at the bottom of LAB5.CPP), which is passed a device context handle, a font name string and the font's point size. This function should call the Windows *CreateFont* function to create a font and return its handle.

   Point size is a traditional measurement used by typographers that specifies a font's height – a single point is 1/72 of an inch. The problem is that *CreateFont* doesn't accept points – it wants the font height in pixels, whose size is dependent on the current display's resolution. The good news is that Microsoft has published a formula to convert points to pixels. You can find the formula in the Microsoft Windows Knowledge Base (article # Q74299), which is part of the Microsoft Developer Library. Anyway, here's the formula:

   height = - (point size * display pixel height) / 72

   You can retrieve the current display's pixel height by calling the Windows *GetDeviceCaps* function and specifying *LOGPIXELSY*.

   Then call CreateFont, passing the font height and the font name string. You can use the default values or zero for all other CreateFont arguments.

Lab 5: GDI 27

7. Then add a *WM_CREATE* case and in it, initialize the *static* variables. Initialize *hfont* by calling the *mycreatefont* function. Since *mycreatefont* requires a device context handle, you will need to call *GetDC* before calling *mycreatefont* and then call *ReleaseDC* when it returns.

   Initialize *hbrGray* by calling *CreateSolidBrush*. Initialize *hpenRed* by calling CreatePen. Please examine Figure 1 to help you code these calls. One hint: to specify a gray color in the RGB model, use equal values for red, green and blue. You should also refer to Chapter 6 in the online course for more information on pens and brushes.

   You should check the returned handles from all of these calls. If they are zero, call the provided *err_msg* function to display an error message.

8. Next, in the *WM_DESTROY* case, call *DeleteObject* to destroy the font, pen and brush.

9. Then add code to the WM_PAINT case to draw the logo, selecting the font, pen and brush as required. The following steps detail what you need to do.

10. Before you can draw the rectangle, you need to determine the text string's width and height. This is not as easy in Windows as counting the characters, since Windows uses pixels. Luckily, Windows includes the handy *GetTextExtentPoint32* call to calculate a string's pixel width and height.

    But before you call this magic call, you first need to select the Times New Roman font into the device context. After the *BeginPaint* line, call *SelectObject* to select the static *hfont* variable into the device context. You should define a variable named *hfontOld* to accept the return of SelectObject (you must cast the return to *HFONT*). If hfontOld is zero, the call failed and you should call the *err_msg* function to display an error message.

    Then define a variable:

    ```
    SIZE  sz;    // string width and height
    ```

    This variable contains two fields, *cx* for the string's width and *cy* for the string's height. Then call *GetTextExtentPoint32* to retrieve the string's width and height into the *sz* variable. Note that the string itself is defined at the top of the file in the *pszName* variable.

11. Still in WM_PAINT, add code to draw the rectangle. You will first need to select the pen and brush (store the returns from *SelectObject* in variables named *hpenOld* and *hbrOld*). Use the *sz* variable and Figure 1 to help you determine the rectangle's coordinates. Remember that the rectangle's upper-left corner should be at (100, 100).

12. Still in WM_PAINT, call *SetBkMode* to set the text mode to *TRANSPARENT*. This tells Windows not to draw the text's background. Then call *SetTextColor* to set the current text color to blue. Be sure to check the returns from these calls.

13. Now finally, you can call *TextOut* to draw the text. Remember that the text coordinates should be (120,150) – by default, Windows uses the coordinate point you specify in TextOut as the upper-left corner of the string's bounding rectangle.

14. At the end of the WM_PAINT case, immediately before the *EndPaint* call, de-select the font, pen and brush by re-selecting the previous handles (you stored the previous handles in *hfontOld*, *hpenOld* and *hbrOld*). This guarantees that when your window is destroyed, the GDI objects you created are not selected. If they were, the DeleteObject calls in the WM_DESTROY case would fail.

Lab 5: GDI

15. Choose *Save All* from the *File* menu, then build your program in the same way you did in Lab 4. If there are any errors, fix them before continuing.

16. Then run your program. Do you see Becky's lovely logo? If you don't, refer to the LAB 4 FAQ in Chapter 6 for hints and modify your code.

17. Congratulations! You are now finished with Lab 5 (and your cousin William owes you some cash). You should continue by taking the review quiz in Chapter 6 in the online workshop.

Lab 6: Window Styles and Information

Note: If you are viewing this with Windows Write, you will get best results if you choose Tabs from the Document menu and set the first three tab stops to .5", 1.0" and 1.5".

Objectives:

- To gain experience with overlapped, popup and child window styles
- To learn how to query information about a window

In the first part of this lab, you will create three windows: a main, overlapped window, a secondary popup window and a child window. In the second part, you will modify the window procedures so that each window displays information about itself, for example, its parent window handle.

Part 1: Window Styles

In this part of lab, you will play around with the three basic window styles: overlapped, popup and child windows.

Most programs use overlapped windows as their main window; overlapped windows always have a titlebar and a border. Overlapped windows also have no parent window, and thus can move anywhere on the desktop.

Most dialog boxes are popup windows. The popup style is quite similar to overlapped – they both are top-level windows and can move anywhere on the desktop. The reason Windows has both kinds is largely historical; if you really want to, you could use a popup window for your main window and overlapped for your dialog boxes.

The final major window style is the child window. Child windows always have a parent window and must stay within the boundaries of their parent. You can think of a child window as subdividing its parent. For example, a typical dialog box is populated with several child windows: buttons, listboxes and so forth.

Your task in the first part of lab is to create popup and child windows – we have provided you with code to create the main overlapped window, since it is the same as in earlier labs.

Steps:

1. Start the Microsoft Developer Studio by choosing it from the Microsoft Visual C++ group. Close any current project by choosing *Close Workspace* from the *File* menu.

2. Create a new project for the lab by choosing *New* from the *File* menu and selecting *Project Workspace*. Then fill in or select the following:

    Type: Application
    Name: lab6
    Platform: Win32

Lab 6: Window Styles and Information 30

        Location: Enter the directory on your hard disk where the online workshop lab exercises are installed, for example:

                          c:\descript\labs\lab6

Note: the *lab6* sub-directory should already exist. Make sure that "lab6" appears only once in the Location directory.

Then click on the Create button to cause the Developer Studio to build the initial project files.

3. To save you some typing, we have provided you with a partially completed source file that you will fill in. Choose *Open* from the *File* menu and select LAB6.CPP. The Developer Studio will display the file. Please examine it so that you understand what has been provided for you. The provided code includes *WinMain* and two window procedures: one for the main overlapped window (*WndProc*), and one that the child and popup windows will share (*AnotherWndProc*).

4. Even though you have opened the file from within the Developer Studio, it doesn't automatically add the file to the current project. To do that, choose *Files Into Project* from the *Insert* menu and select LAB6.CPP. This adds the source file into the project.

5. The provided WinMain registers a class for the main overlapped window. You must add code to WinMain to register another class that the popup and child windows will share. The new class should have the same attributes as the existing class, with these differences:

    window procedure address: *AnotherWndProc*

    classname: "Another"

Be sure to check for errors after the new *RegisterClass* call and call the *err_msg* function if it fails.

6. In a later step, you will create a child window. Windows requires that each child window have an ID – most developers define the ID as a symbolic constant. At the top of the file, immediately after the function prototypes, define an ID:

```
const int IDW_CHILD = 10;
```

The actual value isn't important (Windows does require that if a window has multiple children, each must have a unique ID).

7. In the main window procedure, define *static* variables to hold the popup and child window handles. Note: be sure that you are working in the main, overlapped window procedure (*WndProc*), not the window procedure for the child and popup windows (*AnotherWndProc*).

8. Add a WM_CREATE case to the main window procedure, and in it:

    a.   Retrieve the current instance handle by calling *GetWindowLong*. Store the instance handle in a local variable that you define.

    b.   Create a child window with the following specifications:

title:	"Child"
styles:	WS_VISIBLE, WS_CHILD, WS_THICKFRAME, WS_CAPTION
ID/HMENU:	IDW_CHILD
x,y,cx,cy:	Any values you like (don't use *CW_USEDEFAULT*)
parent:	The main overlapped window

Lab 6: Window Styles and Information

Be sure to check the returned window handle and display an error message if the call fails.

    c.   Create a popup window with the following specifications:

title:	"Popup"
styles:	*WS_VISIBLE, WS_POPUP, WS_THICKFRAME, WS_CAPTION*
ID/HMENU:	0 (no menu)
x,y,cx,cy:	Any values you like (you can use *CW_USEDEFAULT*)
parent:	The main overlapped window. For popup windows, this is really the *owner* window.

Be sure to check the returned window handle and display an error message if the call fails.

9. Choose *Save All* from the *File* menu, then build your program in the same way you did in previous labs. If there are any errors, fix them before continuing.

10. Then run your program. If you don't see all of the windows, refer to the LAB 6 FAQ in Chapter 8 for hints.

    Try the following:

    a. Change each window's size. Can you?

    b. Move each window. Can you move the popup window outside the main window? How about the child window? When you move the main window, do the child and popup window move too? Why or why not?

    c. Move the popup window so it overlays part of the main window. Then try clicking on the popup or child windows, then clicking the main window. Do either "go behind" the main window? Try clicking on an unrelated window. Does it go behind the main window? Why or why not?

    When you are finished playing around, close your window the main window.

Part 2: Window Information

In this part of lab, you will learn how you can query information about a window at runtime. This technique is valuable for at least two reasons: first, it gives you a better understanding of how windows relate to each other, and second, you often need to query window information in "real" programs, especially when you program dialog boxes.

In this part, you will have each window display information about itself, such as its own window handle, its parent's window handle and so forth. You will then be able to look at each window's output and see how they are related.

Since the information display will have the same format for each window, you will write a function to display the output and call it from the WM_PAINT section of each window procedure.

Lab 6: Window Styles and Information 32

Steps:

1. If not already running, start the Microsoft Developer Studio by choosing it from the Microsoft Visual C++ group. If not already open, open the *lab6* project by choosing *Open Workspace* from the *File* menu.

2. At the bottom of LAB6.CPP, write an empty (for now) function:

   ```
   void windowinfo ( HWND hwnd, HDC hdc )
   {
   }
   ```

   This function accepts two arguments: the handle of the window for which to display information, and the device context that indicates where to draw the information. Each of your window procedures will call this function from *WM_PAINT*, passing their own window handle and the DC handle retrieved by *BeginPaint*.

   Then write a prototype for the function by copying its definition to the top of LAB6.CPP near the existing function prototypes. Be sure to end the prototype with a semicolon.

3. Complete the *windowinfo* function:

   a. Allocate a 100-byte character array.

   b. Call *GetTextMetrics* to retrieve information about the current font. You will use the *tmHeight* field of the *TEXTMETRIC* structure to space each line of text that you display.

   c. Use *wsprintf* and *TextOut* to format and display the window information in the following table. The x-coordinate should be zero. The first string's y-coordinate should be zero; add *tmHeight* to each successive string's y-coordinate to space the lines of text. Display the value for each item in hex – you can call *wsprintf* with the *%08X* format specifier. For example:

   ```
   wsprintf ( sz, "hwnd = %08X", hwnd );
   ```

Information	**How to Retrieve**
window handle	passed to function
parent window handle	*GetParent*
first child window handle	*GetWindow*
window style	*GetWindowLong*
instance handle	*GetWindowLong*
window procedure address	*GetWindowLong*

   Hint: the data type for the window procedure address is *WNDPROC*.

4. Call the new function from the WM_PAINT case in each window procedure. Be sure to call it between the *BeginPaint* and *EndPaint* bracket.

5. Choose *Save All* from the *File* menu, then build your program in the same way you did in previous labs. If there are any errors, fix them before continuing.

6. Then run your program. If you don't see all of the information, refer to the LAB 6 FAQ in Chapter 8 for hints.

Lab 6: Window Styles and Information

Examine the output closely. Does it make sense? For example, in the child window, does the parent window handle match the window handle displayed by the main overlapped window?

7. You are now finished with Lab 6. You should continue by taking the Review Quiz in Chapter 8.

Lab 8: The Keyboard

Note: If you are viewing this with Windows Write, you will get best results if you choose Tabs from the Document menu and set the first three tab stops to .5", 1.0" and 1.5".

Objectives:
- To learn how to respond to both alphanumeric and non-character keystrokes
- To learn how to manipulate the caret
- To understand how a Windows program that accepts keystrokes can store and repaint the text that the user enters

Part 1: Accepting Character Keystrokes

In this part of lab, you will write a window procedure that accepts keystrokes and displays them as the user types. You will store the characters in an array so that you can redraw the characters each *WM_PAINT* message. In subsequent parts of the lab, you will enhance the program so it displays a caret and lets the user move the caret by pressing the left or right arrow keys.

To make this program simple, the window will display the characters using the *Courier New* font, which is a fixed-space font. In other words, all of the characters occupy the same width. It's not that much harder to work with a proportionally spaced font, but we'll leave that as an extra exercise for the student.

Also left as extra exercises is to let the user highlight characters, move the caret with the mouse and to support multiple lines of text.

Steps:

1. Start the Microsoft Developer Studio by choosing it from the Microsoft Visual C++ group. Close any current project by choosing *Close Workspace* from the *File* menu.

2. Create a new project for the lab by choosing *New* from the *File* menu and selecting *Project Workspace*. Then fill in or select the following:

Type:	Application
Name:	lab8
Platform:	Win32
Location:	Enter the directory on your hard disk where the online workshop lab exercises are installed, for example:

   c:\descript\labs\lab8

   Note: the *lab8* sub-directory should already exist. Make sure that "lab8" appears only once in the Location directory.

   Then click on the Create button to cause the Developer Studio to build the initial project files.

3. To save you some typing, we have provided you with a partially completed source file that you will complete. Choose *Open* from the *File* menu and select LAB8.CPP. The Developer Studio will

Lab 8: The Keyboard   36

display the file. Please examine it so that you understand what has been provided for you. The provided code includes a complete *WinMain,* and a partially completed window procedure.

4. Even though you have opened the file from within the Developer Studio, it doesn't automatically add the file to the current project. To do that, choose *Files Into Project* from the *Insert* menu and select LAB8.CPP. This adds the source file into the project.

5. In this part of lab, your window procedure will accept and display character keys passed by the *WM_CHAR* message. As you learned in Chapter 10, WM_CHAR messages are optional. So your first job is to modify the message loop in *WinMain* so that Windows generates WM_CHAR messages for your window procedure.

6. Next, when the user types a character key, you will display it, but you also need to store the character in a buffer so that you can re-display all of the characters every *WM_PAINT* message. Since you will manipulate the buffer in multiple messages, define as a *static* at the top of the window procedure:

   ```
   static char ach[BUFFSIZE];            // character array
   ```

   You will also need to define the *BUFFSIZE* constant – please do so at the top of the file. A good size for your buffer is 32 characters.

7. You will also need to keep track of a few other pieces of information. Define the following *static* variables:

   ```
   static      int    i;                 // current character index
   static      LONG   cxChar;            // character width
   static      HFONT  hfont;             // Courier New font handle
   static      POINT  pt;                // current character coords
   ```

8. Now add a *WM_CREATE* case to the window procedure. Here is an overview of the tasks you need to accomplish. We will give you some hints in the next few steps.

   a. Initialize the character index to zero
   b. Initialize the character coordinates to the upper-left corner of the client area
   c. Create a 12-point *Courier New* font and store its handle in the static variable
   d. Select the font into a window DC
   e. Query the font metrics for the new and store the width in the *cxChar* static variable
   f. De-select the font and release the DC, but don't delete the font

   If you want to do these steps on your own without any help, please skip steps 9 and 10 which have hints for completing the steps.

9. Creating a font is not hard, but the code takes a lot of typing. The good news is that you already did the work back in Lab 5, so to save typing, you can copy the *mycreatefont* function from that lab. Choose *Open* from the *File* menu and find the LAB5.CPP file (if you didn't complete Lab 5, you can look in the LAB 5 solution directory). You can then use the mouse or keyboard to highlight the mycreatefont function. Then choose *Copy* from the *Edit* menu. Then press Ctrl-F6 until LAB8.CPP is displayed and move to the bottom of the file. Then choose *Paste* from the *Edit* menu.

   Be sure to write a function prototype for mycreatefont at the top of LAB8.CPP. Before you can call mycreatefont, you need a device context handle -- call *GetDC*. Then you can call the function from WM_CREATE and store the font handle in the static variable.

Lab 8: The Keyboard 37

10. Before you can query the font metrics, you must select the font into the DC. To do that, call *SelectObject*. Then call *GetFontMetrics* to query the font information. Since *Courier New* is a fixed-space font, the average and maximum character widths are the same – you can store either one in the static variable.

    Be sure to de-select the font and release the device context before continuing. Don't delete the font – you will use the same font when you draw the characters.

11. Now add a *WM_CHAR* case to the window procedure. Here are the steps you need to do here:

    If there is room in the buffer:

    a. Store the character in the buffer at the current index
    b. Select the Courier New font into a window device context
    c. Display the character at the current coordinates
    d. Increment the index and add the character width to the x-coordinate
    e. De-select the font and release the DC, but don't delete the font

    If the buffer is full:

    a. Call *MessageBeep* to inform the user that the buffer's full

12. Next, add code the *WM_PAINT* case that loops through and displays all of the characters currently in the buffer. Start displaying the characters at the client's upper-left corner.

    You will need to select the font before displaying the characters and de-select the font after the loop terminates. Again, don't delete the font

    Hint: don't modify the *static pt* variable that holds the current coordinates – if you do, the next time the user types a character, the *WM_CHAR* code will display it in the wrong place. We recommend that you define a temporary *POINT* variable to use in *WM_PAINT* to display each of the characters in the buffer.

13. Finally, in the *WM_DESTROY* case, call *DeleteObject* to get rid of the font.

14. Choose *Save All* from the *File* menu, then build your program in the same way you did in previous labs. If there are any errors, fix them before continuing.

15. Then run your program. Try typing some characters – do you see them? Try covering your window with another window and then resurfacing it – do you still see the characters? What happens if you type more characters than the buffer size?

    Refer to the LAB 8 FAQ in Chapter 10 if you have any problems or questions.

    Close your window. Then continue with Part 2 of this lab.

Part 2: The Caret

In this part of lab, you will show the user when your window gains and loses the focus by creating and destroying a caret. You will not let the user move the caret – that's for the next part of lab.

Steps:

Lab 8: The Keyboard   38

1. If not already running, start your development environment and open the *lab8* project. Then open LAB8.CPP.

2. Add another *static* variable to hold the font's height – your caret will use the height. In WM_CREATE, initialize the static variable from the font metrics.

3. Add a *WM_SETFOCUS* case, and in it, create a caret that has the system-defined border width and the font character's height. You can pass *NULL* for the bitmap argument. Then set the caret's position to the current character's coordinates and then show the caret. See Chapter 10 for hints.

4. Add a *WM_KILLFOCUS* case and in it, destroy the caret.

5. Then develop and test your program as before. Try changing the focus to and from your window. Does the caret turn off and on? Try typing some characters and then repeating the process – does the caret reappear at the current character's coordinates?

   Don't be alarmed if the caret doesn't move as you type characters – you will add that feature in the next part of lab.

   Refer to the LAB 8 FAQ in Chapter 10 if you have any problems or questions.

   Close your window. Then continue with Part 3 of this lab.

Part 3: Moving the Caret

In this part of lab, you will fix your program so that the caret moves as the user types characters.

Steps:

1. If not already running, start your development environment and open the *lab8* project. Then open LAB8.CPP.

2. Modify the WM_CHAR case so that the caret moves to the end of each character as the user types. Here are some hints:

   a. Hide the caret before displaying the character
   b. Set the caret position, then show the caret. Do these steps *after* you update the character coordinates.

3. Then develop and test your program. Does the caret move as you type characters?

   Refer to the LAB 8 FAQ in Chapter 10 if you have any problems or questions.

   Close your window. Then continue with Part 4 of this lab.

Part 4: The WM_KEYDOWN Message

Lab 8: The Keyboard

In this part of lab, you will let the user move the caret by pressing the left and right arrow keys.

You will have to do a bit of range checking so the arrow keys work properly. For example, if the user keeps banging on the left arrow key, the caret should stop when it reaches the beginning of the text and refuse to go any further. Similarly, whenever the user presses the right arrow key, you must not move the caret past the last character in the buffer.

Since the user can move the caret without typing a character, you need to think about what should happen if the user backs up over an existing character and then types a new one. To make this simple, your program will simply overwrite the existing character and replace it in the buffer. A more sophisticated program would maintain an "insert/overwrite" flag based on the Insert key (see the *GetKeyboardState* system call). However, to insert a character, you need to move the rest of the characters in the buffer, which, while not difficult, doesn't really add much to your Windows programming skills. Therefore, we'll leave that as an additional exercise for those of you that are interested in that sort of thing.

Steps:

1. If not already running, start your development environment and open the *lab8* project. Then open LAB8.CPP.

2. So that the user cannot move the caret past the last character in the buffer, you will need to keep track of how many characters have been entered. You cannot use your existing index variable, since you will decrement that when the user presses the left-arrow key. So define a new static variable:

   ```
   static      int     iLast;            // "high-water" index
   ```

   In *WM_CREATE*, initialize this index to zero. Then, in *WM_CHAR*, after incrementing the original index variable, use code like this to ensure that the "high-water" index always contains the maximum buffer index:

   ```
   if ( i > iLast )
        iLast = i;
   ```

3. Then add a *WM_KEYDOWN* case and within it, set up a *switch-case* statement based on the virtual key code. Then add cases within the nested *switch-case* for the left and right arrow directional keys.

4. For the left-arrow case, you need to move the caret one character width to the left (if possible) To do that, update the character index (not the high-water index) and the character x-coordinate. Then move the caret. Be sure that you don't move the caret past the first character!

5. For the right arrow case, you need move the caret one character width to the right (if possible). To do that, update the character index (not the high-water index) and the character x-coordinate. Then move the caret. Be sure that you don't move the caret past the last (high-water indexed) character!

6. Modify the *WM_PAINT* case so the loop displays characters up to the high-water index.

7. Then develop and test your program as before. Can you type characters and then move the caret with the arrow keys? Does the left arrow stop at the beginning of the characters? Does the right arrow stop immediately after the last character?

Lab 8: The Keyboard

Refer to the LAB 8 FAQ in Chapter 10 if you have any problems or questions.

8. You are now finished with Lab 8. You should continue by taking the review quiz in Chapter 10 in the online workshop.

Lab 9: Menus

Note: If you are viewing this with Windows Write, you will get best results if you choose Tabs from the Document menu and set the first three tab stops to .5", 1.0" and 1.5".

Objectives:

- To learn how to create a menu as a resource.
- To process commands from menus.
- To learn how to manipulate menu item attributes, for example, graying-out a menu item.
- To create and process floating popup menus.
- To create and load an accelerator table.

In Lab 9, you will write a program that draws random lines throughout your window's client area. You will provide the user with menu items to start and stop the drawing, and to configure the line's width and style. Just for fun, you will create one of the menus as a traditional menu bar and will create the other menu as a floating popup menu. There's no real justification for splitting up the menus like this – the idea is to give you experience with both kinds.

In the last part of the lab, you will add an accelerator table to your window. That way, users will be able to start and stop the drawing and configure the line in two ways: either by choosing from a menu, or by pressing an accelerator key. As you learned in the online workshop, by providing both menus and accelerators, you make it easy for new users to learn your program, while giving experienced users the ability to bypass the menus.

Part 1: Defining a Menu as a Resource

In this part, you will define a menu as a resource, but will not add any code to respond to menu commands. So after you finish this part, the menus will be simply cosmetic. In the next part of the lab, you will make the menus actually do something.

Steps:

1. Start the Microsoft Developer Studio by choosing it from the Microsoft Visual C++ group. Close any current project by choosing *Close Workspace* from the *File* menu.

2. Create a new project for the lab by choosing *New* from the *File* menu and selecting *Project Workspace*. Then fill in or select the following:

Type:	Application
Name:	lab9
Platform:	Win32
Location:	Enter the directory on your hard disk where the online workshop lab exercises are installed, for example:

    c:\descript\labs\lab9

Lab 9: Menus   42

> **Note**: the *lab9* sub-directory should already exist. Make sure that "lab9" appears only once in the Location directory.
>
> If you cannot remember where you installed the online workshop lab exercises, click on the *Lab Setup* button in the Chapter 9 online workshop Lab Exercise page.
>
> Then click on the Create button to cause the Developer Studio to build the initial project files.

3. To save you some typing, we have provided you with a partially-completed source file that you will fill in. Choose *Open* from the *File* menu and select LAB9.CPP. The Developer Studio will display the file. Please examine it so that you understand what has been provided for you.

4. Even though you have opened the file from within the Developer Studio, it doesn't automatically add the file to the current project. To do that, choose *Files Into Project* from the *Insert* menu and select LAB9.CPP. This adds the source file into the project.

5. The provided code is nothing more than a template for a windows program that has no menus or accelerators. Your first task is to create the menu resource. While it's not difficult to write the menu resource "by hand", you will use the Developer Studio to graphically layout the menu. The Developer Studio will then generate both the menu resource script and the *#define* statements for each of your menu items.

    Choose *Resource* from the *Insert* menu and then select *Menu*. The Developer Studio should display a window entitled "Script 1 - IDR_MENU1". That's not a very useful name for your menu, so click the right mouse button on the window and choose *Properties* from the popup menu. And change the ID to IDM_MAIN. Then press Enter.

6. After you complete this part of the lab, your menu will contain a top-level menu item and two menu items on the pull-down:

    ```
    Draw
        Start
        Stop
    ```

    At this point, the "IDM_MAIN" window should display an empty menu, with the very first item (top-left corner) highlighted in a small rectangle. That rectangle indicates that this is an empty menu item: a pull-down menu in this case. To add a menu item, double-click the left mouse button on the rectangle and fill in the form:

    Caption: &Draw

    The "&" character marks the "D" as the menu-item mnemonic that makes it easier for the user to display the pull-down using the keyboard. Notice since this is a pull-down menu item, the ID field is grayed-out in the form – that's because pull-downs don't have separate IDs.

    Press Enter after you have typed in the caption. The window should now display "Draw" in the previously-empty rectangle, and display a highlighted rectangle immediately below the new pull-down menu item.

7. Double-click on the empty, highlighted rectangle beneath "Draw" and add the "Start" menu item. The keyboard mnemonic should be "S". Enter *IDM_START* for the new item's ID.

    Then repeat the process for the "Stop" menu item, assigning the ID as *IDM_STOP*.

Lab 9: Menus   43

8. Now that you have completed designing your menu, you need to tell the Developer Studio to save the menu script in a resource file. Click anywhere on the "Script 1" window to make sure it's at the top of the Z-order, then choose *Save* from the *File* menu. Enter LAB9.RC as the filename.

    The Developer Studio will now write the menu script and store it in this file. It will also create a file named RESOURCE.H, and in it, write the #define statements for your menu IDs.

9. To ensure that the new resource file is associated with your project, choose *Files into Project* from the *Insert* menu and enter LAB9.RC. The Developer Studio should display LAB9.RC in the *Project Workspace* window pane.

    You can close the LAB9.RC window now if you feel like it – you can always re-open it by choosing Open from the File menu or by double-clicking on LAB9.RC in the Project Workspace pane.

10. Next, choose *Open* from the *File* menu and open the RESOURCE.H file. You don't have to modify this file – the Developer Studio creates and maintains it. However, it's nice to know what's in there, so take a look around in it. Notice that there are symbolic names defined for each menu item and the menu itself (IDM_MAIN). The actual values are not important, but they should be unique.

    You can close the RESOURCE.H window when you are finished looking at it.

11. Now surface or open the LAB9.CPP source file. At the top of it, after any other *#include* statements, add the line:

    ```
    #include "resource.h"
    ```

    This ensures that the menu identifiers are available to your source file.

12. Your next task is to modify *WinMain* so that it loads the menu resource when the class is registered. Please review Chapter 11 if you are unsure how to do this (or look at the solution!).

    Note: since you assigned your menu a symbolic name, you will need to use the *MAKEINTRESOURCE* macro to convert the name into a string:

    ```
    wndclass.lpszMenuName = MAKEINTRESOURCE ( IDM_MAIN );
    ```

13. Even though you haven't added any code to respond to the menu, now's a good time to test your program to see if the menu will appear. So choose *Save All* from the *File* menu, and then develop your program by choosing *Build lab9.exe* from the *Build* menu. If there are any errors, fix them before continuing. See the first lab for a review on editing errors in the Developer Studio

14. Then run your program by choosing *Execute lab9.exe* from the *Build* menu. Do you see your menu? What happens if you select *Start* or *Stop*? Can you use the keyboard mnemonics to select the menu items (press and release the Alt key, followed by the underlined character)?

    Refer to the LAB9 FAQ in Chapter 11 if you have any problems.

    Close your window. Then continue with Part 2 of this lab.

Lab 9: Menus

Part 2: Menu Messages

In this part, you will add code to your window procedure to respond to the menu selection. Of course, you will also have to add code to draw the random lines. In this lab, you will draw the random lines using a timer message – in other words, when the user chooses *Start*, you will start a timer and then draw a single line each time the timer clicks off. When the user chooses *Stop*, you should kill the timer. Thus the user essentially will use the menu to start and stop the timer.

Steps:

1. If not already running, start the Microsoft Developer Studio by choosing it from the Microsoft Visual C++ group. If not already open, open the *lab9* project by choosing *Open Workspace* from the *File* menu.

2. At the top of the file, just above WinMain, add the line:

    ```
    const int ID_TIMER = 1;
    ```

    This will be the ID of your timer to draw random lines.

3. At the top of the window procedure, define the following *static* variables:

    ```
    static HPEN          hpen;     // current drawing pen
    static POINT         pt;       // current position
    ```

4. In the window procedure, add a case for *WM_CREATE*, and in it:

    a. Call *CreatePen* to create a solid, single-pixel-wide black pen and store it's handle in the *static* variable. In later parts of the lab, you will let the user choose the pen, but for now you will hard-code your program to use this pen. See Chapter 6 in the online workshop if you are having trouble creating the pen. Use the provided *err_msg* function (it's defined at the bottom of LAB9.CPP) to display a message box if the *CreatePen* call fails. You should call err_msg after each Windows system call to make debugging easier.

    b. Initialize the current position static variable to 100, 100.

5. In *WM_DESTROY*, delete the pen whose handle is stored in the *static* variable. Again, see Chapter 6 for more information.

6. Add a case for *WM_TIMER* and in it:

    a. Make sure the message is for the *ID_TIMER* ID (see *wParam*).

    b. Retrieve the client area's rectangle by calling *GetClientRect*.

    c. Define a *POINT* variable to hold another coordinate – this one will act as the end point of the line you will draw in a moment. Initialize the point to a random location within the client area. To come up with a random coordinate, you can use code like:

    ```
    ptNew.x = rand() % rcClient.right;
    ```

Lab 9: Menus   45

                The *rand* function is part of the C standard runtime library – it returns a pseudo-random integer. We then use the *modulus* operator (%) to ensure that the random value is less than the maximum x-coordinate of the client area.

       d.   Call *GetDC* to retrieve a window device context handle.

       e.   Select the pen into the DC – save the previous pen handle so you can restore it later.

       f.   Draw a line from the current point (coordinates stored in the *static* variable) to the new point that you just calculated. See Chapter 6 in the online workshop for more details on drawing a line.

       g.   Copy the coordinates from the new point to the current point (the static variable). That way, the next timer message, the new point will be the starting point for the next line.

       h.   Clean up the device context and release it.

7.   Now for the real menu stuff. Add a case for *WM_COMMAND*, and in it, add sub-cases for your *Start* and *Stop* menu items.

8.   In the *Start* menu item case:

       a.   Clear the client area by calling:

```
InvalidateRect ( hwnd, NULL, TRUE );
UpdateWindow ( hwnd );
```

             These two calls send a *WM_PAINT* message to your window – if you take a look at that code, you'll see that it does nothing, which effectively erases the client area.

       b.   Call *GetClientRect* to retrieve the client area's rectangle.

       c.   Choose a random current position and store it in the static variable. See the WM_TIMER case you just completed for code you can copy.

       d.   Call *SetTimer* to start a timer that has a 250-millisecond interval. Use the timer ID constant you defined in an earlier step.

9.   In the *Stop* menu case, stop the timer by calling *KillTimer*.

10. Then develop and execute your program as before. What happens when you choose Start from the *Draw* menu? How about *Stop*? When you are satisfied with your program, close the window and continue on in Part 3.

Part 3: Changing a Menu Item's Attributes

In this part, you will add code to your window procedure so that when the user chooses *Start* or *Stop*, your window will gray-out or enable the menu items so that the user must choose them alternately. For example, when the user chooses *Start*, you will gray-out *Start* so the user cannot choose it again, without selecting *Stop* first. Similarly, when the user chooses *Stop*, you will gray-out *Stop* and re-enable *Start*.

Lab 9: Menus

As an added benefit to doing this, the user will now be able to tell if the program is "running" by pulling down the menu – if *Start* is grayed-out, the user knows that the program is currently drawing. While that might be rather obvious in this program, in other programs, the grayed-out state might provide the user with valuable feedback.

Steps:

1. If not already running, start the Microsoft Developer Studio by choosing it from the Microsoft Visual C++ group. If not already open, open the *lab9* project by choosing *Open Workspace* from the *File* menu.

2. In the *Start* menu WM_COMMAND case, call *EnableMenuItem* to gray-out the *Start* menu item. Then call EnableMenuItem again to enable the *Stop* menu item. You can call *GetMenu* to retrieve the handle for your menu.

    Hint: there's a difference between disabling a menu item and graying it out – be sure that you choose the flag for graying out!

    Another hint: EnableMenuItem lets you specify which menu item to affect two ways: by passing the menu item's ID, or by passing the menu item's position (the positions start at zero). It's probably easiest here to pass the menu item ID (for example IDM_START), but if you do, be sure to "or-in" the *MF_BYCOMMAND* flag.

3. In the *Stop* menu WM_COMMAND case, call *EnableMenuItem* to gray-out the *Stop* menu item. Then call EnableMenuItem again to enable the *Start* menu item.

4. You also need to ensure that the *Start* menu item is initially enabled and the *Stop* menu item is initially gray. There are two ways to do this: you can use *EnableMenuItem* in the WM_CREATE case, or you can set the *Stop* menu item as grayed in the resource definition. If you want to try the latter, open the LAB9.RC file and double-click on the *Stop* menu item to display its properties. Then select the *Grayed* checkbox.

5. Then develop and execute your program as before. Is the *Stop* menu item initially grayed-out? After you choose *Start*, is *Stop* still grayed-out? What happens to the menu if you choose *Stop*? When you are satisfied with your program, close the window and continue on in Part 4.

Part 4: Floating Popup Menus

In this part, you will add another menu to your window that lets the user choose the line style and width that the program uses to draw its random lines. Just for fun, you will create this menu as a floating popup menu rather than as part of the menu bar.

Steps:

1. If not already running, start the Microsoft Developer Studio by choosing it from the Microsoft Visual C++ group. If not already open, open the *lab9* project by choosing *Open Workspace* from the *File* menu.

2. The floating popup menu should have items with text:

Lab 9: Menus   47

>   Dummy
>   <u>1</u> pixel
>   <u>5</u> pixels
>   <u>D</u>otted
>   D<u>a</u>shed

   Note the placement of the mnemonic (underlined) characters.

3. To create the new menu, choose *Resource* from the *Insert* menu and select *Menu*. Then click the right mouse button on the window, choose *Properties* and change the new menu's ID from *IDR_MENU1* (or whatever) to *IDM_POPUP*. This will be the ID of the popup menu itself.

4. Like before, double-click the left mouse button on the highlighted rectangle to create a top-level item that corresponds to the pull-down menu. Enter the caption as: *Dummy*.

   For floating popup menus, the top-level text never appears. Thus you can use any text you like for the caption.

5. Then add the items described in Step 2 to the menu. Use the text as shown in Step 2, but you can assign any menu-item IDs that you want. We do recommend that you use the prefix *IDM_* like you did in the earlier menu (for example *IDM_DOTTED*) – the prefix makes it easier to see that the name is for a menu, rather than for a icon or dialog box or whatever.

6. Open RESOURCE.H and ensure that menu item IDs for your new menu items are consecutively-numbered, starting with the 1-pixel menu item, ranging up to the dashed-line menu item. This is important since you will later use the *CheckMenuRadioItem* call – it depends on the order of grouped menu item IDs. You can close RESOURCE.H when you are finished looking at it.

7. Next surface the LAB9.CPP source file. At the top of the window procedure, add the following static variables:

   ```
   static HPEN      hpen1pixel;       // single-pixel wide pen
   static HPEN      hpen5pixel;       // 5-pixel wide pen
   static HPEN      hpenDotted;       // dotted-line pen
   static HPEN      hpenDashed;       // dashed-line pen

   static HMENU     hmenuPopMain;     // top-level popup handle
   static HMENU     hmenuPopup;       // popup menu handle
   ```

8. In the *WM_CREATE* case:

   a. Delete or comment-out the existing code that initializes the *hpen* variable. You will initialize it a little bit differently in a moment.

   b. Call *CreatePen* to create the four pens and store their handles in the static variables.

   c. Call *LoadMenu* to load the floating popup menu (*IDM_POPUP*) from the resources. Store its handle in the *hmenuPopMain* variable you defined in Step 7. You will need to use the *MAKEINTRESOURCE* macro. **Note**: you can use *GetWindowLong* to retrieve the current instance handle.

      Then call *GetSubMenu* to retrieve the handle of the pull-down menu that's part of the floating popup – it's the only pull-down, so its index is zero. Store this menu handle in the *hmenuPopup static* variable you defined in Step 7. This is the handle you'll need to display the floating popup menu.

Lab 9: Menus

      d.   Choose which pen you want to be the initial pen by storing its handle in the static *hpen* variable.

      e.   Then use *CheckMenuRadioItem* to set the menu item that corresponds to the initial pen as bulleted. See the sample program on page 11-5 in the online workshop for an example of using this call. **Note**: this call is not implemented in Windows NT 3.51 – you can still call it, but it will return *FALSE*, with error code 120 (*ERROR_CALL_NOT_IMPLEMENTED*).

9.   In the *WM_DESTROY* case, first comment-out or delete the code that gets rid of the pen whose handle is stored in the *static hpen* variable. Then delete the pens whose handles are stored in the *static* variables you initialized in the *WM_CREATE* case. Then destroy the top-level popup menu.

10.   In the *WM_COMMAND* case, add sub-cases for the new menu items. In each case, set the *hpen static* variable to the corresponding pen and then call *CheckMenuRadioItem* to move the menu bullet to the corresponding menu item.

11.   Add a *WM_CONTEXTMENU* case to the window procedure. Windows generates this message when the user presses the right mouse button on the client area. You will use this message as a trigger to display your floating popup menu. To display the menu, call *TrackPopupMenu*. Here are a few hints:

      a.   The *WM_CONTEXTMENU* message parameters give you the mouse-click coordinates in screen units, not client units.

      b.   Make your menu left aligned and have it track the right mouse button (use the corresponding flags in *TrackPopupMenu*).

      c.   You can use *NULL* for the last argument of *TrackPopupMenu*.

12.   Then develop and execute your program as before. Try clicking the right mouse button on the client area. Does your floating menu appear? What happens if you select each pen style menu item?

When you are satisfied with your program, close the window and move on to Part 5 of the lab.

Part 5: Accelerator Tables

In the previous parts of lab, you added menus so the user can start, stop and configure the drawing that your program does. However, to do so, the user must either use the mouse or a series of keystrokes, perhaps using your menu's keyboard mnemonics. In this part of lab, you will add an accelerator table so that the user can accomplish these things with single keystrokes.

In addition, you will append the text for each accelerator key to the corresponding menu item's text – that makes it easier for users to learn the accelerator keystrokes (that means less documentation for the developer to write!).

Steps:

Lab 9: Menus   49

1. If not already running, start the Microsoft Developer Studio by choosing it from the Microsoft Visual C++ group. If not already open, open the *lab9* project by choosing *Open Workspace* from the *File* menu.

2. Choose Open from the File menu and open LAB9.RC (it doesn't hurt to open it if it's already open). You should now see LAB9.RC in the *Project Workspace* window pane (if you don't see the Project Workspace pane, choose *Options* from the *Tools* menu and select the *Workspace* tab. Then be sure that *Project Workspace* is selected in *Docking Views*).

3. Create the accelerator table by choosing *Resource* from the *Insert* menu and selecting *Accelerator*. The Developer Studio will open a window entitled *IDR_ACCELERATOR1* or something similar. To change the accelerator's ID to something more meaningful, click the right mouse button on *IDR_ACCELERATOR1* in the Project Workspace and display the *Accelerator Properties*. Then type *IDA_MAIN* as the new ID. Press Enter when you are finished.

4. The accelerator window should now have the title IDA_MAIN. In that window, there should be a highlighted rectangle at the top of the client area. This represents an empty entry in the accelerator table. To add a new entry, double-click the left mouse button on the highlighted rectangle and fill in the properties of the accelerator table entry. For the first accelerator, enter:

ID:	IDM_START
Modifiers:	Ctrl
Type:	Virtkey
Key	S

   Make sure the "S" is uppercase. When you press Enter, the Developer Studio writes the new entry into the accelerator window. You can then double-click the empty rectangle to add more entries to the table.

   Here is what your accelerators should look like:

Menu Item	Keystroke
Start	Ctrl+S
Stop	Ctrl+T
1 pixel	Ctrl+1
5 pixels	Ctrl+5
Dotted	Ctrl+D
Dashed	Ctrl+A

   You can close the accelerator window after you add all of the accelerators.

5. In the Project Workspace pane, expand the *Menu* "+" and edit each menu item (on both menus) so that the accelerator key text is part of the menu item text. For example, the *Start* menu item's text should be:

   Start\tCtrl+S

   The "\t" character inserts a tab into the menu-item text so that the accelerator text lines up nicely.

6. Surface the LAB9.CPP window and modify *WinMain* so it loads the accelerator table by calling *LoadAccelerators*. Use the *MAKEINTRESOURCE* macro to convert the accelerator's numeric ID to the string form that LoadAccelerators expects.

Lab 9: Menus

Then modify the message loop so it calls *TranslateAccelerator*. See Chapter 11 in the online workshop for more information. **Note**: you will *not* need to modify the window procedure! Since you've set the accelerator table to match the menus, and you've already written the menu-processing code, the accelerators are already functional!

7. Then develop and execute your program as before. Can you send commands to the program by using either the menu or the accelerator keys?

8. You are now finished with Lab 9. You should continue by taking the Review Quiz in Chapter 11.

Lab 10: Tool Bars

Note: If you are viewing this with Windows Write, you will get best results if you choose Tabs from the Document menu and set the first three tab stops to .5", 1.0" and 1.5".

Objectives:

- To learn how to add a toolbar window to a program that already has functional menus
- To learn how to use a *STRINGTABLE* for tool-tip text strings

In this lab, you will add code to a program that displays a text string and lets the user choose whether the string is bold, italic, underline or any combination of those attributes. As it stands, the program lets the user choose the attributes by selecting from a menu. Your task is to add a toolbar to the window so that the user can set the text attributes without having to bring down a menu.

In the last part of lab, you will tool-tip windows to your toolbar so that the user doesn't have to decipher the meaning of the toolbar bitmaps. To make your program language-independent, you will load all of the text strings from a STRINGTABLE in the resource file. That way, if you decide to convert your program to work with a language other than English, you will just need to modify the resources.

Part 1: Creating and Programming Tool Bars

To save you typing (and avoid overlapping the material covered in Lab 9), we have provided you with a program that already has working menus. Your job in this part is to add a toolbar window whose commands mirror the menu items.

Steps:

1. Start the Microsoft Developer Studio by choosing it from the Microsoft Visual C++ group. Close any current project by choosing *Close Workspace* from the *File* menu.

2. Create a new project for the lab by choosing *New* from the *File* menu and selecting *Project Workspace*. Then fill in or select the following:

Type:	Application
Name:	lab10
Platform:	Win32
Location:	Enter the directory on your hard disk where the online workshop lab exercises are installed, for example:

   c:\descript\labs\lab10

   Note: the *lab10* sub-directory should already exist. Make sure that "lab10" appears only once in the Location directory.

   If you cannot remember where you installed the online workshop lab exercises, click on the *Lab Setup* button in the Chapter 12 online workshop Lab Exercise page.

Lab 10: Toolbars   52

Then click on the Create button to cause the Developer Studio to build the initial project files.

3. To save you some typing, we have provided you with a partially-completed source file that you will fill in. Choose *Open* from the *File* menu and select LAB10.CPP. The Developer Studio will display the file. Please examine it so that you understand what has been provided for you.

4. Even though you have opened the file from within the Developer Studio, it doesn't automatically add the file to the current project. To do that, choose *Files Into Project* from the *Insert* menu and select LAB10.CPP. This adds the source file into the project.

   You should then repeat this step and add the LAB10.RC file to the project. This file contains the menu definition.

5. The provided code creates a window that displays the string "Lab 10 – Toolbars" centered in the client area. From the menu, the user can choose the attributes of the text: bold, italic, underline or any combination. The program correctly handles the check mark on the menu – a check mark next to a menu item means that the attribute is currently "on".

   Now compile, link and run the program so you can see what it does. Close it after you have played with it for a while.

   Then, carefully examine the LAB10.CPP, RESOURCE.H and LAB10.RC files so that you completely understand the code that we have given you. Pay special attention to the WM_COMMAND code in LAB10.CPP – later on, you will modify this code.

6. Your first step is to create the bitmap that contains the images that the toolbar will display in its buttons.

   Choose *Resource* from the *Insert* menu and select *Bitmap*. The Developer Studio should display a Bitmap editor window containing an empty bitmap. The window has two panes: the pane on the left is a *Preview* pane that shows the bitmap at its true size (blank now), and a *Grid* pane where each square represents a pixel in the bitmap. You should also see a *Graphics* window that lets you choose a drawing tool (such as a line or text) and a *Color* window.

7. The first problem is that the default bitmap size is not what you need for your toolbar. By default, a toolbar button is 16 pixels wide by 15 pixels tall, and that's the size you will use in this lab. Since you will have three buttons on your toolbar, you need three images – therefore, your bitmap needs to be 48 pixels wide by 15 pixels tall. To change the bitmap's size, double-click the left mouse button on the *Preview* pane to display the bitmap properties. Enter the following:

ID:	IDB_TOOLS
Width:	48
Height:	15
Colors:	16

   Then press Enter to dismiss the properties window. The bitmap should change size in the *Grid* pane.

8. Next, draw the background of the bitmap. Most toolbar buttons have a light gray background. Find the *Fill* tool in the drawing-tools window and click it. Then find the light gray color in the color palette and click on it. Then click the mouse anywhere in the bitmap grid – the bitmap should now fill with the gray color, both in the *Grid* pane and the *Preview* pane.

Lab 10: Toolbars

9. You will use this single bitmap to hold the images for all three toolbar buttons – all of the images must be the same size. To make drawing the images a bit easier, I recommend that you draw two vertical lines in the bitmap that divide the bitmap into three images. Set the color to black and then use the *Line* tool and draw two single-pixel-wide lines – one in column 16 and the other in column 32. These lines are temporary – you will erase them after you have finished drawing the images. **Note**: the Developer Studio displays current drawing coordinates in its status bar at the bottom of the Developer Studio window.

10. The toolbar buttons will correspond to the *Bold*, *Italic* and *Underline* menu items. Most word processing programs use the characters "B", "I" and "U" in their toolbars to represent these commands. And to make them look more descriptive, the "B" should itself be bold, the "I" in an italic font, and the "U" should be underlined. The set of images in the bitmap will end up looking something like (temporary lines removed):

    To draw the "B" character, choose the *Text* tool– the Developer Studio a popup *Text Tool* window. In the *Text Tool* window, type "B" and then select the *Times New Roman Bold* font. You should now be able to see the character both in the *Grid* pane and in the *Preview* pane. Then use the mouse to drag the character's image within the *Grid* pane so that it's centered in the left-most section of the three-part bitmap. You may need to change the font's size to nicely fill the image section. Then click the mouse in the *Preview* pane and close the *Text Tool* popup window.

    Then repeat the process for italic and underline image sections. **Note:** you will have to draw the under-line yourself, so you should position the "U" character a little bit higher than the others.

11. Then draw gray lines over the temporary vertical lines to remove them.

12. Choose *Save* from the *File* menu. You can then close the bitmap editor window if you like.

13. Next edit LAB10.CPP. At the top, immediately before *WinMain*, define a constant identifier for the tool bar child window:

    ```
    const int IDW_TOOLS = 100;
    ```

    Of course, the actual ID (100) really doesn't matter, as long as it's different from any other child windows (of which you have none!).

14. Then, in the window procedure, define a *static* variable to hold the tool bar's window handle. You must define it as *static* because you will initialize it during the *WM_CREATE* message and use it in other messages, such as *WM_NOTIFY* (more on this in a moment).

15. Then add a *WM_CREATE* case to the window procedure. In that case, do the following:

    a. Retrieve the current instance handle and store it in a temporary variable (use *GetWindowLong*).

    b. Call *CreateToolbarEx* to create the tool bar window. Here are some hints:

    - Create the toolbar so that it is initially void of buttons (no tool tips yet, either). You will add the three buttons in the next step.

Lab 10: Toolbars 54

- Create the tool bar window without the *WS_VISIBLE* style – you will show the tool bar after adding the buttons.

- Specify the bitmap ID from RESOURCE.H. Also remember that there are three images in the bitmap.

- Use the window ID you defined at the top of LAB10.CPP for the tool bar's ID.

c. Send the *TB_ADDBUTTONS* message to add the three buttons to the tool bar window. Here are some hints:

- Your buttons will have no text so you can use -1 for the text string index.

- All buttons should have the *TBSTYLE_CHECK* button style and should be enabled (*TBSTATE_ENABLED*).

- Each button's command ID should match the corresponding menu item's ID.

d. Call *ShowWindow* to make the tool bar window visible.

16. Add a case for *WM_SIZE* to the window procedure. In it, use *SendMessage* to pass the *WM_SIZE* message to the toolbar window. You can pass on the same *wParam* and *lParam* that are passed to the *WM_SIZE* message itself.

17. Before you can compile and link your program, you need to modify your project's settings so it links to the correct libraries. Choose *Settings* from the *Build* menu and click on the *Link* tab. Add COMCTL32.LIB to the list of libraries. If you don't do this, the linker will fail with an error saying something about "unresolved externals" for the *CreateToolBarEx* call. Close the Settings window.

18. Choose *Save All* from the *File* menu, and then develop your program by choosing *Build lab10.exe* from the *Build* menu. If there are any errors, fix them before continuing. See the first lab for a review on editing errors in the Developer Studio

19. Then run your program by choosing *Execute lab10.exe* from the *Build* menu. Do you see the tool bar window? What happens if you click on one of the tool bar buttons, say the "Bold" button? Does the text change to bold face?

    Now try choosing *Italic* from the menu. Does anything happen to the "Italic" tool bar button? Look at the menu. Do the check marks on the menu items match the state of the buttons? If they don't, don't worry! You will write some code so that the buttons and menu items work together in the next part of lab.

    Refer to the LAB10 FAQ in Chapter 12 if you have any problems.

    Close your window. Then continue with Part 2 of this lab.

Part 2: Controlling Tool Bars

In this part, you will add code to your window procedure so that the menu check marks and the button state stay synchronized. In other words, when the user chooses from the menu, your window procedure will notify the tool bar. What about when the user clicks a button? Do you have to add code so that the menu

Lab 10: Toolbars

item can change its state? Actually, no – that's because the existing *WM_COMMAND* code (generated when the user clicks a button) already does that. So in this part, you only have to worry about the case where the user selects the menu item.

Steps:

1. If not already running, start the Microsoft Developer Studio by choosing it from the Microsoft Visual C++ group. If not already open, open the *lab10* project by choosing *Open Workspace* from the *File* menu.

2. In each *WM_COMMAND* case, send *TB_CHECKBUTTON* to the tool bar window to "check" or "uncheck" the corresponding button. For example, if the user chooses Bold from the menu and the text is not currently bold, you should send *TB_CHECKBUTTON* to turn the button check state "on".

3. Then develop and test your program as before. Try choosing from both the menu and clicking a tool bar button. Does the button state and the menu item check stay synchronized?

   Refer to the LAB10 FAQ in Chapter 12 if you have any problems.

   Close your window. Then continue with Part 3 of this lab.

Part 3: Tool Tips and String Tables

While tool bars give users quick access to commands, they can sometimes be a bit difficult to decipher, especially if the bitmap artist is artistically impaired. That's where tool tips come in – they let you associate a text string with each tool bar button, so the user can get an explanation of the button's purpose by hovering the mouse over the button.

There's a problem with text strings, too, however – they are language specific (for example, English). Bitmaps and icons are nice because (most of the time) they mean the same thing in any language. With text strings however, you must change them if you decide to convert your program for a different national language.

To make conversion easier, you can store the text strings for your tool tips as string table resource. That way, you only need to translate the resources and not modify your source code. Of course, in your lab program, you would also need to translate the text string that the program displays in its client area (it really should be loaded from a string table, too). But we'll leave that as an exercise for the student.

Steps:

1. If not already running, start the Microsoft Developer Studio by choosing it from the Microsoft Visual C++ group. If not already open, open the *lab10* project by choosing *Open Workspace* from the *File* menu.

2. Start by defining the string table resource. Choose *Resource* from the *Insert* menu an select *String Table*. The Developer Studio should display an empty string table in the *String Editor* window.

3. To add a string, double-click the left mouse button on the first (empty) rectangle in the string table. The Developer Studio should display the *String Properties* window, in which you should enter:

Lab 10: Toolbars

> ID: IDS_BOLD
> Caption: Bold

Then press Enter. You have just created an entry in the string table: a string with text "Bold" with the *IDS_BOLD* constant as the string ID. This will be the tool tip text for the Bold tool bar button.

Repeat the process for the *Italic* and *Underline* buttons, giving each its own unique identifier and appropriate text. To add a new string table entry, click on the empty highlighted rectangle.

Then choose *Save* from the *File* menu. You can then close the String Table editing window if you wish.

4. Edit the LAB10.CPP file and find the code in *WM_CREATE* that creates the toolbar window. To enable tool tips, you need to "or" in the *TBSTYLE_TOOLTIPS* flag into the tool bar's window style.

5. Then add a case for *WM_NOTIFY* and in it, look for the *TTN_NEEDTEXT* notification. Probably the best thing to do here is to copy from the sample program in Chapter 12.

   However, your code will be a bit different from the sample, which hard codes the text strings. For each button, your code should set *pttt->hinst* to the current instance handle (use *GetWindowLong*) and set *pttt->lpszText* to the appropriate string table ID. You will need to cast to make the compiler happy, for example:

   ```
   pttt->lpszText = (char *)IDS_BOLD;
   ```

   By specifying a non-zero instance handle and a string table ID, you cause the tool bar window to load the string from the string table and display it in the tool tip window. Of course, you could load the string yourself, but why bother if the tool bar will do it for you? (One reason to do it yourself is that you could load all the strings in *WM_CREATE* and save the time-consuming string table load each time the tool bar asks for the tool tip text.)

6. Then develop and test your program. Do you see the tool tip text you leave the mouse cursor over the tool bar buttons?

7. You are now finished with Lab 10. You should continue by taking the Review Quiz in Chapter 12.

Lab 11: A Simple Modal Dialog Box

Note: If you are viewing this with Windows Write, you will get best results if you choose Tabs from the Document menu and set the first three tab stops to .5", 1.0" and 1.5".

Objectives:

- To learn how to use the Microsoft Developer Studio to create a dialog box resource
- To write a simple dialog function that responds to a pushbutton
- To learn how to use the *DialogBoxParam* call to display a modal dialog box

In this lab, you will create an "About" dialog box that the user can view by choosing from your *Help* menu. Many Windows programs use such dialog boxes to show their version number and their icon and your program will do the same.

Part 1: Creating the Dialog Resource

In this part, you will create the resources needed for your program: an icon, a menu and the *About* dialog box. After finishing this part, though, the menu and dialog will not be functional – you will make them work in the second part of the lab.

Steps:

1. Start the Microsoft Developer Studio by choosing it from the Microsoft Visual C++ group. Close any current project by choosing *Close Workspace* from the *File* menu.

2. Create a new project for the lab by choosing *New* from the *File* menu and selecting *Project Workspace*. Then fill in or select the following:

Type:	Application
Name:	lab11
Platform:	Win32
Location:	Enter the directory on your hard disk where the online workshop lab exercises are installed, for example:

    c:\descript\labs\lab11

    Note: the *lab11* sub-directory should already exist. Make sure that "lab11" appears only once in the Location directory.

    If you cannot remember where you installed the online workshop lab exercises, click on the *Lab Setup* button in the Chapter 13 online workshop Lab Exercise page.

    Then click on the Create button to cause the Developer Studio to build the initial project files.

Lab 11: A Simple Modal Dialog Box

3. To save you some typing, we have provided you with a partially-completed source file that you will fill in. Choose *Open* from the *File* menu and select LAB11.CPP. The Developer Studio will display the file. Please examine it so that you understand what has been provided for you.

4. Even though you have opened the file from within the Developer Studio, it doesn't automatically add the file to the current project. To do that, choose *Files Into Project* from the *Insert* menu and select LAB11.CPP. This adds the source file into the project.

5. Your first task is to create the menu resource for your program. Choose *Resource* from the *Insert* menu and select *Menu*. You should then create a menu that looks like:

```
File            Help
   Exit            About
```

See Lab Exercise 9 for help on creating a menu in the Developer Studio. Assign any symbolic IDs you wish for the menu items. **Note**: you should also assign the menu itself a symbolic ID, for example *IDM_MAIN*. To assign the ID, click the right mouse button on the menu-editing window to display the menu properties.

Write down the IDs here for future reference:

Item	ID
Exit	
About	
Menu	

Note: if you are viewing this document online, write the IDs on a piece of paper.

6. Next, create an icon for your program. Choose *Resource* from the *Insert* menu and select *Icon*. Then create any picture in the icon you wish. See Lab Exercise 4 for help. **Note**: you should assign the icon a symbolic ID, for example *IDI_MAIN*. To assign the ID, double-click the left mouse button on the icon-editing window to display the icon properties. Write down the icon ID for future reference:

Icon ID _____

7. Finally, you can create the dialog. Here is what your dialog will end up looking like (your icon will be different):

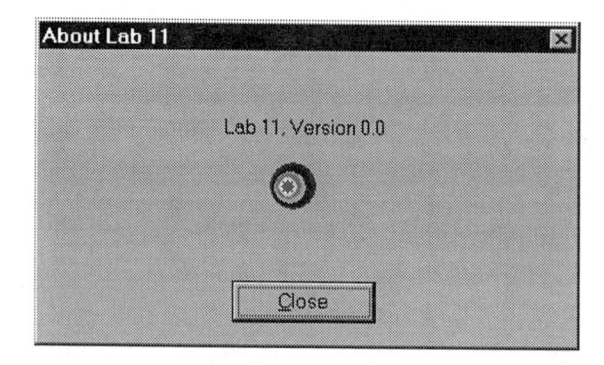

Lab 11: A Simple Modal Dialog Box

To start the dialog editor, choose *Resource* from the *Insert* menu and select *Dialog*. The dialog editor will open and display a dialog that you can use as a starting point for your dialog.

8. Start by assigning an ID to the dialog box itself. To do that, click the right mouse button on the dialog to display the dialog's properties. Enter the following:

    ID: DLG_ABOUT
    Caption: About Lab 11

    Press Enter to dismiss the properties window. The dialog editor should update the dialog's title. The Developer studio will also write a *#define* for the dialog's ID into the RESOURCE.H file. More on that in a moment.

9. You will notice that the starting-point dialog contains two buttons, while yours will have only one – you should delete the *Cancel* button. To delete a dialog control, select it by clicking it with the left mouse button. Then choose *Cut* from the *Edit* Menu.

10. Next you need to change the text (caption) in the remaining button. To change the text, click the left mouse button on the *OK* button to display its properties. Change the caption to "&Close" (don't enter the quotes) and take this opportunity to note the button's ID:

    Close Button ID _____

    To position the button at the bottom of the dialog, make sure it's selected by clicking the left mouse button on it, then choose *Arrange Buttons* from the *Layout* menu and select *Bottom*.

11. Your dialog also needs to display your program's version number. To insert a static text control on your dialog, locate the *Controls* window in the Developer Studio and then hover the mouse over the buttons until you find the one for *Static Text* (you should see a tool-tip window as you let the mouse linger over each button).

    Click on the Static Text button and then click the left mouse button on your dialog – the dialog editor should display a new text control on your dialog. Use the left mouse button to drag the text control so that it's underneath the dialog's title bar. Don't worry about centering the text – you'll do that in a moment.

    To change the text control's characters, simply type your version number message! (See the picture in Step 7). Then press Enter to dismiss the properties window (if visible).

12. To center the text, click the left mouse button on it to ensure that it's selected, and then choose *Center in Dialog* from the *Layout* menu and select *Horizontal*.

13. Your last dialog-editing task is to add the icon to the dialog. In the *Controls* window, find the *Picture* button and click on it. Then click the mouse in the new dialog at approximately where you want the icon to reside (you will center it in a moment). The dialog editor should display a rectangle that marks the dialog's position.

    Double-click the left mouse button on the picture to display its properties, and enter (or select) the following:

    ID: IDC_STATIC

Lab 11: A Simple Modal Dialog Box 60

        Type: Icon
        Image: Enter the Icon ID from Step 6

Then press Enter to dismiss the properties window. You can then center the icon in the same fashion as you did with the static text control

14. Now you need to save your resources in a file. Make sure that the dialog-editing window is the active window and then choose *Save As* from the *File* menu and enter LAB11.RC as the file name.

    Then choose *Files into Project* from the *Insert* menu and insert LAB11.RC into your project. You can then close all of the resource-editing windows if you'd like.

15. Edit LAB11.CPP and add:

    `#include "resource.h"`

    immediately after any other *#includes*. This ensures that your source program can reference the symbolic names for your menu, icon and dialog.

16. Then edit *WinMain* so that when you register the class, you assign the icon and menu that you just created. See Chapter 5: Icons and Chapter 11: Menus if you need help. Be sure to use the *MAKEINTRESOURCE* macro to convert the icon and menu IDs to the string form required in the *WNDCLASS* structure!

17. At this point, it's a good idea to test your program, even though you haven't written any code to support the dialog yet. Choose *Save All* from the *File* menu, and then develop your program by choosing *Build lab11.exe* from the *Build* menu. If there are any errors, fix them before continuing. See the first lab for a review on editing errors in the Developer Studio

18. Then run your program by choosing *Execute lab11.exe* from the *Build* menu. Do you see the menu and the icon? Don't worry if your menu isn't functional – you will add that code in the next part.

    Refer to the LAB11 FAQ in Chapter 13 if you have any problems.

    Close your window. Then continue with Part 2 of this lab.

Part 2: Displaying the Modal Dialog

In this part, you will write a dialog function and update the main window procedure so that the user can exit the program and display the *About* dialog box by choosing from the program's menu.

Steps:

1. If not already running, start the Microsoft Developer Studio by choosing it from the Microsoft Visual C++ group. If not already open, open the *lab11* project by choosing *Open Workspace* from the *File* menu.

2. Edit LAB11.CPP and add a *WM_COMMAND* case for the menu selections. When the user chooses *Exit* from the *File* menu, you should call *PostQuitMessage* to terminate the program.

    When the user chooses *About* from the *Help* menu, you should display the dialog box you created in the last part of lab (call *DialogBoxParam*). Here are some hints:

Lab 11: A Simple Modal Dialog Box 61

- You can ignore the return value of *DialogBoxParam*.
- You can retrieve an instance handle by calling *GetWindowLong*.
- In the next step, you will write the dialog function. It's name (address) will be *AboutDialogProc*.
- Use the *MAKEINTRESOURCE* macro to convert the dialog's ID to the string format that *DialogBoxParam* expects.
- You don't need to pass any application-specific data to the dialog function

3. At the bottom of LAB11.CPP, add a dialog function:

```
BOOL CALLBACK AboutDialogProc ( HWND hwndDlg, UINT iMsg
                              , WPARAM wParam, LPARAM lParam )
{
    switch ( iMsg )
    {
        default:
            return FALSE;
    }
}
```

4. Then write a function prototype for the dialog function by copying its definition to the top of LAB11.CPP and appending a semicolon. Insert the prototype near the other existing function prototypes.

5. Next add a *WM_COMMAND* case to the dialog function. You should have two sub-cases under *WM_COMMAND*: one for the *Close* button and one for an "imaginary" button that has an ID of *IDCANCEL*. The dialog passes this ID if the user closes the dialog box without pressing the Close button (by pressing the "X" titlebar button, for example).

    In each case, dismiss the dialog by calling *EndDialog*, passing the button ID as the second argument. Also remember that in a dialog function, you should return the value *TRUE* for messages that you handle, *FALSE* for messages you do not handle.

6. Then develop your program as before and run it. Try choosing *About* from the *Help* menu. Do you see your dialog box? While the dialog box is visible, try clicking on the main window's menu. Can you? Is the dialog box modal or modeless?

    Press the *Close* button. Does the dialog go away? Then choose *Exit* from the *File* menu. Does your program terminate?

7. You are now finished with Lab 11. You should continue by taking the Review Quiz in Chapter 13.

Lab 12: Dialog Controls

Note: If you are viewing this with Windows Write, you will get best results if you choose Tabs from the Document menu and set the first three tab stops to .5", 1.0" and 1.5".

Objectives:

- To create a dialog box that contains edit controls, a checkbox control and a listbox control
- To write the dialog function to process messages from the control

In this lab, you will write a program that displays an image in its client area. The image will be similar to the output from a Spirograph toy. You will create a dialog box to let the user choose the parameters that the program uses to draw the spirograph.

Steps:

1. Start the Microsoft Developer Studio by choosing it from the Microsoft Visual C++ group. Close any current project by choosing *Close Workspace* from the *File* menu.

2. Create a new project for the lab by choosing *New* from the *File* menu and selecting *Project Workspace*. Then fill in or select the following:

Type:	Application
Name:	lab12
Platform:	Win32
Location:	Enter the directory on your hard disk where the online workshop lab exercises are installed, for example:

   c:\descript\labs\lab12

   Note: the *lab12* sub-directory should already exist. Make sure that "lab12" appears only once in the Location directory.

   If you cannot remember where you installed the online workshop lab exercises, click on the *Lab Setup* button in the Chapter 14 online workshop Lab Exercise page.

   Then click on the Create button to cause the Developer Studio to build the initial project files.

3. To save you some typing, we have provided you with a partially-completed source file that you will fill in. Choose *Open* from the *File* menu and select LAB12.CPP. The Developer Studio will display the file.

5. The provided code contains a function that draws a spirograph image. If you've never played with the actual toy, here's a quick overview of how it works. To use the toy, you use two geared wheels to draw the image. The wheels come in different sizes and have holes in which you can insert a pen. To draw an image, you anchor one wheel to the paper, insert a pen into the other wheel, and roll the second wheel around the first. The second wheel has many pen-holes, each a different distance (offset) from the edge of the wheel.

Lab 12: Dialog Controls 64

We can express this mathematically, using the formulas:

```
x(theta) = (R + r)cos (theta) - (r + O)cos (((R + r)/r)theta)
y(theta) = (R + r)sin (theta) - (r + O)sin (((R + r)/r)theta)
```

where:

```
R = radius of fixed wheel
r = radius of rotating wheel
O = offset from edge of rotating wheel
```

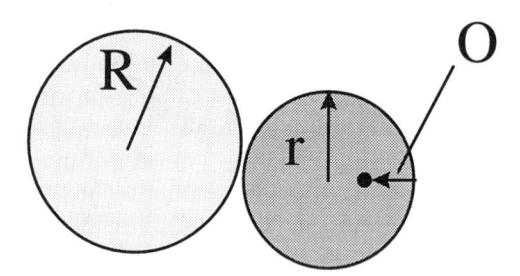

Figure 3 - Spirograph Wheels

You should examine the provided code in LAB12.CPP and see how it calls the *spirograph* function from the WM_PAINT case, passing default values for R, r and O. We also pass an iteration count – the greater the count, the closer together the points will be. In this lab, you will create a dialog box to let the user enter the values instead of hard-coding them.

Note: in lab, you will give the user the option whether or not to offset the pen instead of letting them enter the value for "O" – if they choose "yes", the *spirograph* function calculates a reasonable value for "O". There's no good reason for this except that it will give you practice using a checkbox control.

4. Even though you have opened the file from within the Developer Studio, it doesn't automatically add the file to the current project. To do that, choose *Files Into Project* from the *Insert* menu and select LAB12.CPP. This adds the source file into the project.

5. Your first job is to create the menu for the program. Choose *Resource* from the *Insert* menu and select *Menu*. You should then create a menu that looks like:

Options
Spirograph Parameters

See Lab Exercise 9 for help on creating a menu in the Developer Studio. Assign any symbolic IDs you wish for the menu item. **Note**: you should also assign the menu itself a symbolic ID, for example *IDM_MAIN*. To assign the ID, click the right mouse button on the menu-editing window to display the menu properties.

Write down the ID here for future reference:

Lab 12: Dialog Controls 65

Item	ID
Spirograph Parameters	_____

6. Your next job is to create the dialog. To start the dialog editor, choose Resource from the Insert menu and select Dialog. The dialog editor will open and display a dialog that you can use as a starting point for your dialog. Your dialog should look like:

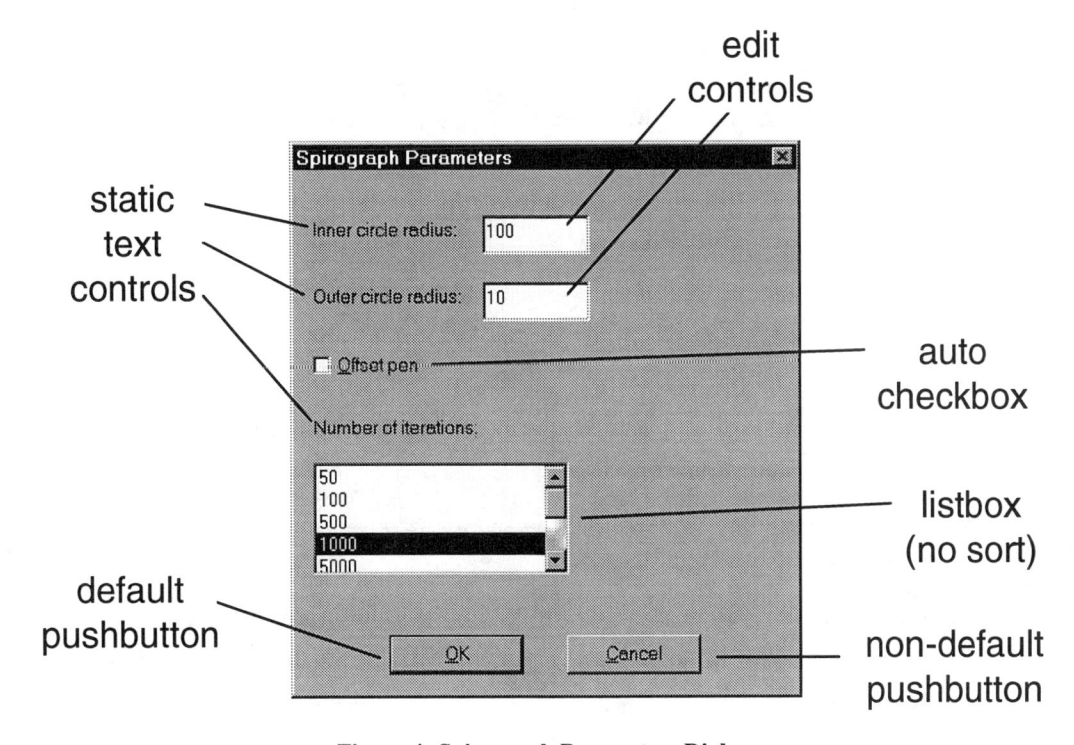

Figure 4: Spirograph Parameters Dialog

See Lab 11 for help creating the dialog. Write down the your dialog's ID and the IDs of your controls here for future reference:

Dialog ID _____

Control	ID
"Inner" edit control	_____
"Outer" edit control	_____
Checkbox	_____
Listbox	_____
"OK" button	_____

Lab 12: Dialog Controls

"Cancel" button   _____

7. Click on the dialog-editing window to ensure that it's active, then choose *Save As* from the *File* menu and enter LAB12.RC.

   Then choose *Files into Project* from the *Insert* menu and insert LAB12.RC into your project. You can then close all of the resource-editing windows if you'd like.

8. Now it's time to edit LAB12.CPP. At the top, *#include* "RESOURCE.H", and then write a *typedef* for a structure (write it outside of *WinMain*). The structure should have a field for each dialog control:

Dialog Control	Structure Field Type
"Inner" edit box	int
"Outer" edit box	int
"Offset" check box	BOOL
"Iterations" listbox	int

   Don't allocate the structure yet – you'll do that in a moment.

9. Then modify *WinMain* to load your menu.

10. At the top of the *WndProc*, allocate a *static* instance of your structure. Make it static so that it will hold its state from one message to the next.

11. Add a *WM_CREATE* case to the window procedure, and in it, initialize the fields of the structure. Sample values: R=100, r=10, offset pen = FALSE, iterations = 1000.

12. Modify the *WM_PAINT* case so that the call to *spirograph* uses values from the structure.

13. Add a *WM_COMMAND* case to the window procedure and in it, a case for the "Spirograph Options" menu item. When the user chooses that item, you should call *DialogBoxParam* to display the dialog. Hints:

    - You will write a dialog function in a moment – its name will be *SpirographDialogProc*.
    - You should pass a pointer to the structure as the last argument of DialogBoxParam.
    - The dialog function will call *EndDialog* to dismiss the dialog when the user clicks a pushbutton. The dialog function will pass the button ID as the second argument of EndDialog.

14. If the user OKs the dialog (check the return from *DialogBoxParam*), you should call *InvalidateRect* to force a repaint of the entire client area.

15. At the bottom of LAB12.CPP, write a skeleton dialog function:

```
BOOL CALLBACK SpirographDialogProc ( HWND hwndDlg, UINT iMsg
                                   , WPARAM wParam, LPARAM lParam )
{
        switch ( iMsg )
        {
```

Lab 12: Dialog Controls

67

```
                default:
                    return FALSE;
        }
}
```

16. Write a function prototype for the dialog function at the top of LAB12.CPP.

17. In the dialog function, allocate a static pointer to the structure you defined in an earlier step.

18. Now for the "hard" part. In the dialog function, add a case for *WM_INITDIALOG*. This will take quite a bit of code, since you have many dialog controls to initialize. Remember that the goal is to have the dialog show the current values whenever the user displays the box – in other words, in WM_INITDIALOG, you must initialize the dialog controls using values from the structure whose pointer the caller passed. The following steps give you some guidelines.

19. Retrieve the pointer for the structure passed by the caller and store it in the static variable you allocated in the last step.

20. Initialize the edit controls by calling *SetDlgItemInt* using the current values for R and r from the structure.

21. Initialize the checkbox by calling *CheckDlgButton* using the current value for the "offset pen" boolean from the structure.

22. To initialize the listbox, you can allocate a static array of character string pointers, with values "50", "100", "500", "1000", "5000", "10000", "50000" and "100000" (more, if you'd like). Note that these are strings, not values. Then code a loop to send *LB_ADDSTRING* to add each string. Also in the loop, after you add a string, send *LB_SETITEMDATA* to assign the new item its value as item data (you can use the *atoi* C-library function).

23. After you have added all of the strings to the listbox, you need to select the string that corresponds to the current iteration count from the structure. Use the C-library function *_itoa* to convert the iteration count to a string, and then send *LB_SELECTSTRING* to the listbox.

24. Call *SetFocus* to set the initial focus to the first edit control Then return *FALSE* from the WM_INITDIALOG case. And you are no done with that case! Whew!

25. Next, add a *WM_COMMAND* case to the dialog function to respond to messages from the dialog controls. The main thing here is to react to the OK and Cancel pushbuttons. If the user presses OK, you need to fill in the structure fields by pulling data from the dialog controls. In either case, you need to pass back the pushbutton ID when you dismiss the dialog – the calling code depends on seeing that ID. The following steps give you some help on coding the WM_COMMAND case for the OK button.

26. Use *GetDlgItemInt* to retrieve the data from the edit controls for R and r. Store the values in the corresponding structure fields.

27. Use *IsDlgButtonChecked* to retrieve the checkbox state. If the button is checked, store *TRUE* in the appropriate structure field. Otherwise, store *FALSE*.

28. Send *LB_GETCURSEL* and *LB_GETITEMDATA* to retrieve a value from the currently selected iteration count in the listbox. Store the iteration count in the structure.

29. Call *EndDialog* to dismiss the dialog, passing the OK button's ID. Then return *TRUE* from the message case.

Lab 12: Dialog Controls

30 In the case for the Cancel, button, pass back the Cancel button's ID. Then return *TRUE* from the message case. Note that Windows does not pass the return value from the message case back to the caller – instead, Windows passes the second argument of EndDialog (the button ID). The convention for returning from a dialog function is TRUE if you processed a message, FALSE otherwise.

31 Add a *WM_CLOSE* case in the dialog function, and in it, dismiss the dialog, passing back the Cancel button's ID.

32 Choose *Save All* from the *File* menu.

33 Then run your program by choosing *Execute lab12.exe* from the *Build* menu. You should see a blue image. Then use the menu to display your dialog. Does it start out with your default values? Try changing a value or two. Did the spirograph image change? Bring up the dialog again. Does it reflect the new values?

Refer to the LAB12 FAQ in Chapter 14 if you have any problems.

Close your window. You are now finished with Lab 12. You should continue by taking the Review Quiz in Chapter 14.

Optional Lab

Add another dialog to your program to let the user choose the image color. Use a listbox to display the possible color strings and use the listbox item data to associate an RGB value with each entry.

Lab 13: List View Controls

Note: If you are viewing this with Windows Write, you will get best results if you choose Tabs from the Document menu and set the first three tab stops to .5", 1.0" and 1.5".

Objectives:

- To learn how to use a list view child window in report view to display a set of records
- To use a C++ Standard Template Library container to store the set of records
- To respond to notifications from the list view

In this lab, you will write a program that displays a list of students. The data for each student will include the student's name, student ID number and a test score. You will use a list view control in report view to display the student records.

To store the student records in memory, you will use the C++ Standard Template Library (STL), which provides a group of C++ classes that act as containers. A container is a C++ object that manages collections of data – in this case, the data will be a set of structures. We will provide you with the STL code, since we don't cover it in the workshop. However, we believe that STL is a very useful and important part of the C++ Standard Library and is very appropriate for this lab where we need to store a list of students.

Steps:

1. Start the Microsoft Developer Studio by choosing it from the Microsoft Visual C++ group. Close any current project by choosing *Close Workspace* from the *File* menu.

2. Create a new project for the lab by choosing *New* from the *File* menu and selecting *Project Workspace*. Then fill in or select the following:

Type:	Application
Name:	lab13
Platform:	Win32
Location:	Enter the directory on your hard disk where the online workshop lab exercises are installed, for example:

   c:\descript\labs\lab13

   Note: the *lab13* sub-directory should already exist. Make sure that "lab13" appears only once in the Location directory.

   If you cannot remember where you installed the online workshop lab exercises, click on the *Lab Setup* button in the Chapter 15 online workshop Lab Exercise page.

   Then click on the Create button to cause the Developer Studio to build the initial project files.

3. To save you some typing, we have provided you with a partially-completed source file that you will fill in. Choose *Open* from the *File* menu and select LAB13.CPP. The Developer Studio will display the file.

Lab 13: List View Controls

4. The provided code creates and displays a window with a menu. When the user chooses from the menu, the program displays a dialog box that lets the user enter information about a student. The provided code then stores the new student's data in an STL *vector* container. A vector is similar to a C++ array, except that it automatically resizes itself as you add items.

   You should examine the provided code and make sure that you understand how it works. Especially examine what happens when the user OKs the dialog box – the code calls an *insert_student* function that calls the STL vector's *push_back* function to append the new student's data to the vector. The code then retrieves an STL *iterator* for the new student. An iterator is a C++ object that behaves like a pointer: you can de-reference it, increment it, compare it to other iterators and so on. The provided code doesn't use the iterator, but you will write some code that does in a moment.

   Take a look at the code in the *WM_DESTROY* case: the program loops through the vector using two more iterators. Each time through the loop, the program de-references the *pstart* iterator to append the record's data to a file name STUDENT.DAT – you can examine this file after running the program to see the student records.

   Finally, examine the *WM_PAINT* case – it's pretty much empty! Thus, as you enter new student records, the program stores them in the STL vector but doesn't display them. That will be your job in this lab.

5. Even though you have opened the file from within the Developer Studio, it doesn't automatically add the file to the current project. To do that, choose *Files Into Project* from the *Insert* menu and select LAB13.CPP. This adds the source file into the project.

   Then add LAB13.RC to the project in the same fashion.

6. Because you are using a common control, you need to modify the project setup. Choose *Settings* from the *Build* menu and select the *Link* tab. Then enter COMCTL32.LIB into the list of "Object/Library Modules".

7. Before you add any code to the program, you should build the executable and run it and try creating some new student records by choosing from the *Insert* menu. Then edit STUDENT.DAT to see the records. Be sure to close the STUDENT.DAT editor window before you try running the program again, or else the program won't be able to open the data file.

8. To display the students, your program will create a list view control. One of the things that a list view displays is an icon for each record. Choose *Resource* from the *Insert* menu and select *Icon*. Then create an icon that represents a student. See Lab Exercise 4 for help. **Note**: you should assign the icon a symbolic ID, for example *IDI_STUDENT*. To assign the ID, double-click the left mouse button on the icon-editing window to display the icon properties. Write down the icon ID for future reference:

   Icon ID _____

9. Next edit LAB13.CPP and add a case for *WM_CREATE*. In that case, create a list view control as a child of the main window. Your list view control should be in report view. Store the list view's handle in the provided *hwndList* static variable. You can set the child window's size and position to zero, since you will re-size the window each time the main window's size changes.

10. Call *GetSystemMetrics* to retrieve the system size for small icons. Then create a small-icon image list to hold one image, using the *ILC_MASKED* flag. Store the image list handle in a static variable that you define.

Lab 13: List View Controls

11. Call *LoadIcon* to retrieve your student icon's handle and then add the icon to the image list. Store the returned image index in the provided *nIndexImage* static variable. You can then delete the icon object since the image list copies it.

12. Still in WM_CREATE, use *ListView_InsertColumn* to configure three columns that have the header text as follows:

    <u>Name</u>   <u>Student ID</u>   <u>Test Score</u>

    Use the *LVCF_WIDTH* flag and the *lvc.cx* field to set each column's width to 100 pixels (you will need other *LVCF_* flags, too).

    You don't need to add any rows to the list view yet, since you will do that after the user closes the edit-student dialog.

13. Edit the *WM_DESTROY* case, and at the top of it, call *ImageList_Destroy* to get rid of the image list. You don't need to destroy the list view child window, since Windows automatically destroys a child window when the parent is destroyed.

14. Find the *insert_student* function near the bottom of LAB13.CPP. The provided code calls this function after the user enters student information into a dialog and then presses OK. The provided dialog function stores the student information in a STUDENT structure – a reference to this structure is passed to insert_student.

    The code that's already in insert_student adds the student record to the STL vector container and retrieves a pointer (iterator) to the new record. The provided code also retrieves the count of records stored in the container. You will use the *ps* and *nIndex* variables in a moment.

15. Your job is to add code to the *insert_student* function so that it also writes the student information to the list view child window. In other words, each time the student OKs the dialog, you need to add the information to the STL container *and* display it.

    Your code will be similar to the sample program in Chapter 15, with one big difference -- in this lab, the student data is already stored in the STL container – why should you "waste" memory by also having the list view child window keep a copy of the data? Instead, you will use a *callback* technique, where the list view container sends a message whenever it needs the data -- you can then supply the student information by reading the record from the STL container. In a way, this is like a promise: when you add an item to the list view, you won't supply the item data, but promise that to furnish the data upon demand.

    To make that easy, whenever you add a row to the list view, you will store the STL pointer (iterator) to the student record as the *lParam* application-defined field in the list view item. Then when the list view asks us for the data, you can use the iterator to access the student record and supply the item text.

16. Still in the *insert_student* function, call *ListView_InsertItem* to add an item that represents a student and corresponds to the first column in the list view ("Name"). Fill in an *LV_ITEM* structure, using these hints:

    ```
    mask          LVIF_IMAGE | LVIF_PARAM | LVIF_TEXT
    iItem         Use the nIndex variable that's calculated from the STL container's element
                  count (size)
    iSubItem      Set this field to zero, since you are adding the data for column zero
    ```

Lab 13: List View Controls

        `pszText`   LPSTR_TEXTCALLBACK – this is the "promise" that cause the list view to send WM_NOTIFY whenever it needs to display the text
        `iImage`   Use the image index passed to the function
        `lParam`   The STL iterator variable (cast to LPARAM)

17. Then add the data (actually the promise) for each of the other two columns by calling *ListView_SetItemText* twice. Use the hints shown above for help, but be sure to pass the correct column number (hint: the "Name" column you added in the last step is column zero).

18. Now for the interesting part. Whenever the list view repaints, it will now ask for the text for each item by sending the *WM_NOTIFY* message with the *LVN_GETDISPINFO* notification code. Back in the main window procedure, add a case for WM_NOTIFY, with a sub-case for LVN_GETDISPINFO. See Chapter 15 for an example.

19. In the *LVN_GETDISPINFO* sub-case, allocate a static character string of 25 bytes or so. Your code will store the "promise" text in this string and then return the string's address back to the list view. You need to make the string static, or else it would be de-allocated when your window procedure hits the return statement, and the list view would receive a pointer to "garbage".

20. Cast the *WM_NOTIFY lParam* value to a pointer to a *LV_DISPINFO* pointer, perhaps naming it *pnmv*. You will use this pointer to return the requested string's address.

21. Retrieve the STL iterator (pointer) to the item in question. Remember that you stored the STL iterator in the item's *lParam* application-defined parameter when you added the item to the list view. Here is the code for this step:

```
// retrieve the STL iterator to the
// item in question
   STUDENT_VECTOR::iterator ps;

ps = (STUDENT_VECTOR::iterator)pnmv->item.lParam;
```

From this point on, you can refer to the student using the iterator. For example, *ps->szName* references the student's name (the *STUDENT* structure type is defined at the top of LAB13.CPP).

22. Write a *switch* statement that chooses the column number (switch on *pnmv->item.iSubItem*) and add a case for each column index, 0, 1 and 2.

23. For column 0, use *strcpy* to copy the student's name from the STL element (using the iterator) to the static string. Then set *pnmv->item.pszText* to the address of the static string (no ampersand). This fulfills the promise for this column.

24. For each of the other two columns, use the *_itoa* C library function to convert the student ID or test score integers to strings, storing the result in the static string. Then set *pnmv->item.pszText* to the address of the static string (no ampersand). This fulfills the promise for these columns.

25. Finally, you must add a *WM_SIZE* case to the window procedure so that you can re-size the list view child window whenever the main window's size changes. In that case, call *SetWindowPos* or *MoveWindow* so that the list view fills the entire client area of the main window.

26. Choose *Save All* from the *File* menu and then choose *Build lab13.exe* from the *Build* menu to develop the program.

Lab 13: List View Controls

27. Then run your program by choosing *Execute lab13.exe* from the *Build* menu. You should see an empty list-view report view window in the main window's client area. Choose from the Insert menu to add a new student. Do you see the student's data in the list view?

    Refer to the LAB13 FAQ in Chapter 15 if you have any problems.

    Close your window. You are now finished with Lab 13. You should continue by taking the Review Quiz in Chapter 15.

Lab 14: Property Sheets

Note: If you are viewing this with Windows Write, you will get best results if you choose Tabs from the Document menu and set the first three tab stops to .5", 1.0" and 1.5".

Objectives:
- To learn how to create property sheet page dialog resources
- To learn how to display a modal property sheet control

In this lab, you will write a program that displays a property sheet to let the user enter information about a student. The property sheet will have two pages: one for the student's name, the other for the student's test score. To simplify the lab, the property sheet will not display an "Apply" button, but if you wish, you can do an optional lab that includes the "Apply" button on the property sheet.

Steps:

1. Start the Microsoft Developer Studio by choosing it from the Microsoft Visual C++ group. Close any current project by choosing *Close Workspace* from the *File* menu.

2. Create a new project for the lab by choosing *New* from the *File* menu and selecting *Project Workspace*. Then fill in or select the following:

    Type: Application
    Name: lab14
    Platform: Win32
    Location: Enter the directory on your hard disk where the online workshop lab exercises are installed, for example:

    c:\descript\labs\lab14

    Note: the *lab14* sub-directory should already exist. Make sure that "lab14" appears only once in the Location directory.

    If you cannot remember where you installed the online workshop lab exercises, click on the *Lab Setup* button in the Chapter 18 online workshop Lab Exercise page.

    Then click on the Create button to cause the Developer Studio to build the initial project files.

3. To save you some typing, we have provided you with a partially-completed source file that you will fill in. Choose *Open* from the *File* menu and select LAB14.CPP. The Developer Studio will display the file.

4. The provided code creates a window that displays information about a student: the student's name and their test score. Currently these attributes are hard-coded – your job is to let the user enter the data into a property sheet.

    Before you get started writing code, you should carefully examine the provided code. Note that we have given you two skeleton dialog functions. Each of these will control a page in the property sheet. You will flesh-out these dialog functions in a later step.

Lab 14: Property Sheets

5. Your first job is to create the resources for your program. Choose *Resource* from the *Insert* menu and create a menu that looks like:

   <u>S</u>tudent
          <u>P</u>roperties

   Write down the menu IDs here for future reference:

   ID of entire menu   _____

   ID of Properties item   _____

6. Next, you will create the dialog resource for the Name property sheet page. Choose *Resource* from the *Insert* menu and then expand the Dialog entry. Then click on the entry for a medium-sized property sheet page (not OLE). This will create a dialog resource that has the proper styles for a property sheet page.

7. Click the right mouse button on the new dialog to display its properties. Enter the following:

   ID: DLG_NAMEPAGE
   Caption: Name

   Then close the properties window.

8. Edit the new dialog to have a static text control and a single-line edit control. The dialog should look like:

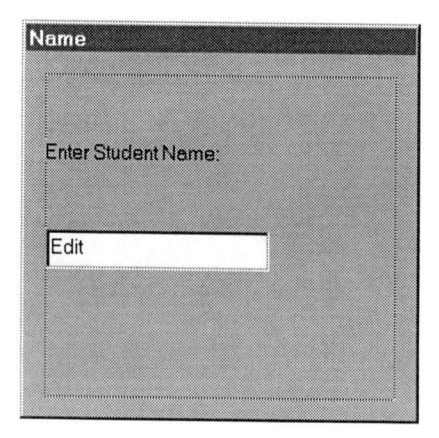

   Figure 5: Name Property Sheet Page

   Write down the ID you assigned to the edit control here: _____

9. Then create another property sheet page dialog that looks like:

Lab 14: Property Sheets

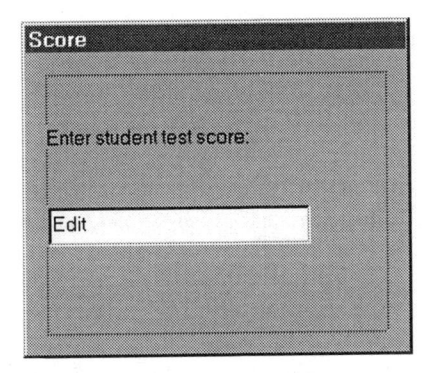

Figure 6: Score Property Sheet Page

Assign IDs similar to the other dialog. Write down the IDs here for future reference:

Dialog ID: _____

Edit Control ID _____

10. You can then save the resources in a file named LAB14.RC and insert that file into the project.

11. Because your lab will use a common control, you need to modify the project setup. Choose *Settings* from the *Build* menu and select the *Link* tab. Then enter COMCTL32.LIB into the list of "Object/Library Modules".

12. Next, edit LAB14.CPP. At the top of the file, write #includes to include the RESOURCE.H file from the local directory and COMMCTRL.H from the system directory.

13. In *WinMain*, call *InitCommonControls* to load the common controls library.

14. Still in *WinMain*, load the menu that you created in an earlier step and assign it to the window class.

15. In the main window procedure, add a case for *WM_COMMAND* and a subcase for the *Properties* menu item. In the subcase, follow the next few steps to display the property sheet.

16. Allocate an array of two *PROPSHEETPAGE* structures. Initialize each page as follows:

`dwSize`	The *sizeof* the *PROPSHEETPAGE* structure
`dwFlags`	You can set this to zero
`hInstance`	The current instance handle (use *GetWindowLong* to retrieve it)
`pszTemplate`	The resource of ID of the dialog for this page
`pfnDlgProc`	The address of the dialog function for this page
`lParam`	The address of the *static* variable that holds the data that this page represents. Note that you will need to specify an & for the score integer

    Since you pass the address of a variable as the *lParam* field, the dialog function will be able to retrieve a pointer to the variable during its *WM_INITDIALOG* message.

17. Allocate and initialize a *PROPSHEETHEADER* structure as follows:

`dwSize`	The *sizeof* the *PROPSHEETHEADER* structure
`dwFlags`	*PSH_PROPSHEETPAGE	PSH_NOAPPLYNOW*

Lab 14: Property Sheets   78

hwndParent	The main window handle
nPages	You have two pages
pszCaption	How about "Student Properties"?
ppsp	The address of the array you filled in during the last step

18. Then call *PropertySheet* to display the property sheet. Since property sheets are modal by default, this call will not return until the user dismissed the sheet. You should check the return value -- if the call fails, call the provided *err_msg* function to display an error message. If the call is successful, call *InvalidateRect* to invalidate the entire main window to repaint with the updated student information.

19. Next, find the *NameDialogProc* dialog function. As it stands, this function is just a skeleton – your job is to complete it so that it handles the *Name* property sheet page.

    Start by defining a *static* character pointer that will point to the caller's student-name string.

20. Then, in *WM_INITDIALOG*, initialize the static pointer to point to the caller's string. This will take two steps, since for property sheet page dialogs, *lParam* points to the *PROPSHEETPAGE* structure – the pointer you need is contained in the *lParam* field in that structure. See the sample program in Chapter 18 for an example of how to retrieve the pointer. You will need to cast the pointer to *char ** to make the compiler happy.

21. Still in *WM_INITDIALOG*, use *SetDlgItemText* to initialize the student-name edit control using the pointer you just retrieved.

22. Then work on the *WM_NOTIFY* case. Add a subcase for the *PSN_APPLY* notification that the property sheet sends when the user clicks the property sheet's OK button.

23. In the *PSN_APPLY* subcase, call *GetDlgItemText* to retrieve the current student-name text and store it in the caller's student-name string (use the static character pointer).

    Then set the dialog message-result to zero to tell the property sheet that you handled the case successfully. Use *SetWindowLong* to do this.

24. Then find the *ScoreDialogProc* dialog function and write similar code to the *NameDialogProc*. The major difference is that the caller passes you the address of an integer rather than a string – you can use *SetDlgItemInt* and *GetDlgItemInt* to write and read the edit control as an integer.

25. Choose *Save All* from the *File* menu and then choose *Build lab14.exe* from the *Build* menu to develop the program.

27. Then run your program by choosing *Execute lab14.exe* from the *Build* menu. You should be able to display the property sheet by choosing Properties from the Student menu. Are there two pages in the property sheet with the correct titles? What happens if you change an attribute and then press OK? What about Cancel?

    Refer to the LAB14 FAQ in Chapter 18 if you have any problems.

    Close your window. You are now finished with Lab 14. You should continue by taking the Review Quiz in Chapter 18. Or, if you wish, you can do the optional lab described below.

Lab 14: Property Sheets

Optional Lab

Modify your property sheet so that it displays an "Apply" button. You will need to modify the *PROPSHEETHEADER* structure flags. You will also need to modify the dialog functions so that they save a copy of the current attributes during *WM_INITDIALOG* and restore them if the user presses Cancel (*PSN_RESET* notification). Finally, you will need to send an application-defined message from the dialog function to the main window if the user presses "Apply" – the main window should repaint when that happens. Use the sample program in Chapter 18 as a guide.